THE PARLIAMENT OF 1621

THE
PARLIAMENT
OF 1621

A STUDY IN CONSTITUTIONAL CONFLICT

by Robert Zaller

UNIVERSITY OF CALIFORNIA PRESS
BERKELEY LOS ANGELES LONDON

1971

University of California Press
Berkeley and Los Angeles, California

University of California Press, Ltd.
London, England

FOR MY PARENTS

"If the House press the King to grant unto them all that is theirs by the law, they cannot in justice refuse the King all that is his by the law. And where will be the issue of such a contention? I dare not divine; but sure I am that it will tend to the prejudice both of King and Subject."

—Sir Walter Raleigh

CONTENTS

ABBREVIATIONS

A.P.C.	J. V. Lyle, ed., *Acts of the Privy Council of England,* Vol. V (London, 1930); Vol. VI (London, 1932).
A.H.R.	*American Historical Review*
Birch	Thomas Birch, ed., *The Court and Times of James the First* (London, 1849).
B.M. Add. MSS	British Museum, Additional Manuscripts.
Cabala	*Cabala Sive Scrinia Sacra: Mysteries of State and Government in Letters of Illustrious Persons . . .* (London, 1691).
C.S.P.D.	M. A. E. Green, ed., *Calendar of State Papers, Domestic Series 1619–1623* (London, 1858).
C.S.P.V.	A. B. Hinds, ed., *Calendar of State Papers Venetian,* Vols. XVI, XVII (London, 1911).
Chamberlain	N. E. McClure, ed., *The Letters of John Chamberlain* (Philadelphia, 1939).
C.D.	Wallace Notestein, Frances Relf, Hartley Simpson, eds., *Commons Debates 1621* (New Haven, 1935).
C.J.	*Journals of the House of Commons,* Vol. I.
D.N.B.	Sir Leslie Stephen and Sir Sidney Lee, eds., *The Dictionary of National Biography* (London, 1885–1901).
Ec.H.R.	*Economic History Review*
E.H.R.	*English Historical Review*
Gardiner	S. R. Gardiner, *History of England from the Accession of James I to the Outbreak of the Civil War 1603–1642* (London, 1883–84).
Harl. MSS	Harleian Manuscripts, British Museum.

H.J.	Evangeline de Villiers, ed., "The Hastings Journal of the Parliament of 1621," *Camden Miscellany*, Vol. XX (London, 1953).
H.L.Q.	*Huntingdon Library Quarterly*
J.M.H.	*Journal of Modern History*
L.D. G.	Henry Elsing, *Notes of the Debates in the House of Lords . . . A.D. 1621*, ed. S. R. Gardiner (Camden Soc. CIII, London, 1870).
L.D. R.	Frances Relf, ed., *Notes of the Debates in the House of Lords 1621–1628* (London, 1929).
L.J.	*Journals of the House of Lords*, Vol. III.
P.D.	Edward Nicholas, *Proceedings and Debates in the House of Commons in 1620 and 1621* (Oxford, 1766).
P.R.O.	State Papers, Public Record Office (Spanish and Paris Transcripts).
Rushworth	John Rushworth, ed., *Historical Collections . . .* (London, 1721–1722).
Salvetti Newsletter	Salvetti Newsletter, Add. MSS 27962.
Spedding	James Spedding, *The Letters and Life of Francis Bacon* (London, 1861–1874).
S.P.	State Papers, Public Record Office. Various series: Domestic, Spanish, German, Holland, Flanders.
T.R.H.S.	*Transactions of the Royal Historical Society*

NOTE: Days and months are given in old style, but the year is dated from January 1.

PREFACE

An historian of the Stuart period, in making his debut, ought first to pay homage to the father of us all, Samuel Rawson Gardiner. That Gardiner is out of date goes without saying; so will this book be, in its turn, and so it should. But those of us who till the soil should not forget the man who cleared the forest.

This particular book owes its existence to Professor J. H. Hexter, who first suggested and long supported it, and to Professors Wallace Notestein, Hartley Simpson, and Frances Relf, the editors of the splendid work on which it is chiefly based: the *Commons Debates 1621*.

I wish to thank the Institute for Historical Research for permission to use its facilities, and the History of Parliament Trust, which allowed me to examine the unpublished files of its parliamentary biographies. The Earl of Dorset very kindly permitted me to inspect the Sackville manuscripts. The help of many friends, colleagues, and teachers has gone into and between the lines of this book.

I will not attempt to thank my wife for what she has done. Thanks are meager, and gratitude is poor, beside what I owe her.

R. Z.

4 July 1970

INTRODUCTION

The existence of a vital cleavage in the political structure of England was far from apparent in the first years of Stuart rule. Rather, all signs seemed to indicate just the reverse. England had, by the seventeenth century, achieved a high degree of social cohesion and national unity, and this unity was universally attributed by her people to the excellence of their political system, the harmonious immemorial balance of the king's power and the subject's right. England's law, wrote Francis Bacon, was "the best, the equallest in the world between the Prince and People; by which the King hath the justest Prerogative, and the People the best liberty."[1] It was almost unthinkable to Englishmen that the loom on which the fabric of unity was woven should break its web, that the tighter the fiber was drawn, the weaker became the frame.

But within a system thus conceived as static and perfected, one body had developed so rapidly and anomalously as to jeopardize the order of the whole. This body was Parliament. The very antiquity of Parliament as an institution helped to conceal the astonishing character of its transformation from a medieval estate to a modern deliberative assembly, asserting its right to legislate every aspect of the national life, confirming or condemning royal policies and ministers, and declaring itself to be uniquely the voice of the nation. The story of Parliament's growth has been ably told,[2] and need not detain us here. Two important results of this growth should, however, be noted.

The first is that Parliament had, by the time of the Stuarts, acquired a powerful sense of corporate consciousness.[3] Its members no longer conceived of themselves as a body sporadically assembled at the king's pleasure, and existing, like the Cheshire cat, only when the sovereign's eye was upon it, but as an ongoing and permanent function of state, a "continuous performance," in Professor Notestein's phrase.[4] This sense of continuity was evidenced in a number of ways. The end of one Parliament had developed the habit of carefully preparing unfinished business against the beginning of the next. The two houses began to keep records of their proceedings, and employed antiquarians to search the yellowed records in the Tower for older accounts. New orders and procedural innovations were scrupulously preserved, and from session to session the manner of transacting business, of reading bills and investigating grievances, became more fixed, exact, and efficient. The importance of this body of rules and records in creating a corporate consciousness cannot be overestimated. They were as much a part of the idea of Parliament as the halls of Westminster or the Chancellor's woolsack. As the bridle and bit presuppose the rider, so they implied the absent assembly.

As a corollary of this new consciousness, the House of Commons began to seek control over the determination of its membership. In 1604 it won the right to validate its own elections, a right it exercised vigorously thereafter, and in 1621 to expand itself by creating new parliamentary boroughs.[5] It also sought to annex the "privileges" of free speech and immunity from arrest, which the king traditionally granted at the beginning of each session, as "rights" inherent in the institution of Parliament and inseparable from it. Such a development would tend to convert Parliament into a kind of chartered body, independent of the sovereign will. The only seeming parallel to such independence was the judicial system; and it is significant that Parliament began increasingly to justify its assumption of power by reviving, in a drastically altered context, its ancient functions as a court.[6]

The second result of Parliament's growth was the development of the idea of Parliament as the voice of the nation. The notion that Parliament "spoke" for the nation, not merely as representing particular interests but as a quasi-religious embodiment of the whole, was actually a platitude of long standing. "The regiment of England," wrote John Aylmer in 1559,

> is not a mere monarchy, as some for lack of consideration think, nor a mere oligarchy, nor democracy, but a rule mixed of all these . . . the image whereof, and not the image but the thing indeed, is to be seen in the Parliament house, wherein you shall find these three estates: the king or queen,

which representeth the monarch; the nobleman which be
the aristocracy; and the burgesses and knights the democracy . . . .[7]

But when Peter Wentworth claimed in 1576 that Parliament
must discuss whatever "seemeth good to our merciful God to put
into our minds" without limit or impediment because the Commons were "chosen of the whole realm . . . to serve God and all
England,"[8] he was turning an old idea to very new uses. Free
speech and parliamentary immunity might be justified by reference to the nation—it could be argued that unless every member
could freely speak his mind, neither the public business nor the
king's duty could be done—but they did not derive from it. Had
the Commons desired these freedoms the better to perform their
business, they should have been satisfied with the assurance that,
though their privileges came from the king, the king would always grant them. What firmer bond could the sovereign give his
people than his own word? But the Commons were not so satisfied
in 1604, nor ever after. They argued, not utility, not necessity,
but right. Their privileges were part of that fore-existing juridi-
cal entity, Parliament; indeed, they were identical with it, for
tyranny might abrogate them for a time, but a Parliament that
denied its privileges was no Parliament at all.

Wentworth in his famous speech justified his claims by virtue
"of a special trust and confidence . . . reposed in us" for the
maintenance of the subject's right and the welfare of the state. It
might be supposed that this was precisely the function of the
king. But princes, no matter how wise and just, might err, and
when they did, said Wentworth, it was the duty of their subjects
in Parliament to correct them. This granted, it was readily apparent that the privileges of the House of Commons were of the most
critical importance to the commonwealth. But it was a good deal
to grant indeed. It was most of what Parliament was to struggle
for, through two revolutions, for the next hundred years.[9]

Thus, the sense of a corporate identity led to the notion of inherent rights, and the idea of Parliament as the voice of the nation
to a concept of general responsibility for its welfare. These latter
concepts in turn formed a self-proving system. The existence of
inherent rights was justified by responsibility to the nation, and
that responsibility justified those rights—for why else should they
exist but for such a purpose? Thus, each clarification of Parlia-

ment's rights was a pretext for the extension of its responsibility, and vice versa. There was no logical end to this cycle but a total assumption of sovereignty, and this was exactly the position to which Parliament was led in the 1640s.

The result of Parliament's making such new claims for itself was a steadily worsening crisis of authority in the first four decades of the seventeenth century which brought vital governmental functions to a standstill. Foreign policy was virtually impossible under the first two Stuarts. Parliament was no less frustrated. It was scarcely able to pass bills any longer; the parliaments of 1610, 1614, 1621, 1625, 1626 and 1628–29 were dissolved in anger; and finally, for eleven years, there were no parliaments at all.

Nothing could have been more plain than the failure of the Stuart political system. Despite goodwill and even grim determination, Parliament after Parliament came to grief. Yet most MPs throughout the period continued to see no contradiction between being good parliament men and good subjects, between duty to the king and responsibility to the nation. They blamed their troubles on projectors and papists at Court, and, after 1621, on the Duke of Buckingham. The Crown too sought an explanation in personalities. James and Charles believed that a willful faction in the Commons that "would have all donn by Parliament" had deliberately sown disharmony between king and people, and they tested their hypothesis empirically by punishing or removing those whom they identified with it. The most drastic of these purges occurred in 1626, when Charles excluded virtually every prominent figure of the preceding Parliament. The result was that the new Parliament, hydra-like, sprouted new heads, and was even more unruly than the one before.

What this suggests may be stated simply. As individuals, the 450-odd members of the House of Commons were sincerely loyal men. As a body, they were subversive and revolutionary.[10] Put another way, this is to say that a fundamental incompatibility had developed between the institution of Parliament and that of monarchy, and that any resolution of that incompatibility would require the radical modification of one or the other.

The full unfolding of this conflict awaits a detailed examination of all the parliaments of the period under study. The Parliament of 1621, however, though neither the beginning nor the end of the story, presents an ideal vantage point for a preliminary study. Both King and Parliament were painfully conscious of past disharmony, and both came to this session, clouded as it was by crisis at home and abroad, prepared to bend over backward for unity. If the system still had a chance to work, if ever it needed to work, it was here. But the Parliament failed, and in its failure revealed the collapse of constitutional government in the most vivid and conclusive way. The story of that failure is the subject matter of this book.

I

THE SUMMONING
OF PARLIAMENT

Antigonus: Thou art perfect then, our ship hath touched upon
The deserts of Bohemia.

Mariner: Ay, my Lord, and fear
We have landed in ill time; the skies look grimly,
And threaten present blusters. In my conscience
The heavens with that we have in hand are angry
And frown upon's.

—The Winter's Tale, Act III, scene 3

On a May morning in 1618, a pair of Imperial regents were pushed out a castle window in the faraway city of Prague, the ancient capital of Shakespeare's imaginary isle. The chain of events precipitated by this act was fated to bring Europe at last to the war that a generation of diplomats had anticipated. That conflict closed the era of the Reformation and secularized European history; it remapped the Continent, and left scars that are still visible today.

For England, however, safe in its waters, the Thirty Years' War was little more than the rumor of battles and the pillaging of place-names. Prices fell, trade slumped; but, for all most Englishmen were directly affected by it, Shakespearean geography was all they needed to know.

Yet the war was profoundly to alter England's history as well, for the greatest Protestant and maritime power in Europe did not evade the struggle from casual choice or disinterest. England was crippled by deep internal division, a division exposed, exacerbated, and made irreparable by the pressure of diplomatic responsibility upon the mechanism of state.

In the first decade of the war, England's statesmen vainly strove to conduct the foreign policy her position demanded of her. But the mere sending of a peace mission, let alone the provisioning of an army or fleet, was a grave strain on the restricted revenues of the king; any serious diplomatic excursion could be financed only through Parliament. This fact resulted in the rapid succession of parliaments in the 1620s. Five sat within seven years where there had been but two in twenty before.[1] With such close continuity, Parliament matured leaders, programs, legislative technique, and above all, the crucial consciousness of power, that might have taken much longer to fully evolve under less favorable conditions. By the end of the decade, the old constitution had utterly broken down in operation, and civil war lacked only circumstance. But in the very first of those five parliaments, the ultimate struggle of King and Parliament had already been fully rehearsed, the ultimate issues laid bare. Twenty years before York, the Parliament of 1621 had brought the Stuart monarchy face to face with its final dilemma.

The guiding policy of James I, though as King of England the acknowledged leader of Reformed Europe, was rapprochement with the Catholic powers. To this end he had determined to marry his son and heir, Prince Charles, first to a Bourbon, and finally to a Hapsburg princess. James saw himself not as the leader of a bloc, but as a mediator impartial in the interests of peace. To his mind the pursuit of peace was the most exalted function of Christian kingship; and it was his dream that Spain and England, the leaders of Christendom's two camps of faith, could, acting in concert, preserve the peace of Europe.

Yet James was no dreamer. While courting Spain, he retained hegemony among his fellow Protestants. If he proposed to marry Charles to a Catholic, he had matched his daughter Elizabeth to a Calvinist, the Elector Palatine Frederick V. James had learned to blend factions well in his powerless Scottish youth, and the faculty continued to serve in the great world. As King of England he had made an honorable and statesmanlike record. For fifteen years he had kept his country at peace, and served the wider cause of Christendom. He hoped to end his reign with no greater glory. But there was one flaw in his reckoning: Prince Frederick was

his son-in-law. It was this fact finally that James, for all his dex-
terity, could not escape.

The position of Frederick's dominions, known collectively as
the Palatinate, was one of the more striking geographic anomalies
of the Holy Roman Empire. They consisted of two fairly compact
areas of roughly equal size, separated by about two hundred miles
on an almost exact line of latitude. The Lower (western) Palatinate, a quick march from France, was bisected by the Rhine;
while the Upper (eastern) lay just above the northernmost thrust
of the Danube. On one side, Frederick was athwart Spain's route
to the Netherlands; on the other, he fronted Bavaria, the most
powerful Catholic state in the Empire, and Bohemia, a Protestant
nation with a Hapsburg king. Between the two Palatinates lay a
tangle of princedoms, constituting what was called the Lower
Saxon Circle. These were the states of the Evangelical Union, the
military alliance of the Protestant princes of Germany. Thus a
bloc of Protestant states bookended by the two Palatinates stood
wedged between the two major storm eyes of Europe: Spain's
overland supply line in its briefly remitted struggle with the
Dutch, and the explosive triangle of Bohemia, Bavaria, and Austria. Elementary prudence dictated extreme caution to a ruler
such as the Palatine; instead, the young and weakly willful Frederick plunged headlong into the rashest adventure imaginable.

Frederick was one of the seven electors who chose the Holy
Roman Emperor. Three of these were Catholic bishops, three
secular Protestants, and the last, the King of Bohemia, who had
for a hundred years been the Emperor-designate himself, to wit,
the senior male representative of the House of Hapsburg. It was
evident, therefore, that any disturbance in the orderly succession
to the Bohemian crown would immediately jeopardize the traditional Hapsburg claim to the Imperium. With this in mind, the
Hapsburgs had quietly replaced the failing emperor Matthias
on the Bohemian throne with Ferdinand of Styria. But within a
year of his accession, Ferdinand was faced with a revolt of his
Protestant nobility. Unsubdued in fifteen months, the rebels declared Ferdinand deposed, and offered his crown to Frederick.
But before this news could reach Frankfurt, where the seven
electors had convened to choose a successor to the now defunct
Matthias, Ferdinand had been raised by unanimous consent to
the Imperial throne.[2]

No other ruler in Europe would have taken up a crown proffered by rebels. Frederick, who had openly solicited it, was now hesitant himself. He must first, he said, have the advice of his father-in-law.

Of James's reaction there could scarcely be doubt. The inviolability of thrones was the first principle of his political philosophy. An Ahab, a Nebuchadnezzar, a Nero, once lawfully instituted, was a people's true ruler under God, for though he be "an idolatrous persecuter, a forraine King, a Tyrant, and usurper of their liberties; yet in respect they had once received and acknowledged him for their king, he not only commandeth them to obey him, but even to pray for his prosperitie, . . . because in his prosperitie stood their peace." James needed no more than a bookmark to answer his son-in-law, for the words he himself had written twenty years before could not have been more exactly applicable to Bohemia.[3]

Moreover, James had already made his position clear. As long as a year before, he had been asked by Spain to use his influence in Germany to help settle the Bohemian affair.[4] James eagerly accepted: it was precisely the role, with precisely the partner, he had conceived for himself on the international stage. In the spring of 1619, he dispatched a Scottish nobleman, Viscount Doncaster, to open negotiations between the disputants. It was the first of three embassies James was to send in successive years to the capitals of Germany, and one of the most opulent diplomatic expeditions to leave English shores since the Field of the Cloth of Gold. Doncaster's instructions reflected the presupposition of Hapsburg centrality in Europe: he was to vigorously support Ferdinand's candidacy at the pending Imperial Diet, and his kingship in Bohemia. The rebels were to be guaranteed religious freedom and a general amnesty, nothing more.[5] When the Dutch put out a feeler for them, James replied severely than any assistance to the rebels would disqualify his mediation, in which undertaking his honor was "deeply engaged."[6]

It was therefore a considerable disillusionment when Doncaster discovered that neither side had any serious intention of coming to terms. Even the Spanish had done nothing to dispose their Imperial cousins to the English mission, and their ambassador in Vienna but scantly excused himself for it.[7] To crown the debacle, Frederick had no sooner submitted the Bohemian offer to his father-in-law's wisdom than news came that he had accepted it without waiting for a reply.[8] His doing so put James in the inelegant position of demanding satisfaction from Madrid for its inaction while convincing the Spanish that his own mediation had been in good faith, for a shrewd world was unlikely to believe that the English King was innocent of Frederick's adventure. The Palatine had publicly consulted James: immediately thereafter he had accepted the crown: what conclusion was any sane man to draw? James was furious. "I never saw his Majestie more sensible of anything than he is of the cleering of his honour in this point," wrote John Digby to Francis Cottington in Spain.[9] The imputation of double-dealing was not only a disparagement of the King's self-professed role as a peacemaker and of his sworn word in international affairs; it imperiled the good relations with Spain which were the cornerstone of his entire foreign policy and his only hope for heading off the general European crisis which clearly impended in the autumn of 1619.

Under these circumstances, it might have seemed that James's best course was to remain aloof until such time as the antagonists in Germany should be ready for genuine negotiation; but Frederick's assumption of the crown, far from entitling England to withdraw, had drawn her inextricably into the maelstrom of continental diplomacy. The Palatine was in open rebellion against the Emperor, a situation that invited retaliation against his own dominions. James might shun Frederick's speculation in kingship, but could he idly watch his son-in-law and daughter driven into exile?

The logical executor of such an attack, moreover, would be Spain. She was already providing the chief financial support of Ferdinand's war in Bohemia. From Flanders she could easily deploy an army against Frederick, and have for recompense the acquisition of a new springboard against the Dutch. Such a move would force James's hand; and an Anglo-Spanish confrontation in the Rhenish Palatinate could irreparably sunder the alliance of the two countries.

This, of course, was precisely the calculation of Frederick and his advisors; and the Dutch, eager backers of the Palatine from the outset, made the same mental note. It was England's potential weight in the balance of war, and not the sincerity of her desire for peace, which made her a factor—inevitably, a party—in the reckoning on all sides. This hardening of attitudes clearly presaged the drift to general war. In England as well, opinion favored a "strong stand"; the Privy Council pressed James for a firm commitment to Frederick, and the Archbishop of Canterbury envisaged a crusade.[10]

But James kept his own course. If most accepted war as inevitable, that only made greater the responsibility of those who still sought peace. England's policy would be to champion her coreligionists on one side, while offering friendship to the Hapsburgs on the other. Thus James offered Spain closer ties, while warning her that he would be obliged to defend the Palatinate against any invasion.[11]

Spain, too, was slowly deliberating her responsibilities in light of the new situation. The great imperial power of the modern world, whose dominions embraced three continents, was weary, overextended, gone flat with bureaucratic fatigue. The last chapter of her long struggle with the Dutch impended, and her statesmen wished to commit a supreme effort to this task. But the plight of Austria could not be ignored. It had been hoped that Ferdinand could subjugate the Bohemians with money and the loan of a famous general; but the Elector Palatine's acceptance of the rebels' crown—in effect, a second aggression against the Empire—had greatly widened the issue. "Germany" was now the problem, not merely Bohemia; what had been a stubborn but localized rebellion was now a direct challenge to the constitution of the Holy Roman Empire, a threat to any general sovereignty in Germany whatever, and indeed to the very existence of the Austrian Hapsburgs. The conclusion was inescapable. Ferdinand could not survive alone. How the neutrality of England could be kept in the face of a Spanish intervention in Germany was impossible to say; but the risk had to be taken. Spain must enter the war directly; Frederick must be stopped at his source.

Spain's decision to invade the Palatinate had been reached by the end of 1619, and a treaty formally committing her to it was signed with Ferdinand in February, 1620.[12] Technically, the Spanish commander who was to lead the invasion—Ambroglio Spinola, Europe's finest general—would fight under Imperial banners: Madrid felt it best to spare what offense it could in matters of form. Spain had no territorial aims in Germany. She fought to pacify, not to conquer. She would enter the war solely in the just cause of the Emperor, and she would withdraw when that cause had prevailed.

At the same time, Spain sent back to London its resident ambassador, Diego Sarmiento de Acuña, Count of Gondomar, after a diplomatic recall of twenty months. The resumption of his embassy was no more than a gamble against odds that peace with England could be kept despite the invasion of the Palatinate; but if any man could work the miracle, it was Gondomar. It was he who had created the Anglo-Spanish alliance.

Recent studies[13] have begun to scrape the barnacles of legend off the celebrated relationship between James and Gondomar. A scandal to contemporaries, it long outlived the protagonists, and became a caution to posterity. William Prynne noted it in his *Hidden Works of Darkness,* and John Rowland wrote at the end of the Protectorate that "Gondomor is yet fresh in the memory of many men who knew him when he lay leiger here from the King of Spain."[14] The scurrilous histories of Wilson and Weldon, which appeared in Cromwell's time,[15] perpetuated the traditional picture of "the gulling of a fool by a knave,"[16] and three centuries of scholarship have done little but embroider it.

Charming and courtly in society, poised and adroit in diplomacy, Gondomar was the model ambassador. He had made a brilliant study of King James, and slowly won his respect, confidence, and intimacy. When Gondomar first arrived at the English Court in 1613, Spanish influence was at a nadir, and Charles, the royal heir, matched to a French princess. Five years later, Spain was the pivot of English policy, Charles' bride was to be an infanta, and Gondomar was on a footing with the King of England such as few foreign diplomats had ever enjoyed with a sovereign before. In public he was accorded signal precedence over all other ambassadors at the Court; in private, free access to the King, open perusal of his correspondence, and the jesting intimacy of a close personal friend. The King and the Ambassador drank and hunted together, exchanged Latin quips and argued theology, and called themselves "the two Diegos."[17]

There was, no doubt, an element of genuine social pleasure in all this, but the relationship between James and Gondomar existed solely by light of the political interests which bound England and Spain. These, it is true, had been largely of the

Ambassador's forging, but they accorded well with James's own predilections, and would never have prospered otherwise. The peace of Christendom and the prestige of England were his standing objectives in foreign policy, and a Spanish alliance would serve them better than any other diplomatic combination. If Spain were the more imposing power of the two, she was also the more vulnerable, as her rulers, with memories of Drake and Hawkins still nightmare-fresh in their minds, were unlikely to forget. It was to be an alliance between equals: neither side need yield its other interests or allies. In this flexibility, indeed, would lie its chief value and strength.

Such an alliance must be based above all on candor, and James made this the theme of his relations with Gondomar. The King opened his dispatches to him because his intentions were wholly above board; he had nothing to hide. He demanded the same frankness in return—a demand that Gondomar, a mere emissary, must often have found difficult to meet—and tested it by regularly intercepting his correspondence. In a sporting sense, the two men must have relished the game of "candor," for it made their encounters a continual duel of wits whetted by high stakes. Indeed, in this relationship without precedent, where protocol was waived but never forgotten, and the rules were an elaborate artifice of equality, a high style was everything. What is really to the Spaniard's credit is that he could have held his own so well at close quarters with a man who could, after all, have broken his career as he would have snapped a twig.[18] Gondomar could press his intimacy with James to an extent and with an audacity that might astonish outside observers; but their dialogue was ultimately at the King's behest, by his sufferance, on his terms, and Gondomar never forgot it.

At Madrid the proposed alliance was viewed in a more negative light. It was less that England's partnership was desired than her hostility feared. The rulers of Spain knew that unless English power were neutralized, the Dutch provinces were irrecoverable; therefore, they welcomed the friendship of James, though they were no doubt embarrassed by the warmth of his embrace. Gondomar's original task had been to wean England from a French alliance, which was perforce an anti-Spanish one; he had succeeded almost too well. If the two nations were to fall out now, the rift would be all the graver for the preceding amity. There was not much hope in sending Gondomar back, but none at all in anyone else. Relations had already deteriorated under his proxy, Lafuente. The English complained of neglect and delay in the marriage talks, the Spanish of Puritan insolence and the persecution of Catholics.

Gondomar himself begged to be discharged from the embassy. He was being sent to preside at the ruin of his own work, and to bear the hatred of heretics. In a particularly baleful moment he told Ciriza, the secretary of state, that the best thing that could happen to him would be to die en route to London.[19]

Gondomar's first audience, however, on his arrival in March, 1620, was like the welcome of royalty. James sat in state on a dais, surrounded by the household and the Privy Council. He came forward and hugged the Ambassador, and "said aloud to those who were near him, that I was very like a good gentleman, a great friend of his called the Count of Gondomar; and I answered, also aloud, how glad I was to see what a resemblance he bore to the King of Great Britain, that I had formerly known, and I entreated him to tell me if he was the same person: he put his hand on his breast saying that he was the same, the very same, as I should experience, that I should see him, hear him, and touch him with my own hands."[20]

But more private talks probed the sore spots of Anglo-Spanish relations. The King was greatly disappointed that Gondomar had not brought a "final resolution" from Madrid on the marriage treaty. Digby, the principal English negotiator, had expected to leave immediately to conclude it. The English were frankly suspicious of King Philip's sincerity: "They suppose that your Majesty's intentions are to delay matters, and not content yourself with any conditions." This impression must be removed: for only if the English were firmly convinced of Spain's determination to ratify their alliance could Anglo-Spanish relations hope to survive the shock of the Palatinate. As it was, Gondomar gloomily reported, *los puritanos* throve, thirsting for war with Spain, and only James himself stood in their way. Should he come to doubt the match, the last impediment would be removed, and a rupture might not even await the invasion of the Palatinate.[21]

In the next months, the Spaniard was hard pressed by English demands for Philip's "real terms." Yet the truth was that both sides recognized how injurious excessive candor might be at this stage. Gondomar observed that whenever Digby caught a whiff of what terms Spain would demand for the security of Catholics in England, he would beg him not to push matters that could only come to pass gradually. The English were determined not to be dallied with; but what they really wanted to learn was more the spirit of Spanish intentions than the letter of their demands.[22]

Meanwhile, in Flanders, the preparations for Spinola's campaign went forward. This was a subject handled between London and Madrid with great delicacy. The Spanish did not deny what Frederick's aggression might force them to; the English gave notice what their reaction would be. Here gesture served better than argument. Roger North, one of Raleigh's old captains, put out past a lax naval guard at Plymouth for Guiana at the end of April; Gondomar called down fury for this breach of the line, and James blandly disavowed the expedition; but the ships were at sea. In July a small force of English mercenaries led by Sir Horace Vere crossed to Germany to help garrison the Palatinate; nominally volunteers and under Frederick's command, they tokened English presence on the Continent: James paid them, and Vere reported to him every week. Finally, and most forcibly, James ordered the long-projected, long-delayed expedition of Sir Robert Mansell against the Barbary pirates to be readied for sailing. In a vague and dilatory way, the English and Spanish governments had for several years discussed a joint naval attack against these pirates, who preyed on the shipping of the western Mediterranean, and the waxing or waning of this project was at any given moment a tolerable index of the state of Anglo-Spanish amity. Now James served peremptory notice on Madrid that his fleet was on its way. The Spanish were aghast. In the state of Spain's naval preparedness such a fleet could bombard her coasts at will; to acquiesce to James's demand was to give carte blanche to the English for another Cadiz.[23] Despite Gondomar's frantic efforts to stop it, the fleet sailed September 8. By that date in the year it was normally impractical for any voyage to set out, and the Spanish had begun to hope for luck when, in midautumn, Mansell suddenly appeared, leaving them to simulate courtesy as best they could.[24] His movements were uniformly correct and peaceable, but in a wider sense the Spaniards had good cause for alarm: for beyond either the avowed purpose of the mission or the implied threat behind it, it marked historically the first tentative assertion of English naval presence in the Mediterranean.[25]

But playing cat-and-mouse with Spain did not exhaust James's diplomatic resource. With or without Madrid, he was determined to assert his interest in Germany, spread his intention to assist Frederick in case of attack, and sound for possible allies to support the calling of a Diet of the Empire to deal with Bohemia. It was primarily for this latter end that he dispatched two envoys, Sir Edward Conway and Sir Richard Weston, on a long tour of German states in the summer of 1620. The embassy was a comic disaster. Street satire greeted their attempts to build a peace party. The princes of Germany all deplored the war and assiduously armed for it; the Duke of Saxony, whom James had most hoped in, made virtual hostages of the envoys, and rummaged their trunks for gold. At last reaching Frederick, they were dining with him when Prague fell, and had to flee for their lives.[26]

As an eleventh-hour peace effort, the embassy of Conway and Weston was thus a total failure; as a fact-finding mission, almost wholly negative. English influence alone could accomplish nothing: that much was finally clear. As a combatant, James might still be reckonable; as a peacemaker, he spoke calm to a whirlwind. England was thrown back with redoubled dependence upon her ally. Germany could not save herself, nor England save her, nor France: Spain remained the key.

Then, on the next to last day of August, after an ominous week of feints and marches along the Rhine, Ambroglio Spinola hurled a force of twenty-four thousand men into the Rhenish Palatinate.

Report of the invasion produced a commotion in London, but King James, still on his annual summer progress, received the news with calm. He continued the wonted circuit of his country estates; from Wanstead to Havering, from Havering to Theobalds, and a week later to Hampton Court. Badgering him at every step was Frederick's desperate envoy, Achatius von Dohna, who, at last given audience, burst out theatrically that he did not know whether his master had at that hour a single foot of land left in the Palatinate. But James's only concrete reply was to send a courier to Frederick to inquire if he were now willing to come to terms with the Emperor.[27]

The King's reaction was that of a man who has so long fore-
seen calamity that he is almost relieved to see it come. His next
move was clear, however, and no longer to be delayed. Gondomar was summoned to Hampton Court. James greeted him with
a tirade. For months, he raged, the Spanish had led him to believe that Spinola was bound for Bohemia, not the Palatinate.[28]
Did they think he would swallow this perfidy? He was not going
to allow his children to perish or his religion to be ridden under,
whatever the cost.

James had overplayed his hand. Gondomar, wrapped in
offended grandeur, denied coldly that he or his government had
ever guaranteed the Palatinate. Quite the contrary, he had
warned James, and repeatedly, that his master was prepared to
stake all on the recovery of Bohemia.

The King was unable to deny this. Pressing his advantage,
Gondomar demanded, and got, a letter of retraction confessing
that Spain had "never affoorded other or better hope" for the
Palatinate, Frederick persisting in his aggression.[29] It was a triumph of coolness and nerve, but James played the next round
better. When he summoned the Ambassador again, it was to
stonily inform him that he had just issued a public declaration
pledging to go to war for the Palatinate in the spring if diplomacy had not restored it by then.[30]

The declaration uncapped a long-pent burst of patriotic joy.
James's policy of neutrality in Germany and alliance with Spain
was wholly unintelligible to the great mass of his countrymen,
for whom Frederick's cause was a glorious adventure and Spain
the inveterate national enemy. His own ambassadors complained
of public ridicule: Trumbull in Flanders wrote that he was
"looked upon lyke an owle, [and] interro[g]ated upon such
termes . . . as I am compelled to hyde my head, and . . . dare not
appear in the streets."[31] Now at last the King had thrown off his
long lethargy and taken manly action. "There was never so ioyfull a Courte here as this Declaration hath made," wrote Sir
Benjamin Rudyard. "I see mens hartes risen into theyre faces."
James himself, the long strain of repressing his subjects' zeal re-
laxed, entered into the spirit of the occasion, and spoke ebul-
liently of leading his own armies.[32]

"The King has come round now," remarked Sir Robert Naunton, one of the more aggressively "Protestant" of the councillors,

with quiet satisfaction.[33] But Naunton was wrong. If the King had moved at all, it was straight along the same path. The declaration had been logically dictated by events; for as North's voyage, Vere's levy, and Mansell's fleet had kept measure to Spain's invasion buildup in Flanders, so now the invasion itself called for a stronger equivalent from England. James could not well have responded with less, but he refused to do more. He remained as aloof as ever from Bohemia; and if he were committed now to defend the Palatinate, the door to negotiation was still pointedly open. Gondomar considered James's reaction quite moderate; it was no more, after all, than what the King had publicly advertised all summer through Conway and Weston, and far less than had been originally feared in Madrid. Indeed, no sooner was diplomatic ritual decently complete, than James privately reassured the Ambassador that if Spain were ready to rescind her conquests upon a settlement in Bohemia, the Anglo-Spanish alliance need suffer no lasting impediment from the episode on the Rhine.[34]

The declaration, however, stood before the world, an irrevocable step, a commitment of honor. Nor did James, in soothing the Spaniards, wish to blunt his threat. For Spain to cease to believe either in England's desire for the alliance or her firm resolve to abandon it unless her vital interests were respected, would be equally fatal for James.

It was not enough, however, to make a declaration; it was necessary to take the steps that would make it credible as well. A decision to act was, perforce, a decision to arm. That meant money, and money meant a Parliament. At the beginning of October, therefore, James ordered his lord chancellor, Francis Bacon, to lay plans for a Parliament quietly with a commission of judges consisting of two chief justices, Henry Hobart and Henry Montague, Sir Edward Coke, and Ranulph Crew, Speaker of the preceding Parliament.[35]

Only inescapable necessity could have brought the King to call Parliament again. He had been more than six years without one and, despite continual financial stringency, there had been no indication that he intended to call one in the foreseeable future. A new Parliament meant another tug of war with the prerogative; and in this dangerous game the Crown, while not yet seriously worsted, had already reached a point at which, apparently, grants of supply could be had only by concessions of power. And if there was one sure thread of principle in the mind of James, one fixed resolve in his politics, it was not to yield one jot of the full sovereignty that had descended to him with the crown of England.

But even now, James had not yet fully resolved to call, or perhaps reconciled himself to calling, a Parliament. While Bacon's commission sat, a benevolence for the Palatinate was launched with loud publicity. Prince Charles subscribed ten thousand pounds and the privy councillors followed suit. A swift yield of nearly thirty thousand pounds from such redundant sources tricked out the campaign with a gaudy illusion of enthusiasm. It was expected that every earl would contribute one thousand pounds, each bishop and baron, five hundred pounds; and royal pursuivants dutifully scoured the country, pricking sheriffs and assigning muster calls among the recalcitrant gentry.[36]

The Palatine's needs were indeed exigent, and parliament money would take long both to grant and collect: to that extent the benevolence was plausible. But it was widely interpreted in the country as an attempt to forestall the calling of Parliament, and perhaps a precedent for its quiet demise. It was feared that soon "all men shalbe rated and pay by way of subsidie as yf it were don by parliament, and those that refuse their names to be certified, that order may be taken with them." "This," reported John Chamberlain, the old London gossip, "hath quite put downe the speach of a parliament for the present, and perhaps the name of yt for hereafter." [37]

If such were the King's intentions, his subjects shut an iron door on them. Letters of apology, pleas of poverty, polite refusals piled up in the Privy Council registers.[38] The entire campaign, outside London, realized the sum of six thousand pounds.[39] The country was determined to force a Parliament.[40] James made a flying trip to London on All Souls' Day, but left still undecided, his ministers following him into the country. At noon on November 3, "never a Lord of the Council could say we should have a parliament, but after a long debate with the King, it was concluded upon before night, and the writs are now writing."[41]

Bacon's commission was already well into its work. Its principal tasks were to draft a proclamation for the Parliament, to place councillors, courtiers, and well-disposed country gentlemen in it, and to frame some good "commonwealth bills" to address the problems and grievances of the kingdom. These, said Bacon, must be "not wooing bills to make the King and his graces cheap, but good matter to set the Parliament on work, that an empty stomach do not feed upon humour."[42]

Bacon, with his omnibus mind, had a remarkably clear and broad overview of the problems of governing England. Nothing escaped his interest, and his papers are a kind of *catalogue raisonné* of Stuart administration. The cloth trade must be given more encouragement, he noted, old draperies as well as new. The supply of corn should be regulated. The outflow of specie must be checked. There was not enough ordnance and gunpowder on hand, the castles of the realm were in disrepair. The abuses of paid informers were a source of discontent. Reforms were wanted in Ireland. There were few matters the Parliament of 1621 would find to complain of which had not already been remarked by Bacon.[43]

Bacon was particularly sensitive to the defects of justice. His lifelong dream was a general codification of the laws. Antiquated statutes so overlay and contradicted one another, he complained, that "our laws endure the torment of Mezentius: the living die in the arms of the dead." From this root problem grew the whole malefic labyrinth of legal practice, insecure titles, interminable suits, a vast officialdom. The uncertainty of the law too often left justice to the judges' discretion, and bloated the dockets of equity. The Lord Chancellor was a sharp critic of his own court. In his inaugural address he spoke bitingly of the "excess or tumour" of Chancery. Altogether too many suits determinable at the common law were brought to it, too many specious appeals from other courts were accepted by it, too many injunctions against normal process issued from it. The Chancery, he lectured his colleagues and subordinates, was ordained to supplement the law, not to supplant it.[44]

But reform itself was not Bacon's forte. Years passed, the paper projects came and went, and things remained pretty much the same. The Chancellor's originally clear perception of the abuses in his court was gradually blurred by identification, and an unmistakeable note of bureaucratic complacency crept into his attitude. Presented now with the opportunity of making a grand review of the grievances of the kingdom, he found remarkably little to suggest. His bills of grace were a lusterless lot, little differing from those of 1614 or even 1610; and of the "good commonwealth bills" of which he spoke, no written record remains.[45] In fact, the only councillor to present a genuine program of reform to the House of Commons in 1621 was Sir Lionel Cranfield, the master of the wards. To Cranfield, reform was urgent; to Bacon, the Stuart bureaucracy, of which he had become so wholly a part, was fundamentally sound; and the changes he envisioned for it were the gradual renovations one makes in any good, well-founded house. Significantly, he and Cranfield were barely on speaking terms by the autumn of 1620,[46] and Cranfield's work appears from all internal evidence[47] to have been entirely his own.

In immediate terms, however, it was plain enough what the great issue of the Parliament would be. The whole land cried a single grievance: the abuse of patents. And to this question Bacon and his commission bent their chief study.

Patents were, in the broadest sense, grants or commissions to private persons conferring upon them certain privileges, exemptions, or delegated powers. Most of them involved control of a particular trade or industrial process; these were known as "monopolies." Other kinds were designed to promote or execute certain governmental functions. Historically, the patent system represents a stage in the growth of the modern state. The patents of monopoly enabled the government to exercise a closer surveillance of the economy, while those granted for administrative purposes extended central authority into the lairs of local goverment.

Of more concrete interest, however, was the monetary potential of the patents, whether in the profits of a protected industry or the proceeds from licenses sold to country inns and alehouses. Some, indeed, had no other end in view, such as the one for uncovering defective land titles that might be reclaimed by the Crown ("concealments"), or those that had created the new subnobility of baronets. And on the other side of the ledger, patents were a costless way of rewarding courtiers for their good service, or at any rate good connections. To the chronically insolvent Stuart exchequer, no source of revenue, or dam for expenses, was to be despised.

Naturally, the system was wide open to abuse. It soon became

more or less an appendage of patronage. Many monopolies had
nothing more to recommend them than their patentees' desire
to be rid of competitors; and the administrative patents, with no
systematic supervision from above, tended to degenerate into
mere licensed freebooting. The Privy Council was inundated
with complaints. The councillors duly studied them, made
reports to each other, and did nothing.[48] The most notorious of
the patents had been sponsored by the Marquis of Buckingham,
and rash would be the man who made an enemy of the royal
favorite. Nor were the councillors themselves wholly guiltless.
Bacon, and most of the other high legal officials of the Crown as
well, had at one time or another taken part in the drafting or
approving of patents that, in operation, reflected very dubiously
on their devisers. The situation was hopelessly inbred, and it was
clear that only a violent external stimulus could alter it.[49]

That stimulus was the advent of Parliament. To allow the
House of Commons to pounce on a wholly unrectified scandal of
such proportions was to invite serious trouble from the outset.
The government was spurred to action at last. Bacon's commission undertook an exhaustive review of the patents. His recom-
mendations were balanced and sensible. To take all objection-
able patents "away now in a blaze will give more scandal that
such things were granted, than cause thanks that they be now
revoked," he wrote. Moreover, to rescind them all by Act of
Council would bring "a flood of suitors" to Court seeking compensation, whereas to do so in Parliament would annul them
without redress. Let, therefore, "some grave and discreet gentlemen of the country" make a "modest motion" in the Commons
against certain patents, and the King might then give them his
assent.

But the main point was to keep the initiative against the patents in Crown hands at all times. This would be possible only if
that initiative were decisively undertaken before Parliament met.
The most noxious patents must be withdrawn at once, without
shuffling but without ceremony either, as if the Council merely
kept its "wonted centinel" over the well-being of the kingdom,
and "thought not of a Parliament." An occasion might be made
of revising the King's "Book of Bounty," a proclamation of 1610
against monopolies, or the recent case of Sir Henry Yelverton,
the attorney general, committed to the Tower for surreption in

drafting a patent for the city of London.[50] If the Council could draw the fangs of the issue now, an ideal result might be hoped for: revocation of the worst patents would deflect attention from the government, yet leave popular indignation scope to work itself off against the patentees themselves.[51]

But Bacon's plan faced a very problematic obstacle: Buckingham. The Chancellor, who had been the young man's political mentor since his first rise to favor, wrote him privately. His brother Edward's patent of alehouse recognizances, he told him, and Sir Giles Mompesson's patent for inns, "are more rumoured, both by the vulgar and by the gentlemen, yea and by the Judges themselves, than any other patents at this day. Therefore," he continued,

> I thought it appertained to the singular love and affection which I bear you, upon so many obligations, to wish and advise, that your Lordship (whom God hath made in all things so fit to be beloved) would put off the envy of these things (which I think in themselves bear no great fruit), and rather take the thanks for ceasing them, than the note for maintaining them.[52]

Buckingham refused. Should he quail at a Parliament, and turn coward to his friends and family at the monitions of a graybeard tutor? At that very moment, he was engaged in promoting yet another patent for his younger brother, Kit Villiers, to establish an office "for the sole engrossing of wills in the prerogative court of Canterbury." Bacon himself certified this patent, which passed the royal seal on December 30, along with Sir Robert Naunton and Sir Henry Montague, now Viscount Mandeville. The only adjustment he made in it was to exempt the smaller diocesan courts of Canterbury from its jurisdiction.[53]

What Bacon really thought of this patent one cannot say; he was merely asked for an opinion on its legality, not a conjecture on its probable outcome in practice. Certainly he must have regretted the timing. But it should be borne in mind that neither Bacon nor anyone else dreamed of abandoning the patent system as such. It was a question of gleaning a few bad apples from the bushel, not giving up the whole orchard.[54]

When Bacon presented the report of his commission's work to a full-dress Council meeting in mid-December, he stood by his opinion, and argued for an at least token revocation of patents. These were dangerous matters, he warned, to allow a Parliament to meddle with; and at the least it would divert men from "the main errand." Others objected that it was already too late to make any reform credible. To act now, "in the Calends of a Parliament," would seem a mere sop to public opinion. Would anyone believe that the patents would not return as soon as the session was over?[55]

The objection was cogent, but the debate itself was merely academic. Buckingham's veto had already settled the issue. James came to the meeting, but sat silent, listening without comment. If the King gave no sign, who would risk incurring the displeasure of the Marquis? No decision was come to, no strategy agreed; the bomb was left to tick away, the dust to settle where it would.

Bacon made a final effort with Buckingham. He had yielded to the arguments of his fellow councillors, he said; yet still he remained "a little doubtful" about the patents, and suggested "that if way be given . . . to the taking away of some of them, it will sort to your honour."[56] Whether this wistful appeal ever received a reply we do not know.

Yet it is questionable how far Bacon himself was really alarmed. The intransigence of the Marquis would certainly make things more difficult. But there was no indication that Bacon's defeat on this point led him to despair of prospects for the Parliament in general. He continued busy about it, watching election results, sketching bills, anticipating grievances, and at the end of his labors, heaved a small sigh of contentment: "Methinks there is a middle thing between art and chance: I think they call it providence, or some such thing; which good servants owe to their sovereign, specially in cases of importance and straits of occasions."[57]

That Bacon's preparation for the Parliament of 1621 was to prove wholly inadequate is less to our point than that he considered it, emasculated as it was, a satisfactory piece of work. The discrepancy lies not in negligence, but in Bacon's very notion of what a Parliament was.

Bacon was the last of the great statesmen reared under Elizabeth, and his conception of Parliament remained essentially that of a Tudor bureaucrat. Parliament's function was to point out popular grievances; it was the Crown's part to redress them. Parliament might suggest, might initiate reforms, but it was the Council, the day-to-day administration of the kingdom, that would have to carry them out. Therefore, for the government to present a "program" in Parliament, except insofar as it was found convenient to embody conciliar reforms in statute, or to keep the Commons out of mischief, was a reversal of logical procedure. One may fault Bacon for being blind to the extent of abuses in the government and for seriously underestimating the intensity of grievance in the country; one may perhaps fault him as well for failing to perceive that a dose of old Tudor nostrums—a few bills of grace, a few solemn promises, and a fine speech from the throne —would no longer go very far with the House of Commons. But he can hardly be blamed, on his own terms, for not coming to Parliament with a root-and-branch program of reform.

Bacon, unlike his master, had no antipathy to parliaments. James had found them at his accession as an institution he was "obliged to put up with," but Bacon, like any native Englishman, accepted them as a normal and necessary part of the state; he even liked to think of himself, a bit patronizingly, as "a good parliament man."[58] To James Parliament was an uncertain threat; it had no real place in his political philosophy. Such fears were wholly foreign to Bacon. If Parliament proved refractory, or attempted to exceed its powers—a chronic habit, and one certainly not new to the present reign—it was to be gently but firmly reproved and the principal offenders, if necessary, punished. But no matter what its pretensions, it could never cause serious harm: its power was inherently limited. It might prove inconvenient, but it could never threaten the Crown. The prerogative of the King was absolute and inalienable: it could neither be given nor taken away by any power on earth.

In this, Bacon was certainly less perceptive than James. The King, though his view of prerogative was a far more exalted one than his Chancellor's, had a very lively sense of its vulnerability. *Sub specie aeternitatis*, of course, the powers of a king were immutable; but in earthly practice they were subject, like everything else, to the vicissitudes of the temporal: assassinations, conquests, revolutions, and the insidious encroachments of aristocracy or "popularity."

Yet James himself, by his failure to act on the patents, did more to invite "a maine attack" on the prerogative in Parliament than anyone else. His was the authority that had granted them, his the only one that could revoke them. Doubtless he was ill-informed; it is clear, from his repeated exclamations of surprise later on that he was taken unawares by the extent of the monopoly scandal. Some complaints did reach him,[59] but most died in the Council: Buckingham barred the way to the throne. In any event James was not overscrupulous about how his servants made their fortunes, nor very attentive to the tedium of domestic affairs in general. Administration bored and rather bewildered him. He had none of his predecessor's penny zeal, and in matters of the heart he knew no stint. "Christ had his John," the King summed up his weakness, "and I have my George."

As it was, James seemed well pleased with Bacon's work. The Chancellor became, in January, 1621, Viscount St. Albans, at a ceremony of great splendor attended, in a rare mark of favor, by the King himself.[60] At the ripeness of sixty, Bacon was a serene and happy man. Statesman, jurist, philosopher, historian, moralist, the best and busiest mind of his age, he was at the summit of his fame and worldly fortune. No hero of Attic tragedy was ever more primed for a fall.

The summoning of Parliament released a wave of anti-Spanish sentiment in the country; memories of 'eighty-eight mingled with indignation over the Palatinate, renewed instincts of Elizabethan rapine with relief at the King's final waking from his Spanish trance. From sermons in the pulpit to catcalls in the street, a unanimous opinion expressed itself, the same in substance at every level of sophistication: imperial Spain and antichrist Rome had planned together the conquest of the world, and England's answer must be to drive the priests back to their pope, and Spain home to her ports.

The most gifted of a spate of pamphleteers was the Norwich divine Thomas Scott, who bearded the Spanish Council of State in a brilliant satire called *Vox Populi,* which purported to be a transcript of its proceedings on the eve of Gondomar's departure for England. The Ambassador was limned with special verve. He painted an England "effeminated by peace and luxury," a Court that "gaped wide for Spanish gould," and a King who, though otherwise "one of the most accomplisht princes that ever raign'd, extreamly hunts after peace, and so affects the true name of a peacemaker, as that for it he will doe or suffer any thing." A councillor objects that a Parliament may still rally the land: "A Parliament! (sayes the Embassadour) nay, therein lies one of the chieftest services I have done, in working such a dislike between the King and the lower house, . . . as that the King will never endure Parliament again but rather suffer absolute want, than receive conditional relief from his subjects."[61] James was enraged at the tract, and Naunton's cosecretary, Sir George Calvert, added a manhunt for its author to his many duties, while Sir Walter Aston, in Madrid, transmitted formal apologies to the Spanish.[62]

Gondomar himself bore a difficult time with aplomb. He penned descriptions of the droller efforts of Puritan draftsmanship to Ciriza, and said he could send an armload of seditious prints to Madrid every day if he had a courier.[63] At Court he still met open hostility, though the King was once again gracious. One day at Whitehall pictures of Henry VIII triumphing over the Spanish at Kinsale, which decorated one of the galleries, were found mutilated. Even James joined the general uproar. Gondomar replied simply that he knew of no Spaniard cowardly enough to fight with a picture.[64]

At the end of November, however, tidings of disaster arrived from Brussels. The Bohemian army had been utterly routed on the heights before Prague, and Frederick himself, with his wife and infant family, had fled a fugitive, no one knew whither.

James received the news at Royston without marked emotion, but in London it provoked incredulity and despair. The air, reported the Flemish agent Van Male, is full of "soupirs lamentations [et] exclamations contre les Catholiques avec mille livretz séditieux qui s'impriment à toute heure . . . ."[65] A cloaked informant warned Gondomar of a plot against his life the day the news of Prague arrived, and the Ambassador sat up armed all night with his family and servants. The next day, Advent Sunday, a guard of 300 men was sent to his house in Holborn. In the streets his litter was pelted with garbage, and the apprentices yelled after him, "There goes the devil in a dungcart!"[66]

As Christmas approached, the anti-Spanish sermons multiplied in number and violence, until, in mid-December, the Bishop of London ordered his clergy by the King's command to cease all reference to Spain or any other "matter of state" in their preaching. The Bishop's injunction had little effect; that Sunday

the Paul's Cross preacher "spake very freely" about Prince
Charles's impending marriage on the text, "thou shalt not plow
with an ox and an ass." Not even imprisonment spiked the
tongues of London pastors.[67]

The result of this ferment was the "Proclamation Against Excess of Lavish Speech of Matters of State," which was published
the day before Christmas. In it the King issued strict warning to
his "loving subjects . . . from the highest to the lowest to take
heed how they intermeddle by pen or speech with causes of state
and secrets of empire either at home or abroad."[68] Whig historians considered this proclamation a classic example of James's bad
public relations, coming as it did on the eve of a Parliament, but
to the King and his councillors it was a serious cautionary step
against an outbreak of public disorder. Bacon wrote it, and his
draft was approved without alteration. The judicious Salvetti,
the Florentine resident in London, applauded its appearance:
"It cannot," he wrote, "but have the best effects: beside somewhat restraining the people . . . it will, above all, set limits to the
MPs, who perhaps were once more in the mood of talking too
much and making unpleasant requests, as is their bad habit."[69]

Members for Parliament were now being chosen, and the heat
of local election contests spread London's excitement into the
countryside. James watched the weekly trickle of returns closely;
he said that when he knew the men and the elections he would
guess at the success of the Parliament.[70] The "prognosticks," confessed Bacon, "are not so good as I expected."[71] Calamity abroad
and a trade depression at home had created a radical climate, and
James seemed about to get his fill of "wrangling lawyers" in the
Parliament.[72]

The nature of the elections, of course, varied greatly according
to the custom of the constituency and the sway of local magnates;
county and freehold elections might be fiercely waged, while
those in boroughs controlled by a great lord or a town corpora-
tion, or beholden economically to the government, were often
decided at the stroke of a pen. At the latter extreme, for example,
were the two seats at St. Albans, where Bacon was high steward
and had a country estate. The mayor of the town journeyed to
London "to knowe the Lord Chancellors pleasure who should
be Burgesses." Bacon gave him the names of two Court-affiliated
lawyers, Thomas Richardson, whom he also chose to be Speaker

of the House of Commons, and Robert Shute. Not only did neither candidate ever visit the town, but upon their election, the mayor and chamberlain were obliged to trek to London once again to swear them.[73]

Still, nothing was ever certain where the commonalty had a voice, as at Sandwich—normally a safe admiralty borough—where Sir Edwin Sandys "interloped" in 1621. Sir Edwin was perhaps the most exemplary of that generation of "parliament men" whose public lives spanned the crucial decades between the Armada and 1629.[74] To James he was a pariah. He had been hailed before the Council to explain his conduct in the Addled Parliament, and when, a few months before contesting Sandwich, he was running for reelection as treasurer of the Virginia Company, the King had intervened personally against him. "Choose the devil if you will," he told the directors, "but not Sir Edwin Sandys."[75] The electors of Sandwich risked the choice, however, after a vigorous canvass by Sandys, who "uttered his affections to the place" and promised to plead the case of its impoverished port against the great London merchants in Parliament. The actual poll was a tumult. The frightened mayor tried desperately to put over the government nominees, but was shouted down by the voters who, according to an unfriendly witness, "raved of breach of liberties."[76]

Nor was a seat at the disposal of the "government" always at the disposal of the Crown. Edward Lord Zouch, who, as lord warden of the Cinque Ports, controlled a number of seats, resisted attempts from Whitehall to encroach on what he considered a power perquisite of his own office. It was thought best not to press the question. "The King would have been glad to have the men whom he recommended placed," wrote Buckingham to Zouch, "but will be content with your Lordship's appointments, not doubting that you will choose persons serviceable to his Majesty."[77]

The unpopularity of the government was reflected in its attempts to place privy councillors in the House of Commons. All eight of the commoners on the Council were instructed to stand: there had never been more than four at any one time in James's previous Parliaments, and bitter experience had proved their insufficiency. One councillor, the old courtier-poet Fulke Greville, had enough influence of his own in Warwickshire to secure one of the prestigious county seats. But Secretary Calvert pulled through in Yorkshire only thanks to the blatant pressure of the locally powerful Wentworths, and Sir Thomas Edmondes and Sir Julius Caesar, treasurer of the household and master of the rolls, respectively, were rejected outright in Middlesex. Henry Cary was returned for Hertford by grace of the Earl of Salisbury. Only three councillors therefore were able to win county seats; the rest, including Edmondes and Caesar, found safe boroughs instead. As a final insult, Sir Henry Yelverton, who still lay in the Tower, was returned unsolicited by the electors of Northampton. Yelverton had ostensibly been committed for malfeasance, but the real reason was widely guessed: his stubborn opposition to Buckingham.[78]

The meeting of Parliament in 1621 was bound up with the hopes and fears of the entire politically conscious public in England to an extent perhaps unique in the nation's history. The international situation was the gravest of a century. England herself was not yet directly menaced, as in 1588, but the very existence of the Reformed faith seemed in dire jeopardy. In the east and west of Germany it was now under direct military attack. The United Provinces were protected by an uneasy truce whose expiration date was only three months away. In France, a generation's experiment in toleration was rapidly failing, and the government of Louis XIII was preparing a campaign of reduction and—who could tell?—perhaps extermination against the Huguenot minority. In Switzerland the Protestant cantons were being overwhelmed by Spanish armies. And what Providence would exempt England from the fate of all Protestant Europe if she continued to lie supine and inactive? Indeed, was not an unseen army of priests already preparing by internal subversion the day when the Antichrist should once again establish his dominion in England?

The opening of Parliament, once postponed by an unexpected French embassy and a second time by the King's gout, came finally on Tuesday, January 30.[79] Early on the crowds began to line the short few hundred yards from Whitehall to Westminster. Old John Chamberlain said he had never seen more people. Two scaffolds collapsed under the crush. At eleven o'clock the King emerged on horseback, emblemed with his sovereignty, a great crown of state on his head, and all the Lords spiritual and temporal and all the justices of the realm about him. The slow procession began with drums and fifes beating the march. James was "very cherefull all the way," chatting with his peers, and calling out to the crowds, "God bless ye! God bless ye!" At Westminster Abbey, Lancelot Andrewes preached. Meanwhile, the Duke of Lennox, lord steward of the household, appeared before the members of the Lower House, who waited in the Court of Requests, and administered the oaths of supremacy and allegiance, according to the Act of 1563. After having sworn about sixty men, he deputed some forty of them to swear the rest. As soon as sworn, the MPs went to the Lords' Chamber, where the Parliament was formally to be opened. The space allotted the Commons behind the bar of the Upper House was wholly inadequate to their number, and they were normally obliged to compete with the crowds in the street as well: in 1604 and 1614 they had found their places taken by spectators who managed to slip or storm in in the general crush of entry.[80] But this time things were better run: sergeants stood ready at the doors to expel all outsiders.

At three o'clock the royal procession left the Abbey and crossed the Old Palace Yard to the Lords' Chamber, where the House of Commons was now assembled. The Prince appeared first, wearing a coronet, and beside him walked the Marquis of Buckingham. Then came the earls of England,[81] their heads uncovered, Rutland bearing the Cap of Maintenance and Cumberland the Sword, Arundel and Oxford side by side immediately before the King. James was borne in a chair under a high canopy, "beeing so weake in his leggs and feet," reported Chamberlain, "that yt is doubted he will find little use in them hereafter." Baron Digby, the vice chamberlain, carried the royal train, and behind him came again the array of prelates, justices, and lesser peers. At the door of the Lords' Chamber the Prince took his father's crown in his hands and bore it aloft through the entry. James was set down in the accustomed place at the head of the hall, with the Prince at his left hand and the Lord Chancellor on his right. The final order of persons and places complete, and "silence being made," the King began his speech.[82]

James had prepared his address with great care. It was not merely a directive to action, but a concise statement of his constitutional views and a kind of apologia for the reign. As such it is one of the most characteristic and interesting of his mature writings.

The King began with a long introduction in which a strain of bitterness was immediately apparent. He had given his subjects, he said, "a true mirror" of his mind and heart, especially those of the House of Commons; but some, "through a spice of envy," had turned all his speaking back "like spittle against the wind upon mine own face." Therefore, he promised, "I mean never to weary myself nor you with such long tedious discourses [as] I have done heretofore." A strange prologue, certainly; but James was a man in whom emotions rose easily to the surface. Face to face with his adversaries after seven years, he could not keep them wholly back.

James now passed on to a consideration of the general nature of Parliament. Parliaments, however called, wherever found, were "nothing else but the head that calls the body together," that is, an emanation of sovereignty. The function of Parliament was given in the writ of summons, *"ad deliberandum et consultandum de rebus arduis et magnis nos et regnem nostrum tangentibus,* to advise and deliberate with the king upon the high and urgent affairs of the kingdom"; or, more plainly, "to give your king your best advice in such errands as he shall crave of you, either in things proper to yourselves or in such other things as it shall please the king to ask." Things proper to parliaments were the enacting of laws, the reporting of grievances, and the granting of supply. On the first point James was graphically explicit. Parliament was to pass the laws the king called for; of its own it had no legislative right. The king was the "maker" of the laws; "ye are the advisers, councillors, and confirmers of them."

The second office of a Parliament was to inform the king of the state of the realm, it having the best knowledge of "the particular estate of the several countries." Yet here too it was merely limited to pointing out defects and abuses; it was the king's part to remedy them.

Lastly there was supply, and James was "not ashamed to speak it, that all People owe a kind of Tribute to their Kings, by way of Thankfulness to him for his Love to them." But at this point he proceeded no further into that tender subject.

The King then turned to the reasons for the present Parliament. His first words were addressed to the bishops. For religion no new legislation was needed: "God be thanked we have laws enough so that the true intent of them [be] followed." It was in the execution of those laws, and the propagation of the faith generally, that zeal was wanting: "If our Church were as busy to persuade the right way as the bold Jesuits and puritans and other sectaries are to supplant and pervert, we should not have so many go astray on both sides." God's work, James warned, must not be done negligently. This work was not the making of martyrs, "as papists and puritans think." "I mean not to compel mens consciences," said James, "for that I ever protested against." Only God could ultimately instill faith; but His laws were not to be flouted, and if men could not be forced to belief, they must at least be kept to obedience.

Here was the essence of James's latitudinarian faith, the argument against fanatics of whatever persuasion—and James was personally as far from Geneva as he was from Rome—who would "compel men's consciences." His present meaning was clear. Parliament was not to meddle with religion. There were laws enough. Those laws required conformity to the outward dignity of the Erastian church; if its ministry failed, force could go no further.

With a skillful elision, James moved from religion to politics. Some had intimated that because of the Spanish match he would "grow cold in religion and suffer the papists to triumph over us." The King reminded Parliament of his long pamphlet war with the Jesuit Bellarmine, and how for the forwardness of his faith he had "been a martyr . . . in the mouths of many idle fellows." If he did not marry his only son for the glory of God and the furtherance of religion, then, said James, "I am not worthy to be your king." And should any papist turn "insolent" in expectation of the marriage, he would soon be set to rights.

Here James walked on narrow ground. If the laws against Catholics had lapsed, it was not the bishops' fault. James had always thought them too harsh; they could make only hypocrites and desperate men. Never enforced very systematically as a result, under pressure from Gondomar they had been virtually dispensed, and what the Spanish would ultimately demand was nothing less than complete tolerance, ratified by Parliament. Far from that, the King could at best hope to bluster the zealots at

Westminster into relative quiescence. Ground between these two extremes, he could only make his promises as vague as possible. But the immediate problem was Parliament, for any attempt in the Commons to revive the anti-Catholic statutes would gravely embarrass his entire diplomacy.

Finally, James came to supply. No king had ever demanded—or received—less from his subjects: in eighteen years he had had only six subsidies and four fifteenths, and not a penny in the last ten. Queen Elizabeth might nearly have spent such a sum in a year during the Irish troubles.[83] "I will not say I have governed so well as she did, but I may say that we have had as much peace in our time as she in hers." If that were a fault—here a hit at the war party—"I pray you pardon me; but I ever took it as an honor unto me to be a peaceable king, that everyone might live quietly under his own vine and fig tree." But now he must ask relief from his subjects: "I have labored as a woman in travail, not ten months but ten years . . . and therefore [am] now full Time to come to be delivered of my Wants."

Beyond the debts of the Crown, however, there was, as all men knew, one great urgency that had brought this Parliament together: the state of the Palatinate, that "miserable spectacle that no man can look upon without a weeping eye." James sketched the background of the invasion rapidly—the original quarrel, his attempts at mediation, Frederick's precipitate acceptance of the Bohemian throne. He would give his son-in-law the advice he had asked but never waited for: Rebellion against established thrones on the pretext of religion he left to the Jesuits and the devil, "from whence it came"; for his own part, he declined to dispute kingships and "toss up and down crowns like tennis balls." Yet he was bound by blood to defend the Palatinate, and with blood he would, if other means should fail him. Already, however, he had spent, in embassies and arms, more than £200,-000, "And now"—suddenly James was bitter again—"I am to provide for wars . . . and nothing can be expected of you *without begging as a man would beg an alms* [italics mine]." But he quickly recovered. If his subjects would give him the means, he would maintain English honor. "And now if we could all speak at once and all people hear at once, I persuade myself I should read and hear from all their tongues one general acclamation. . . ."

This was the crest of the speech. On the downward slope, James picked up justice and trade. Let those with grievances speak: "I have chosen Judges of Learning and Integrity, the best I could find: if they prove unjust, I will not spare them." The King noticed a "want of money" in the realm—the beginning of the long trade crisis of the 1620s—and attributed it to an unfavorable balance of trade. Some, he knew, would blame it on his excessive bounty. In previous parliaments men had been bold enough to say that they would not stint their giving if they could believe their money would reach the King's pocket. It was true, he confessed, that he had been abused; but a thorough reform of the household had been begun—figures were exhibited—and the Court had learned now that "every day was not to be a Christmas." Others complained of monopolies, and "it may be, I have in some Grants hurt myself, and in others my Subjects." If he were rightly informed, he would give speedy redress, as befit a just king. But, he warned, men were not to forget the *raison d'être* of the session, and "hunt after Grievances." Those who trenched on affairs of state, or tried to breed distrust between king and people, could expect their desserts. James continued:

> I know that this Parliament hath been of great Expectation, and so was that at my first coming. Then I knew not the Laws and Customs of this Land. I was led by the old Counsellors that I found, which the old Queen had left; and, it may be, there was a misleading and Misunderstanding between us, which bred an Abruption. And at the last Parliament there came up a strange kind of Beast called Undertakers (a Name which in Nature I abhor) which caused a Dissolution. Now you have that Advantage, that I call you out of my free Motion; and my Trust is in your good Offices, for the good of my Estate, even all and every one of you.[84]

With a brief peroration, the King ended. His speech was well received; Tillières, the French ambassador, called it "une belle harangue et forte éloquente."[85] Certainly it was James to the life: the sudden tempests of feeling, the alternation of cajolement and raillery, of candor and guile; the wit and learning; the pungency, the sputter, the force. But it was also, all agreed, a strong and a "royal" speech. It dealt directly with the major problems of the nation and spelled out the themes of the session. It set limits to the Parliament which its more aggressive members might refuse to accept, but could scarcely claim to mistake. To be sure, the passive and purely consultative body James described bore scant relation to the twenty-five score men who sat before him. But it was his function to describe, not what Parliament was, but what it ought to be. It had strayed: he was recalling it to its duty. That, indeed, was his duty.

II

'THE HAPPIEST PARLIAMENT
THAT EVER WAS'

Parliament assembled before the King on February 3 to present
its Speaker, who made the traditional requests for free speech,
the personal immunity of its members, and allowance for their
grievances. Replying for the Crown, Bacon assured the Commons full security of the first, "so as they kept themselves within
the compass of dutifull Subjects"; cautioned them not to abuse
the second; and bade them not to look for grievances, but to
prefer only those they brought with them from their counties:
"Ye are to represent the people: ye are not to personate them."[1]

The session began in earnest on the Monday. The House,
alarmed by the restriction on debate suggested in the speeches of
James and Bacon, plunged immediately into the questions of
free speech and the flourishing of popery. Sir Edward Giles, a
prominent Devonshire gentleman and member for Totnes,
moved to petition the King on both points, and young Sir Robert
Phelips, the son of a former Speaker, dovetailed him in an obviously well-concerted speech. Sir James Perrot, a stout Pembroke-
shire Puritan and, it was said, the illegitimate son of a royal
bastard, proposed that the members receive communion, which
would be, among other things, "a meanes to knowe the faith of
those of the Howse."[2] Debate grew steadily more passionate; Sir
Jerome Horsey followed with a denunciation of papists and had
to be silenced by the House when in the sweep of his wrath he
fell upon the Anglican episcopacy itself.

Secretary Calvert then rose to speak. But so, at the same moment, did Sir Edward Alford of Sussex, who without ceremony
began a heated speech: "God be merciful to the Realm of Eng-

land. Never so much Cause for any Parliament—." Calvert gra-
ciously gave place. The Speaker attempted to interrupt Alford,
only to be sharply rebuked by Sir Thomas Roe, who told him he
had no right to speak unless called upon by the House, the first
of many such incidents in the unhappy speakership of Serjeant
Richardson.[3]

When Alford had finished, Calvert tried to put things back on
the rails. He retraced the outlines of the King's speech: the wants
of the treasury, the exemplary frugality of recent years, the lavish-
ness of Elizabethan subsidies, the exigencies of the Palatinate.
The King had convoked a Council of War, whose estimate of a
year's maintenance for an army in the Palatinate was £300,000.[4]

Calvert's appeal was echoed by Sir William Cope and Sir
Thomas Edmondes. But Serjeant Davies, poet as well as jurist,
bored the House into unconcealed irritation with a rambling
speech, and gave is leaders a chance to catch their breath. Sir
George More, a veteran of many parliaments, led the counter-
attack. More "shewed how fit it was to have our privileges free,"
and suggested that grievances and supply go together, "like twins,
as Jacob and Esau . . . for though grievances go first, yet the blessing may be upon subsidies."[5]

This metaphor, passing through many hands, became at last
a formula for compromise. That afternoon, in grand committee,[6] the House broke down the matter of its first debate. Calvert
tried to reassure the House that the King's recent proclamation
"was intended against such as make ordinary table talk of state
matters in taverns and alehouses, and not against parliament
men." But Sir Robert Phelips was unconvinced. He recalled the
four members committed to the Tower in 1614; this breach of
privilege was still outstanding. "The Prerogative of Kinges
growe every daie; liberties of subjects are at a stand."[7] The House
appointed a subcommittee to draft a petition for confirmation of
free speech.[8] Another subcommittee was delegated to frame a
petition against recusants. The grand committee itself reserved
grievances and supply for the end of the week. The next day the
House waded into the trade crisis and the abuse of patents.
Lionel Cranfield had already urged an investigation of the courts
of justice; thus, within the first two days of business, the major
themes of the Parliament had been sounded.

New procedural orders were made, which facilitated business

but had more covert aims as well. The House agreed to read no public bills before nine o'clock, to put up none for passage before that hour, and required that a day's notice be given of all third readings. The Speaker might choose the order in which bills were to be read, as traditionally, "if the house call not for any in particular, but if the house doe so then those must bee reade." The effect of these resolutions was to strip the Speaker's chair of most of its discretionary power over bills.[9]

The House quickly picked up where its predecessors had left off. The unfinished legislation of 1614, the grievances of 1610 were fetched in. Sir Thomas Roe called attention to the dispersal and loss of the records of the House, and orders were subsequently made for their safekeeping.[10] Sir Henry Poole complained of the time lost each Parliament in examining disputed elections, and the House appointed a committee to draw a bill to standardize voting procedures, as far as the anarchy of English electoral practices would allow.[11]

John Chamberlain worried if Parliament were not going too fast. "I know the eyes of all Europe are now upon us and our parliament," he wrote to Sir Dudley Carleton, the English ambassador in the Hague, "but I pray God yt fall not out that *parturiunt montes,* for they undertake so much business at once that it wilbe hard *demesler* so many *fusees.*"[12] Others thought so too. The subcommittee's draft of a petition for free speech, brought in on February 9, was criticized by Sir John Glanville as so vague and sweeping as to court rejection. Sir Edwin Sandys complained that the whole matter of the petition had been insufficiently debated and unclearly defined by the House.[13]

But the irresolution of the Commons was more than a question of haste. The original debate and referral had been inconclusive rather than unthorough, and a week later the House knew its mind no better. The first draft of the petition, reread, was "disliked altogether."[14] Perhaps, it was argued, a verbal request would be safer, for if the written petition omitted something or expressed it badly, the House might be tied to the defect forever. A bill was suggested, with its greater leisure for preparation and precedent-searching. George Chudleigh summarized the objections to all three approaches: "If we go by message we can have but a verbal answer, (which) cannot be a precedent, neither can it equal an act of parliament. If by writing you may peradventure have an answer, which who knows whether it will limit us more than we are already. If by a new act it pass, it is doubtful whether it be better than the old."[15] Sir Edward Coke urged that the whole matter be gracefully dropped. Free speech in Parliament was the right "to speak what we think good for government either in church or commonweal," said Coke, and as for that, "in my conscience I make no doubt but we have freedom." The limit of free speech was, firstly, each man's discretion; second, the censure of the House; and finally, for those "malicious and exhorbitant" speeches hatched in faction to embarrass the state, or for statements "tending to treason," judgment must be reserved to the King and his ministers. If, therefore, they had freedom, and knew its limits, what could be gained from going to the King? What result would there then be of the long debate? It had served its purpose by simply voicing men's fears and clearing the air on the matter; and "now we have long debated it and duly considered it, we have done well though we let it fall."[16] Calvert praised his fellow councillor's remarks and called for business: "I pray hasten to the matters of the commonwealth."

Coke's unguent logic, however, failed to sway the House. Its fears were vague, but deep. It was not meant to rake over the mishaps of 1614, nor to question what was past, declared a member. "Our dissolution last was an evening sorrow, this parliament is a morning joy." But the recent proclamation hung over their heads, and one MP, Henry Lovell, had already been threatened by an official of the Wards. Alford, too, had received warning, and he touched the common nerve by declaring that "there were Eyes over him to observe." But, maintained the plucky Essex radical, he must be free to speak his conscience, "though he displease the King."[17] "I never spake with less assurance than at this present and truly I am much perplexed," said Sir Edwin Sandys. "We are loath to lose the fundamental privileges of parliament and loath to give just offence to the King. It were worth thanks to him to shew how we may preserve the one and avoid the other."[18] Without a specific breach of privilege to complain of, a petition would virtually mean a lack of trust in the King. Yet such in fact was the feeling in the Commons. The memory of the members sent to the Tower after the last Parliament, the untimeliness and ambiguity of the December proclamation, had created a need for positive reassurance from the

Crown. The King's speech and Bacon's reply had not only failed to provide this reassurance, but had actually deepened suspicion.[19] But now, after another frustrating and inconclusive debate, most of the House wished the subject had never come up, and Sir John Finch's suggestion probably best expressed their hope: "I like a signification hereof to his Majesty by some of these honorable persons about the Chair, and I hope we will receive some such gracious assurance from his Majesty as will give us all content."[20]

The councillors took the hint, and, three days later, on February 15, Calvert came into the House with a statement from the King. James "marveled" that the Commons should fear for its privileges, but "to give the Howse the greater confidence," he would willingly declare "That wee neither have by any Acte or Speech of ours heretofore, nor intend by any hereafter, any way to lessen or diminish, the lawfull and free libertie of speech, which appertaines unto the howse of Commons, and hath bene hertofore allowed unto them, by anie of our Noble Progenitours." Sir Nathaniel Rich jubilantly moved that Calvert set down the gist of the King's message in writing; and, as John Pym noted succinctly in his diary, "This speech set an end to that matter." Without even the decent burial of a motion, the subcommittee for free speech, its just-read report, and its just-drawn bill, simply ceased to be.[21] And with it went the speech that Sir Edward Alford had prepared for the expected debate: "O fatall weeke and desmall day . . . ."[22] The House turned its attention again to the menace of Rome.

The other subcommittee appointed on the first day of business, that for recusants, was more than doubled in number by interested members when it met on Wednesday the seventh.[23] Feeling ran high. Papists were practicing their superstition openly. The statutes against them were unexecuted, the fines uncollected, the courts so demoralized that they dared not even receive indictments for recusancy. And while popery flourished, the true religion suffered from insufficient preaching, from plurality and nonresidency. "This is the 63 yeare that without interruption wee have professed here the reformed religion," Sir Robert Phelips observed. "I praye god that for our sinnes it prove not the clima[c]tericall yeare of it." With a pointed reference to Spain's expulsion of the Moors, he remarked that "It is not long

since a wise state for reason of state did thrust out 600,000 people
at once," and in a thrust sharper still, "Papists dare now at Tables
maintain Transubstantiation; and . . . now they begin to maintain also the Pope's Authority at Board, and we are in love with
the Toys of other States, that we think love us. I pray God they
do."[24]

Sir Edward Coke denounced the open resort of London Catholics to the Spanish ambassador's house for Mass. In Spain, said
Coke, should any Spaniard attend a service at the home of the
English ambassador, "he should be quickly had into the Inquisition." He moved to petition that the King issue a proclamation
"to lymitt the Priviledges of Ambassadours to themselves." Then,
"asked of one why he was so bloody minded in seeking to execute
the bloody laws against priests," he replied with a litany of Catholic crimes, "and instanced in the particulars further, saying that
some men in the House did more hurt than 10,000 men would
do good in ten years."

At these remarks, Secretary Calvert's normally slow temper
ignited. He snapped back that the English ambassador in Spain
enjoyed greater liberty in Madrid than Gondomar in London,
and asked Coke if he meant to imply that the government "con-
nived" at protecting recusants. The committee chamber dissolved in uproar. Several members shouted at once that Coke
had used no such word, and there were wild demands that Calvert be expelled from Parliament. Other things were said in
heat; and, if we may trust the report of the Lando, Venetian ambassador, some would even have asked the King for a declaration
"of the way in which he proposed to effect the Spanish marriage
without prejudice to religion, not to speak of its increase."[25]

Another incident soon caused an even greater disturbance, and
actually did lead to an expulsion. On February 15, the perennial
sabbatarian bill[26] came up for a second reading, and seemed
safely home to a perfunctory commitment when Thomas Shepherd, a young Lincoln's Inn lawyer, unexpectedly seized the
floor. With "a greate deale of scorne and Malepeirt gesture," he
derided the entire body of the bill. It was made, he charged, in
defiance of the King's Book—James's so-called "Book of Sports"[27]
—and not only of King James, for did not King David bid the
godly to dance as well, *gaudate et exultate*? "The occasion of the
Bill growes from a kind of Cattle that will not submit them-

selves to the Ceremonyes of the Church. It savours of the spirrit of a Puritan. . . . Shall we make all these engines and Barracado's[28] against Papists and not a Mouse-trappe to catch a Puritan."[29]

Shepherd bundled through his tirade like a man giddy for his doom, but the shouts of the House at last silenced him. He was brought to the bar, and, when the wrath of the House was interrupted by a conference with the Lords, remanded to the Serjeant. The next day, John Pym pilloried him in his first formal speech in the House of Commons. But the punishment suggested by Pym—expulsion, a fine, and the Tower at pleasure—was too harsh for most members, whom a day's respite had cooled down considerably. "A young Man, never of the House before, so busy in such a Matter," observed Sir William Strode, a veteran of many sessions. "We should do him a Pleasure to put him out."[30] And simple expulsion was the verdict.

The incident provoked much comment, and echoes of it were still audible a month later.[31] As the editors of the *Commons' Debates* remark, "The punishment proves how limited was freedom of speech for those who crossed prevailing opinion."[32] Government spokesmen supported the expulsion, and their reasons are interesting. Sir George Chaworth discovered that Shepherd was "one of the busy young Lawyers, in the Proclamation, and ought not to have been elected." Solicitor Heath argued that he had clearly abused the privilege of free speech, and "we therefore must punish; else the King no reason to trust us with the Punishment of any Member of the House." Calvert agreed with the majority that Shepherd was guilty of "petulance and profanity," but he quietly pointed out that the sabbath bill did in fact annul a royal proclamation.[33]

The following week, the subcommittee for recusants presented its draft petition, which the House quickly approved. It differed little from the petition of 1610. All recusants were to be expelled from London and confined to within five miles of their homes, except by special royal license; all arms were to be denied them, and the use of Catholic embassies for Masses forbidden; priests and Jesuits were to be closely imprisoned, and the statutes "straitly" executed against all noncommunicants.[34] Sir Nathaniel Rich, one of the godlier parliamentarians, complained of the clause for royal licenses, but wiser heads kept silent; to attack a dispensation was one thing, to deny the power to dispense, another.[35]

The Commons next secured the support of the Lords,[36] and on February 17, the two houses presented the petition to the King at Whitehall. James was hard-pressed to keep his temper. Spain had at last dispatched her emissary to Rome to seek the papal dispensation for the match. Lord Digby was on the point of departure for Brussels to open a new round of negotiations on the Palatinate. James had bent all his graces to encourage and accommodate the Spanish, and the not normally sanguine Gondomar felt able to boast that "aqui se han ganado y ganan cada dia convirtiendose y declarandos Catolicos infinitos con il silencio de la persecucion."[37] Into this fragile harmony the Commons bugled their petition.

The King began his reply by thanking both Houses for their zeal in religion, and for the opportunity to spike the rumor "That the Papists looke for a kind of *Connivance* [italics mine]" from the state. "I wish the world may knowe I needed noe spurr For a Peticion may seeme to import that I was slacke of my selfe. ... I dare say there hath beene noe slacknes neither in pruneing nor plantinge nor rootinge out the weedes."

James then read his Commons a lecture in policy. "The Pallatinate is nowe in the hands of an enemye to our Religion. He yet useth them fairely And it is best for him soe to do. Yf we begin any newe or stricter course against the Papists, It is like to induce him to the like against our Religion there." The same peril faced the Grisons in the Valtelline, the Huguenots in France, the Dutch on expiration of their truce. "Considering all theis distempers, we must take care to keepe Religion a foote in other places And not by raiseing newe pressures here make them of the other side more violent in their advantage. ... Theis things considered, I graunte the substance but not the waye [of the petition], soe as yow may enioy the effect and I proceed in such fashion as best suites with the State both forreigne and Domesticall."[38]

"God forbid, that I should compel Men's Consciences," James had told his Parliament two weeks before, and for him this was a watchword of statecraft, as well as a statement of conviction. It was the sectarian, papist or puritan, the man foresworn and dangerous, who was abhorrent to him. "A difference is to be made betwixt Papists," he told the petitioners, "Those that Maynteyne the Oathe of Alleadgance, and such other Traytors as refuse it." Peaceable Catholics who wanted to remain loyal Englishmen were rejected by both sides, and (James did not say) the wise monarch would conciliate such subjects rather than drive them to desperation.

"Yow of the Lower House," he commented, "I heare yow gave yeasterdaie a severe Sentence uppon one for speakeinge against Puritans." He would not object to this, but admonished the Commons "that as they looked on the right hand to the Papists, so they should look on the left hand to the Puritans."[39] His audience was so visibly ruffled by this passage that Calvert was instructed to emend it in the House on Monday. Shepherd's expulsion "was iust, for it medled not in the iudicature," the Secretary explained. But the King would have them careful how they gave passage to their "Sundayes bill," for as it stood it was "*ex diametro* opposite" to the "Book of Sports." "[H]is Majestie had upon mature deliberacion writt an edict against Puritanes," Calvert said, and repeated (doubtless James was pleased with his metaphor) the King's admonition to punish extremists with both hands.[40]

The formal report of the King's reply was deferred by the House on the pretext that the Lord Chancellor, the "common messenger" of the two houses, had not yet made his report to the Lords. When a text of the speech came down from the Upper House, it was received with complete silence.[41] The Commons read a bill to enforce the penalties against recusant lands at the end of the week.[42]

The King was further embarrassed by another petition from the House. English ordnance, forged in the great ironworks of Sussex, was highly prized on the Continent, and its export was a royal monopoly, permitted only by the King's license. So lucrative was this trade to the Crown that Elizabeth had sold ordnance to Spain even while at war with her.[43] A license had been granted to Count Gondomar, and, though long dormant, had been recently renewed. A hundred pieces of ordnance lay on the Tower wharf ready for shipment to Spain; and Sir John Jephson, an Irish privy councillor, excitedly reported this to the House. Calvert assured the Commons that the King was merely honoring an old promise, and that the guns were bound directly for Portugal,

for use against the Barbary pirates. But the House was thoroughly aroused. "How can we believe it?" Sir Edward Giles asked
bluntly. The Spanish would use the ordnance where they most
needed it. The King asked for supply, and yet armed his own
enemies. William Towerson, the merchant adventurer, exclaimed that the ordnance was indeed bound for Portugal, for
the King of Spain was fitting out a fleet against English com-
merce in the East Indies. Sir Thomas Roe charged that another
hundred guns had already been smuggled out under Gondomar's
warrant.[44] If these arms were taken too, it would be a national
calamity. The councillors in the House were dispatched on the
instant to request the King to halt the shipment. To emphasize
the gravity of the situation, it was ordered that every man sit in
his place until they returned.

Treasurer Edmondes brought James's reply. A promise had
been made to the King of Spain, "And therefore he prayeth you
that you would suffer him to be a king of his word. If he keep it
not with others, how can ye think he will keep it with you." The
transaction was of no "material prejudice" to England, and the
arms were not to be used against the Protestant cause. But the
King promised to authorize no further sales, and invited the
House to draw up a bill on the subject.[45] This was no doubt a
mere gesture. Elizabeth had vetoed such a bill in 1601, and
Charles's ministers stoutly defended the ordnance monopoly in
1628. James was no less chary of his prerogative than they, and
the draft of a later speech by Edmondes indicates that he fully
intended to retain control of the monopoly.[46]

From these beginnings it was easy to conclude that King and
Parliament were bound for an early rupture, and so many foreign observers in London thought. Parliament "wavers about
with great bitterness," reported the Venetian ambassador, while
"his Majesty proceeds with a harshness which may seem excessive
and not a little dangerous." Salvetti, the Florentine news gath-
erer, deplored the intransigence of "these violent Calvinist Puritans," and predicted that "nothing but ruin and breach can be
its outcome." The French ambassador declared flatly that "if they
do not soften their tone, the said Parliament will be dissolved,
that is my opinion."[47]

But these observers were pessimists by profession, and none
of them, be it remembered, had ever seen an English parliament

before. Unaccustomed to the phenomenon, they perceived that the Commons were sharply at variance with the King on substantive questions of foreign and domestic policy, but they misconstrued the tone of discussion. What one is struck by in these early debates is their guardedness and restraint. The matter of the ordnance, which was no secret to the House,[48] might never have come up had a Crown servant not broached it; and, carried away as they were by their debate, the Commons subsided obediently at the King's reply. The virtual rejection of the petition for religion dismayed the House, but it was not disputed. James's words on free speech gave the House nothing new, but they were eagerly and gratefully accepted. In each instance, the Commons bent over backward to avoid serious contention with the King.

The Commons' most positive gesture of goodwill was a speedy grant of two subsidies, an amount—estimated at £160,000— greater than any ever levied on England in one year before.[49] The government had pressed for supply on the very first day of business. Sir Edward Coke, who had taken the chair—apparently by stratagem[50]—at the grand committee for grievances and supply that afternoon, had purposely deferred the question of supply.[51] This proved the wiser course. When supply was put on the agenda, ten days later, the House was fairly launched into business, and readier to entertain the somewhat unorthodox idea of a supply at the beginning of a session. That very morning, moreover, the King's message on free speech had come down, and the House was in good spirits when it met in committee after dinner.

Sir George More, chancellor of the Garter, a parliament man of forty years' standing, and one of the most respected voices in the house, began the debate. "What greater grievances can there be than the King's wants?" asked More. "I am persuaded every one here is willing to give. . . . I will not take upon me to say how much it should be. But I will spare from my back and belly rather than be wanting in it." Sir Edward Sackville eloquently pictured the plight of the King's daughter. "Who can hear this," he concluded, "and not be ready to give?" "To give liberally will procure more frequent parliaments," added Sir Thomas Edmondes.[52]

Various sums were conjectured on the floor, but Christopher

Brooke, member for York, was the first to make a specific proposal. Brooke called for two subsidies, and two subsidies prevailed, though not without opposition. "Let us not make too
bold with our countrymen's purses till we bring them some
good news," Sir Henry Poole grumbled. The Crown was also
dissatisfied. Sir Julius Caesar said that two subsidies would not
equip an army, and called for two fifteens to go with them—an
additional sixty thousand pounds. This, he said, would "do ex-
ceedingly well." But the House was skeptical. "Yf we go to
the Pallatinate, a Million will not dischardge the Armye," said
Phelips; and whether he spoke on a tip or simply an educated
guess, his figure was very near that which had just been submitted
by the Council of War to the King.[53] The discrepancy between
the official figure and knowledgeable estimates damaged confidence in the government's word and created suspicions of the
real purpose of the levy. Phelips suggested that "we goe to the
Lords and consult with them touching the proportion and the
manner of making warre," to which Calvert retorted tartly,
"Methinks it's a very strange thing for a king to consult with
his subjects what war he means to undertake." But Coke intervened and headed off the argument. A solution was at last put
forward by Sir Edwin Sandys, who was to turn so many debates
in this Parliament with timely good sense and moderation. Considering that two subsidies were "no proportion for the regain-
ing of the Palatinate, and therefore instead of terrifying our
enemies it will but hearten them," but also that the country
could afford no more at present, he suggested that they "proceed
as a present of love to the King without any other consideration,"
to be spent as he saw fit. This formula was eagerly embraced,
and two subsidies voted by the committee "neither for Defence
of the Palatinate, nor yet for relieving the King's Wants, but
only as a free gift and present of the Love and Duty of his Subjects."[54]

The next day the vote of the grand committee was reported
to the House by Coke. He brought with him a message from
King James.

> I wish yow had all heard the king or all England. I went
> to the king and acquainted him with it: some had done it
> before it was all accepted. I read the votes of all the house

that none should have thankes more than the other. Whereon his Message retourned was this, mark his Epithet:

"That this their free, noble, and no merchantlike dealing should produce two notable effects, first, his Honour and Credit abroad; secondly, that it should breed such good blood in him, as he would strive, nay hunt to find out the Grievances and Oppressions of his Loving Subjects, and relieve them, and that therein he would meet with his Subjects more than half way."

The King, said Coke, had bidden his councillors to tell the Commons "that I accept the fairness of their gift more than the gift itself.[55]

Edmondes, Calvert, Greville, and Cranfield all followed in the same strain. The House then voted unanimously to confirm the grant of the committee. Only Alford, like the bad fairy at the party, struck a less than magnanimous note. The councillors, he said, "should not have related unto the King what was done for granting of the Subsidies at the Committee, till they had been past in the House, because it might have been overruled in the House notwithstanding the Opinion of the Committee." The House agreed, and made an order for it.[56]

But what most encouraged the Commons was the attitude taken by Crown councillors in the House toward grievances. From the first day, Coke and Cranfield had placed themselves in the forefront of reform, naming the abuses, urging inquiry, directing activity. Coke's first speech was striking, and, for a councillor, certainly novel in tone. The House must have been pleased to hear him say of its privileges that "they were like a circle of which if any part be broken the whole is broken," startled at his citation of a statute of Edward III: "A Parliament to be holden every Year, that the People may complain of Grievances." Among present grievances he forthrightly placed religion and monopolies. It was Coke who led the Commons' delegation to the Lords for the recusancy petition, and Coke who, having presided over the original grand committee, naturally retained the chairmanship of its permanent successor, the committee of the whole for grievances. This chair was the pivotal position in the House of Commons, and Coke promised to be a very active occupant. The King having shown his readiness to redress the ills of the commonwealth, said Coke, "My motion is to strike while the iron is hot and to appoint two days every week to hear grievances." Mondays and Fridays were assigned on the spot, but the committee's business was soon virtually co-extensive with that of the House.[57]

Cranfield also had a program—justice, trade, and patents, as he said on the first day—and never ceased to hammer at it. On the fifteenth, he expounded his headings in detail, and made a sweeping review of grievances. On the twenty-first he chided the House on its slowness to act, and moved that a separate day and committee be assigned for each point of his triple platform. Actually, the committee for courts of justice was already functioning, having been appointed at Cranfield's motion on February 8; and on the twenty-sixth, a committee for the decay of money was a last designated, of which he became chairman.[58]

Like his colleague Coke, Cranfield considered the petition for free speech a waste of time, though for somewhat less sophisticated reasons. In the debate on the twelfth, he broke down the issue bluntly and with characteristic pragmatism: "The Question, what free Speech is. If that be, to speak home to any Grievance, they may assure themselves of it.[59] Cranfield seemed to want every window thrown open wide. When Henry Lovell, unhappily involved in a suit at Wards, "shewed the wonderful abuses" of Cranfield's own court, he applauded the motion, welcomed an investigation, and declared himself "ready to make satisfaction in his person or estate or both" to any man wronged in his jurisdiction.[60]

The House soon showed its appreciation of Coke and Cranfield. "Sir Lionell Cranfield . . . hath got great commendation for divers good and honest speaches," wrote Chamberlain. Coke was praised publicly in the House as early as February 8 by Alford, who rejoiced in his progress "like a Parliament-man in Queen Eliz. Time." "In good faith (my lord)," wrote Dudley Digges, who had taken his seat in the Commons late, "the privy councillors are as forward as any of us." And after a brilliant exposition of patents by Coke on the nineteenth, Alford exclaimed the sentiments of the House: "That this was the first Parliament that he ever saw Councillors of State have such Care of the State."[61]

It became gradually apparent, however, that there was a certain lag between the two front ministers and the rest of the councillors of the House. A sharp eye would have noticed it the first day, over subsidies. Calvert's initial call for supply had been couched in the most drastic terms: "The busines of the Pallatinate is a pressing and bleedinge busines. . . . It will admitt noe delaye. The Spring Approacheth, Spinola hath overrunne all the countrie." Equally necessitous was the relief of the King's debts, "that greate Lumpe which is soe greate a Corasive to his Majestie." Despite all economies, revenue remained small while expenses were "vast." Several smaller fry echoed the same note; but Coke simply rebutted these breathless assertions of crisis: "God be praised, his Majesty's cause was neither *causa deplorata,* nor yet *causa desperata.*" The insufficiency of revenue was not a shortage in the source. It was a leak in the conduit that might easily be plugged. " . . . I know that if all the water came home to the mill that should, the ordinary charge and the ordinary receipt would be near at one."[62]

From Cranfield, too, came no exhortation to supply, but another discourse on grievances, and the advice "Not to hinder the Business by going too fast."Again in the subsidy debate of February 15, he declined the subject and took the occasion to deliver a speech on grievances: "I will not speak for money. I see everyone is so free as that no spur need be added.[63] This courting of easy popularity did not make Calvert's task any simpler.

But far more damaging to the Crown than lack of policy coordination or displays of personal antipathy was the attitude which Coke and Cranfield took toward the investigation of the patents of monopoly. Great tact and skill would be required to manage it, for as Bacon had predicted, nothing was more potentially dangerous than a Parliament run off the rails on this subject.

But instead of maintaining a common ministerial front, Coke and Cranfield plunged ahead into the patents. They bluntly rebuffed their fellow councillors' efforts to limit the scope of the investigations, and gave the Commons the most unreserved encouragement to probe for scandal up to the very highest levels of government. With deliberate indiscretion they played up the evils of monopoly and maximized the embarrassment of the government.

The differences between Coke and Cranfield and their fellow ministers were very pronounced. What was a good deal less obvious was the difference between the two men themselves. It has long been recognized , of course, that Coke "defected" to

what is conventionally called the opposition in 1621. But it is
not as a renegade from the King's cause that he is generally remembered, but as the white knight of parliamentary liberty;
and, indeed, his name is deservedly writ large in the history of
the English constitution. But to those in the House of Commons
who watched the transformation, Edward Coke was a privy
councillor; they had no reason to suppose that he was acting as
other than a privy councillor; and they followed him as one.[64]
Later on, as it became increasingly apparent that Coke was walk-
ing a different road, and James vented public displeasure at his
conduct, the image of the privy councillor insensibly faded away
and merged with the new prestige Coke had won in his own
right as the leading figure in the Commons. But while he was
still regarded as a spokesman for the Crown (and often was one
in routine, carrying messages, preferring bills of grace), he emboldened many to follow him in the naïve and happy belief that
there was a single concord in the state. It was not until the full
force of the monopoly scandal broke that it became clear that
Edward Coke had, to all intents and purposes, walked out of the
King's Council of State.

Coke's motivation was complex. He was sixty-nine years old
in 1621. Dismissed from the bench at the height of his career,
humbled by disgrace to a courtier, he had waited four years for
royal favor in the limbo of a minister without portfolio; his lifelong rival Bacon had climbed past him to the Chancery; and
when in December of 1620 the long-vacant treasurership had
gone to the mediocre Mandeville, he at last realized that he
would wait forever: James would never trust him with high
office.[65] The thread of opposites which had woven his long
career, ambition for place against judicial probity, had come
out on a short skein: and what seemed left was either stolid
soldiering in the Privy Council to an undistinguished end, or
embittered retirement. But the occasion of a Parliament suddenly offered Coke a new sphere of activity. By what rapid
process of disillusion, sensed opportunity, and resuscitated pride
he passed into permanent opposition to the Crown in the winter
of 1621, we can but vainly conjecture. In Parliament, however,
he returned to the theme that had always redeemed an often
sordid career.

What Coke as a legist had always sought was to create a bulwark that could protect the subject and his precious legal rights from the inroads of government; having failed to achieve this on the bench, he now strove to accomplish it in Parliament. The reign of the common law was both the aim and the sanction of his lifelong activity. The agency was basically indifferent. If the Court of Common Pleas would not serve the turn, the High Court of Parliament must be made to do so. Without conceiving the least disloyalty to the Crown as an institution, Coke set about to rectify what he considered a dangerous imbalance in the constitution. If in the process he was to lead Parliament to a radical assumption of new powers, it was from a political philosophy essentially conservative.

Coke's more personal animus tends to cast shade on the purity of these professional motives. That a so suddenly and fortuitously reawakened concern for the right of the subject embodied Coke's own frustrated drive for power is, I think, beyond question. Yet we need not doubt his conscious sincerity. That he dared to arrogate to himself the function of setting the English constitution to rights might in itself be held, in a mere subject, a profoundly illegal act: James thought so. Here was a new species of the overmighty subject, and one all the more dangerous because he fought not with the weapons of anarchy but of law. And yet, in a man of such force, aim and motive are so often fused that no distinction can justly separate them. When Coke protested in December on behalf of the Commons "that we have done nothing but in the Duty of the most dutifull Subjects," he spoke what he believed to be the truth.[66]

Coke assuredly knew what he was doing. Lionel Cranfield was his own dupe. Although Cranfield, far from deserting the service of the Crown, soon prospered in it to the extent of a peerage and the lord treasurership, his role in Parliament was only scarcely less damaging to its interests than Coke's. Historians have made sharp criticisms of Cranfield's performance in the House, but their censure has dwelt on the manner rather than the matter of it. Despite his early attempts to charm, Cranfield's bearing was arrogant, dogmatic, and domineering. "One may read in his face," D. H. Willson muses, "a certain irrepressible effrontery." As the session wore on, he exchanged hot words with one after another of his fellow members and, not scrupling to invoke his office, threatened several with punishment after the end of Parliament. Such altercations gradually eroded his influence, until in May Sir Edwin Sandys told him bluntly that "those that come into the Howse must leave both their greatnes and meaneness at the Doare."[67]

Cranfield's most significant quarrel, however, was to be with Bacon, with whom his relations were already embittered.[68] Cranfield's rancorous attacks on Bacon were not merely, as Willson points out, "utterly destructive of any party loyalty or cohesion" among government forces.[69] In the atmosphere that was soon to develop in the Commons over monopolies, they were like land mines planted under Bacon's reputation.

But even the best of Cranfield's intentions were disastrous. He had long nurtured the program of administrative, economic, and judicial reform which he presented to the Commons in the first weeks of the session. Such reform and economy as had been achieved in the government since the fall of the Howard clan was largely to his credit. But in Parliament Cranfield saw his real opportunity. He had long argued for, long anticipated a Parliament, and as James himself testified in 1624, was later to beg on his knees that it not be dissolved with all its good work left hanging.[70] And Cranfield looked to it not merely as a legislator: he was not averse to giving some of his colleagues a good, salutary shake-up as well. From this stemmed his invitation to the Commons not merely to remedy abuses but to publicly expose those responsible for them. But what Cranfield totally failed to perceive was that one could not thrust new swords into the hands of a Parliament and expect them to be tamely sheathed in the government's scabbard when their work had been done. Far too little and far too late did this gifted administrator begin to suspect that he had laid his lamb of reform to bed with the lion of revolution.

Thus the two councillors, though paired together by their fellow parliamentarians, worked quite independently of one another, and for radically different ends. Yet their separate purposes converged on at least one point: a common repugnance for Francis Bacon. Coke's seasoned antipathy to Bacon calls for no comment: it was one of the great standing facts of thirty years of English public life. Cranfield's was of more recent date, but it made up in rancor what it lacked in vintage. The attitude of these two men bears crucially on the question of Bacon's fall, the most consequential and spectacular event of the Parliament of 1621. Neither, of course, could have planned—they could scarcely have imagined—the Lord Chancellor's impeachment. Nor does the evidence suggest that they acted in concert against Bacon in the House at any time. But both Coke and Cranfield, I believe, in their separate paths, worked consciously and directly at bringing Bacon to the greatest possible discomfiture; and both, faced with the opportunity of securing his public disgrace and actual removal from office, seized it gratefully and joyously with both hands. When their work was done, a power had been put into Parliament's hands which was to be invoked many times again, until in its ultimate extension it claimed the life of a king.

The issue of the patents of monopoly, broached by Cranfield on the first day of the session, was quickly taken up. The next day, February 6, Alford moved for a committee to examine all patents concerning bullion, in view of the notorious scarcity of coin in the kingdom. His motion was seconded by Sir Edward Sackville,

> and extended further, That inquirie might be made towchinge his Majesties referments of the Peticions uppon which such graunts ensued, and soe the faults might be taken from his Majestie and lye uppon the Refferrees who misled his Majestie and are worthie to beare the shame of their owne worke.[71]

The King, Sackville explained to the House, unable to examine personally all the suits brought before him, referred them to "those of place and trust about him who by reason of their places in all presumption should best understand the business," and would not grant any until they had been certified by these officers as "both lawefull and convenient for the common weale."[72]

Thus the referees had come under fire as early as the sixth of February. But the moment was premature. The Commons were wholly absorbed with their two petitions, and in the tedious unsnarling of disputed elections. It was not until the fifteenth that an impatient Cranfield led the House back to the subject. He spoke with disgust of the plausible schemers who came to Court: "What patent hath not had a fair pretence, I know something because I have been a Master of Requests." The King "was ever jealous" of the welfare of his subjects; therefore, the blame for obnoxious patents lay with his legal experts, and "if the referees be in fault, can he do himself more honor than to call them to account?"[73]

Four days later, the subsidy passed and the petitions disposed, the committee for grievances, under Coke, turned at last to monopolies. William Noy opened the meeting with a long exposition of patent procedure, carefully stressing James's innocence of any fault: "The Kinge hath sufficiently exprest that Greivances are not originallie from him . . . the King by his Book[74] hath published his Distaste of these importunate Suitors." Let them be taught "more Manners"; and let the referees be examined as well, as "is most fit."[75]

Coke himself followed. He would not examine the King's own prerogative. Yet the King had, besides his personal or "absolute" prerogative, which no subject might question, a "disputable" prerogative, that is, one actionable in the law courts. To this latter category belonged dispensations and grants of patents. Some grants were legally acceptable but proved harmful in practice: "These things have [been] alwaies holpen by Parliament." But there was another kind of grant, good neither in law nor execution, and for this, "the sole Fault . . . lies in the Referrees." Such obnoxious monopolies had multiplied of late like Hydras' heads, said Coke; and Alford added, significantly, "This exorbitant time makes all the Kings officers secure and carelesse."[76] One could not wish for clearer statements of the concept of Parliament's watchdog functions in the state, and the necessity for frequent and regular sessions.

The patent of inns was then considered. This patent was one of those Bacon had urged Buckingham to rescind before Parliament. Solicitor Heath explained its terms. The presumptive aim was to regulate inns by issuing licenses to innkeepers through a commissioner, Sir Giles Mompesson, and two assistants. Justices of the peace, it was argued, were not empowered to grant such licenses, and justices of assize were too busy. Mompesson and his co-commissioners were to receive one hundred pounds per annum for their labors, and Mompesson, in addition, one-fifth of the total receipts; the rest was to go into the Exchequer. Three men, in short, were by the terms of this patent to supervise the erection and maintenance of inns in all the counties and shires of England. The result had been merely a hit-and-run shakedown operation. Mompesson, a member of Parliament, was called before the committee the next day. Who, it was demanded, had cleared this patent? Mompesson testified that it had been twice referred, first for law to Justices Crooke, Winch, and Nichols, and to the then Attorney General Bacon; second, for "convenience," to Lord Treasurer Suffolk, Secretaries Lake and Winwood, and Serjeants Montagu and Finch; and was thereupon drawn up by Bacon, Finch, and Solicitor Coventry. "If these did certify it," ejaculated Coke, interrupting the narrative, "no king in Christendom but would have granted it." And, he added, careful to point the inevitable moral, "Therefore his Majesty is free from all blame in it."[77] The patent of inns was the first of the monopolies to be condemned in 1621.[78]

The related patent of alehouses was dealt with next. In reporting it to the House on February 22, Coke explained

> . . . the justices take the recognizance, but these projectors take the profit. Nay, they have put in their patent a command upon the justices of peace to be assistant unto them. What a base thing is that. Nay, there is a command to judges to send out process for them into all England (which is not fit, except they did see a good cause). If we had branded this in the execution only, the commission might have start up again in a short time. Therefore we branded the very institution of it likewise.[79]

The judgment of the committee was confirmed. Thus the House, led by Coke, had taken the significant step of condemning not only the abuses of the patentees but the patents themselves, thereby passing an implicit judgment on those who had drawn and approved them: the referees.

The tactics of Coke in the committee were revealing. Kit Villiers, the younger brother of the favorite, was involved in the alehouse venture, and Edmondes tried to shield him. But Coke insisted that all the subscribers of the patent be brought as delinquents to the bar, "alleadging playnely that hee would not spare . . . the quality of the persons." Cranfield backed him: "I see not how you can exempt any except you mean to overthrow the whole business." There was a considerable uproar: it was the first move against an important courtier, and the King's servants rushed to his defense. The erratic Sackville, this time marching in step, wrested the concession of counsel for Villiers. But it was a major victory for Coke. His control of the committee was clearly affirmed. And the rift among the councillors showed wider than ever.[80]

Yet men hesitated before the path chalked out by Coke and Cranfield. Who would undertake the responsibility of calling the "great ones" to account, who would run the risk? The skittishness of the House had already manifested itself in the debate on free speech. More than one member felt "eyes over him to observe."

It was the impulsive Sir Francis Seymour who, for the first time since Sackville's original motion, raised the question of the referees before the full House. He found no takers. Three days later, on February 24, he broached the subject again, but again there was no response. On the morning of the twenty-seventh, he entered the House quaking: "I came to the House to learn. My first lesson shall be to do my King and country service. I was questioned the last day for speaking my mind touching referees. I am now come to renounce and recant the same." But Seymour did not recant. Flushed and on his feet, he renewed and amplified his former statements; and the longer he spoke, the bolder he became. An order had been made in the committee to question the referees, "but it is asleep and my fear tells me that it will not awake." Yet how was it possible to avoid the plain facts of the case? The patents had been certified by the referees, and they could not plead ignorance of their legal defects, "for then they should deny that profession wherein they have spent most of their time." He concluded by calling for a day to be set aside "to hear what these referees will speak for themselves." If they should prove as guilty as others, "I see no cause why they should not be punished as well as others."[81]

Such a speech, and especially the report of a threat to a member, could have been normally expected to throw the House into pandemonium. But there was no response—nothing at all. After a moment's embarrassed silence, the House began to discuss Mompesson again. It was Cranfield, as in the Lovell incident, who retrieved the thread: "We have a projector and a patent. The projector had had no patent if the referees had not certified both the lawfulness and the conveniency. Let these things be considered." He moved to have the referees named and examined as a matter of course in every patent investigated, beginning with those for the patent of inns.[82]

Cranfield had practically declared open house on the government in this statement. Yet even with such a daring and unequivocal lead, the Commons hesitated to act. They had on hand Mompesson, the master monopolist, and a projector in hand was worth any number of shadowy prey in the bush.

For the next three days the House busied itself with Mompesson and his associates. There were difficulties enough in this affair. The patient and painstaking Coke realized that the steps must be laid out one at a time. Although Mompesson might be punished as a member of the House, he pointed out to the Commons, the maximum penalty they could inflict on him would be to send him to the Tower: hardly an adequate recompense for his depredations. William Noy and William Hakewill were appointed to search precedents "to show how far, and for what offences, the power of this House doth extend to punish delinquents against the State as well as those who offend against this House." Coke announced the solution the next day: on the basis of precedents ranging from Edward I to Henry VI, it was found to be warranted that by joining with the House of Lords, Mompesson might be punished not merely for an offense committed within Parliament, but for a matter of "general grievance."[83]

The antiquity of the precedents cited was a key to the novelty of the proposed indictment. The House of Lords had exercised judicial functions during the Middle Ages, but most of these had long since fallen into abeyance. It had not served as a criminal court since the mid-fifteenth century. To resurrect it now as a judicial body of uncertain limits and pretensions would amount to a radical innovation in the state. Moreover, as Gardiner points out, "The House of Lords was, with the single exception of the House of Commons, the most unfit body in existence for conducting a political trial."[84] Few of its members had a serious knowledge of law. Yet Coke's stratagem worked, and it was one of the decisive events of the Parliament of 1621. The case of Mompesson laid the ground for that of Bacon; for had it not revived the judicial functions of the Lords, Bacon could never have been brought to trial before the Upper House.

The first month of the session had been a turbulent one in the Lords too. The older nobility of England had been profoundly aroused at James's lavish creation of new titles: forty-three since his accession. Many of these had been created for Scottish retainers or royal favorites, some—Salisbury, St. Albans—to reward merit. But from 1615 it had been government policy to sell patents of nobility outright. In the following thirteen years the peerage of England was raised by over fifty percent; this "inflation of honors," in Professor Stone's phrase, amounted "to one of the most radical transformations of the English titular aristocracy that has ever occurred."[85] Ireland was Buckingham's special province and his ennoblements exceeded all restraint. Irish viscounts jostled English barons for precedence in the parliaments of the 1620s. As the Commons were incensed at the use of royal proclamations and the grant of the dispensing power for private purposes, so were the Lords at the favorite's power to create peerages. This "English Alcibiades"[86] with his upstart title of marquis had it in his power to derogate the honor and pride of every peer of England, to cheapen the very concept of blood.

From the government point of view, the new policy recommended itself on a number of counts. It was a lucrative income source—nearly £25,000 a year on average between 1603 and 1629[87]—and a profitable way, like the monopolies, to reward service. Carried to excess, however, it was bound to prove self-defeating. New as well as old peers joined to protest the sale of titles in the House of Lords in February, 1621. Meeting at the homes of the earls of Salisbury and Dorset, they drafted a petition to James, which, though scrupulously acknowledging his undoubted power to "collate what you please, upon whom, when, and how you please," begged leave "that we may take no more notice of these Titulars than the Law of this land doth, but that we may be excused, if in civil courtesie, we give them not the respect or place, as to Noblemen strangers, seeing that these be our Country Men," merely translated "into foreign names, only to our injury."[88] The petition was subscribed by thirty-three peers, about a third of whom were of pre-Stuart origin.[89]

James was furious when he heard of it. He commanded Dorset

to bring the petition to the Council, but Dorset held by a promise he claimed Prince Charles had made him to obtain access
to the King for the delivery of the petition. Charles, however,
told the Earl that he had misconstrued his words, and that he
was now ordered to deliver it to the Council. Dorset conferred
with his cosignatories. It was decided to deliver the petition to
the Prince in Council, that is, *qua* Prince and not councillor,
with the request that Charles carry it immediately to the King
without letting the Council examine it. The Prince agreed to
this scheme. But Digby observed that it went against the King's
express instruction that the petition be delivered simply to the
Council, and suggested it might set a precedent. The lords hearing this refused to surrender the petition to anyone but "the
Prince in Councell." After some ado—Dorset coming to the
Council, refusing to present the petition except by this formula,
and returning to the Lords—Calvert suggested that the lords
deliver it to the Prince *and* Council, "which the Boarde liked
well if they could gett it so delivered." They did so, and the
petition was carried to the King without being seen.[90]

The incident illustrates how quickly the Lords had learned
the fine art of legal hairsplitting from the Lower House. As
James kept "counsel" attached to their body to resolve disputed
points of law, so a party of disgruntled lords retained the services
of John Selden and others as private legal aides. Selden produced
a manuscript on parliamentary procedure in 1621 which was
ultimately adopted as the permanent standing rule of the House,
and appropriately titled *Remembrances of Methods . . . in the
House of Lords*.[91] At the beginning of the session, the Lords, in
imitation of the Commons, set up a standing committee for privileges and a subcommittee for precedents. Moreover, the relations of the leaders of the Upper House—Henry, Earl of Southampton; Henry, Earl of Oxford; Robert, Earl of Essex; Richard,
Earl of Dorset; Robert, Earl of Warwick; the lords Say and
Spencer—with the leaders of the Lower were close and coopera-
tive.[92] Thus the Lords, feeling threatened as a body and as a
class by the debasement of the peerage, were highly susceptible
to an approach from the Commons on the retrieval of their
ancient jurisdiction.

Bacon found the Lords increasingly difficult to control. On
February 16 they went into committee as a whole—another

device adopted from the Commons—to debate the recusancy petition. The Chancellor spoke first, and from the close resemblance of his words to those of James at Whitehall the next day, we may readily infer who was responsible for drafting the King's reply. But despite Bacon's lead, and the strong seconding of Charles, Buckingham, and Archbishop Abbot, the Lords, led by Saye and Spencer, voted support for the Commons' petition. Four days later, in the heated argument over the Lords' own petition, Bacon found himself as helpless as poor Richardson in the Lower House. Unable to stem or divert the debate, he tried unsuccessfully to adjourn the House, and then to read a bill. But the debate went on. The tactics that controlled earlier parliaments were no longer of avail in the 1620s.[93]

Meanwhile, a groundswell had begun to gather under Bacon himself. At the meeting of the Commons' committee for courts on February 28, scandalous abuses were revealed among the registrars of Chancery who, to augment their income from fees, had falsified and sometimes simply invented orders, "fathering" them on some attorney who was known to practice in the court. A long-smoldering feud between Chancery and Wards for jurisdiction in the case of a disputed benefice[94] erupted in an envenomed clash between Cranfield and John Finch; and on the same busy day, Cranfield outlined to the committee a sweeping eight-point program for judicial reform. Coke, two weeks before, had introduced a bill of his own "For Limitation of Actions in Chancery," and the attack on that court was to be one of the major themes of the session.[95] This confluence of wind and wave against the person of Bacon was already attracting notice; on February 25, Dr. Mead wrote to his country correspondent, Martin Stuteville, "It is said, that there are many bills ready to be put up against my lord chancellor."[96]

Suddenly, on the third of March, it was discovered that Mompesson had escaped from his confinement in the Tower and perhaps already fled the country. The Commons immediately requested that the Lords have warrants sent out for his arrest. Coke had not yet prepared his case, and at a stroke he and the House had been balked of their prey. But this left them all the more resolved to punish him fittingly in absentia.

The unforeseen rapidity with which the matter of Mompesson had been broached to the Lords brought another figure into the arena: Buckingham. The favorite's name was notoriously coupled with that of the monopolist. For two weeks rumor and accusation had thrashed through Westminster; and now, with Mompesson's name formally laid before the Lords, all eyes turned upon the first peer of the realm.

Buckingham joined his name to the warrant, and spoke at some length of his association with Mompesson. He "never loved to loose a freind for adversity, for hee thought that whosoever did so would never have a freind." Yet if it were shown that Mompesson had deceived the King and done wrong, his hand would be the first to be raised against him. The Marquis admitted that he had introduced Mompesson to the King, but any man might be deceived, and Mompesson's patents had not been sealed before being certified by "the best and most learned." Only the previous Monday, on hearing reports of complaints about the execution of the patents, Buckingham had questioned Mompesson at Newmarket in the presence of the King, and "told him that his Majestie had called a Parliament and if he had done any wronge hee would heare of it; and therefore bid him advise well with himselfe, and, if hee had, that he would confesse it in tyme."[97] Thus the royal favorite, frank-faced and open, determined to defend a friend or punish a malefactor, as the case might be. But the real significance of his statement was not lost upon his audience: that he would stand aside, if need be, and sacrifice the referees.

Two days later another scandalous patent emerged from the committee for grievances. This was the patent for gold and silver thread. The source of the committee's information about it was Sir Henry Yelverton, formerly the King's attorney, now lodged in the Tower.[98] The project had been promoted by Sir Edward Villiers, the older brother of the favorite. Yelverton testified that he had thought the scheme dubious and advised the King not to grant a patent but only to make an indenture between himself and the projectors as agents, "whereby, if found inconvenient, the King might easily put it down." James referred the project to Bacon, Suffolk, and Yelverton, who approved it in this form. A clamor was raised against this at Court, however, by "some that would have had a hand in it"; and the King, actuated by his zeal for the common good, referred it again to the same examiners, "who certified as before." The indenture was made for the manufacture of gold and silver thread in the kingdom, and a supplementary patent later conferred control of imports on the same parties. The goldsmiths bound to this monopoly opposed it violently, and the King was petitioned for a proclamation of enforcement on behalf of the patentees. But before he granted it James referred the entire question once again to Yelverton and Sir Robert Heath, then recorder of London. "Thus you see the King's care, how he never passed anything before he referred it to learned and judicious persons."

Sir Edward Villiers then prevailed upon Yelverton to imprison on his authority as attorney those who resisted the patent. Yelverton bowed to this "but with this caution, that he would release them presently if my Lord Chancellor did not confirm it. But my Lord confirmed it. And Mr. Attorney said he feared to release them because of Sir Edward Villiers and Sir Giles Mompesson." After three weeks' confinement in the Fleet, they were allowed a hearing before Bacon, "but they remaining obstinate were sent back." At last the wives and children of the prisoners petitioned the Lord Mayor of London; the King was thereby apprised of the affair, and immediately ordered their release: "So that you may see it is best to go to the fountain."[99]

A wave of revulsion and dismay passed through the House at this relation. Coke was the first to comment. The imprisonments had violated the twenty-ninth chapter of Magna Carta. He corrected Phelips, who had made the report of Yelverton's testimony, on one detail: Yelverton had committed the goldsmiths not in his capacity as attorney, but as a commissioner for the patent: "Sorry, the Attorney general should be a Commissioner, or this be countenanced by greater Persons."[100]

Sir Dudley Digges rose to move for a bill against the patents, and a declaration for all the suitors, projectors, and certifiers, "that they may be damned to posterity." Let us, he said, "brand those who shall presume to certify any thing on the References of such Business to further them; and to declare such Men unworthy to be near the Person of the King, be they never so great."[101] The House applauded.

The dam burst. Sir Edward Giles fulminated against "those blood suckers of the kingdom, these vipers of the King. The King's Attorney must be afraid of Sir Edward Villiers and Sir Giles Mompesson, what a shame is this. The more examples we make of great men, the more good we do to the country." Sir Hamon L'Estrange made a zestful and biblical speech: "Theis the Jesabells that lye in the eares of kyngs, wormes that breed of the crudityes of ill digestions. Away with Achitophells, the kinge needeth not their counsell." Heath tried to clear himself, and submitted his actions to the judgment of Parliament. But Cranfield tried to indicate the permissible limits of enthusiasm. He carefully pointed out, "That Sir Edw. Villyers had no Encouragement or Comfort from the Marquis. That Sir H. Yelverton confessed, my Lord of Buck' never did write, speak, or send to him about it."[102]

Second thoughts began to creep in among other members too. Harry Vane, a government man, agreed to the investigation of the referees, "Not that he thinks that we may punish them that are great, but yet to examyne it that the King may have his dew honor." Sir John Walter made an impassioned speech. Let all patents be called in and suppressed, and have none granted hereafter. Let all projectors henceforth incur praemunire for preferring suits; and let the House now send to Convocation to have a curse put on them! Yet he concluded with the advice "not to look back to the Referrees; whereby we may draw Opposition, and a Crossing of the Proceedings for hereafter."[103] But at this critical point Sackville stiffened the Commons' back again. The House must not shrink before any, "howe great or in what place soever." Guy Palmes firmed this into a motion and called for a vote, upon which the House at last agreed to call the referees.[104]

The House had been scheduled to present "divers heavy grievances" to the Lords—the Mompesson indictment among them—that very afternoon; Secretary Calvert, who had been in the Upper Chamber securing permission for the requested conference, found the debate on the referees in full swing when he returned. It was clear, however, that the House was not ready to make its presentation, especially now that it had decided to incorporate the referees into it. The conference was put off for three days.[105]

In the interim, the House worked hard to put together its case. The core of it remained the proposed action against Mompesson. The House would not merely ask, as customarily, cooperation in framing a petition to the King for redress of grievances. It was to present what was, in effect, a legal indictment, and to attempt to persuade the Lords that by law they could and of right they should prosecute upon that indictment. Coke now took the lead as never before. This, he knew, was the decisive moment. The argument of the House was distributed among six speakers. Digges was to open with a general introduction; Thomas Crew, Finch, and Hakewill to discuss the specific patents, naming the referees for each; Sandys to summarize; and Coke, in the key role, to press home the precedents, and conclude.

On the morning of the conference, March 8, the Commons staged a dress rehearsal. Digges and Coke went through their paces, but, at ten o'clock, Speaker Richardson suddenly rose from his chair, declared the House adjourned, and strode resolutely out the door, with a tumultuous and protesting mob at his heels. It was a crude and high-handed trick; but its effect was disaster on the conference. Digges and Coke performed ably, and the weight of the latter's precedents sank home ("And thus I leave you to tread in the steps of your noble progenitors"), but the intermediate speakers faltered sadly and, catching fright from one another, not one of them mentioned the referees.[106]

Next morning, the leaders of the House were fuming. Man after man attacked the Speaker. It was the greatest indignity, said Henry Withrington, that he had ever seen in Parliament. The omissions of the middle speakers in the conference were deplored. It dishonored the House, declared Roe. If the House had commanded it, Giles avowed, he would have named his own greatgrandfather. The referees must not be spared. Their souls had "made a wilful Elopement from their Bodies" when they certified the patents; they were "criminal, yea capital Offenders." But as for Coke, he was "the Hercules of this House; of the Honour and Justice of it." Almost singlehandedly he had redeemed what would otherwise have been a complete fiasco, and it was of this moment that Chamberlain spoke when he wrote that Coke "hath won his spurres for ever."[107]

The truth of the matter was, however, that the Commons had gone to the Lords too soon and in too great haste. "Never saw Parliament so out of Order," remarked Alford disgustedly. Hakewill, Crew, and Finch, in defending themselves, had all the same excuse for not having named the referees: there had been no reliable proof of who they were. "I saw no certificate, no petition, and therefore had no ground to speak of them," said Crew, "of which I had a purpose to certify the House, but that it arose at an unlawful hour and therefore could not." The identification of the referees depended solely on the statements of Mompesson and Yelverton. No one was willing to risk his skin on that.[108]

Coke spoke soothingly. Like a paterfamilias, he assured the House that it had not done so badly. "Sir D. Digges did excellently;—*apte, distincte, et ornate, dicere; breviter, et perspicue:* The second gravely and discreetly, like a Common Lawyer: For the third, would not have him blemished, but would have him supply what he forgot: For the last; he also did well." Let the House not consume its time in recrimination, but state what had been omitted at a new conference. Coke reminded the House that he had told the Lords there would be more to say at another time.[109]

James had followed this sequence of events anxiously from its inception. After the Commons' conference with the Lords on March 8, he decided to take direct action. On the morning of the tenth, James appeared unexpectedly in the Lords. The King came straight to the point. "The errant that brought mee hether was this, I have herd of greate discourse among you touching delinquents upon patents granted by me. Bycause I am the giver of all patents, yt can not but reflect on mee." The King wanted to stress that the concept of the Crown in Parliament was for him not merely a symbolic one, but that his presence at the head of the great council of his kingdom was as natural as his presence at the Privy Council: "In former tymes kings sate not in Parliament by representacion but person, as I doe now, both houses makinge then but one." He had come before the Lords to speak because there was a stronger bond between the King and his nobility: "I thought, my Lords, that all the world, especially yee, shold know my hart." First, however, he bade his Lord Chancellor recall the points made by the Commons in their conference two days ago, "to the end I may speake to what appertaineth to myselfe."

Bacon stepped down from his chair, moved to his place as a peer, and, in a barely audible voice, summarized the points of the conference.

James then dealt in detail with his role in the patents. It was a most embarrassing performance. He complained that he had been so beset with pleas and petitions against the patent of inns that they had been brought to him in his very bed. As for the thread patent, "I willed my attorney, Sir H. Yelverton, that there shold in them be a clause of ceasing yf I found them inconvenient. If there be not such a clause it is his fault. . . . If yt [gold and silver thread] were a trade before, I was wronged by my referrees; and both I and they by such as do now blame it and did not then enforme my referees."

The King's worst enemy could hardly have made out a more damaging case. Yet it would be unjust to judge James simply by the undoubted laxity of his administration. As Ranke recognized long ago, he ruled in a sense by corruption. Graft, indulgence, favor, and intrigue—by these skeins the suspicious monarch had sought to tie men to him, to control them by obligation where he dared not trust to love. About his person he kept only the creatures of his own making, the Somersets and Buckinghams. This complex and ambiguous character, in whose conduct and policy his strengths and weaknesses were so inextricably woven, had picked his way through alliance and intrigue for forty years with a sagacity that was half vacillation, a vacillation half sagacious. Yet it seemed now that the credit he had drawn, as it were, on his own character, had at last come due. Abroad, his honor and reputation were being slowly dragged down into the morass of the Palatinate, while at home, they were impeached by revelations of scandal. Corruption James expected, but corruption on such a scale as Parliament had revealed might well destroy that which he prized above all else in life, his good name.

It was for this reason that James had come to the House of Lords. But the King was caught in a cruel dilemma. If he was to save his good name, he must place himself at the head of reform; yet to do this, he must see his great officers of state deposed by Parliament and the royal prerogative profoundly subverted, for this was by now the clear drift of events. To protect his other ministers, he might have sacrificed Buckingham. But such a course, aside from the personal reasons against it, would have the worst result of all. The old aristocracy could not have wished a greater or a sweeter victory than the fall of the Marquis. It would also have encouraged the warhawks in both houses for whom Buckingham was the leader of the Spanish party. The King therefore drew the line at the favorite. He praised Buckingham's administration, and asked the Lords to clear his honor as well as the Crown's, thus firmly associating the two.

How, then, was the King to deal with his dilemma? His decision was not yet fully taken, but its direction was sufficiently clear. For the monopolies, "I am contented (as Sir Edward Coke moved) there should be a lawe made against theis thinges." "As for the thinges objected against the Chancelor and the Treasurer," said James, "I leave them to answere for themselves and to stand or fall as they aquitt them selves, for if they cannot justifie themselves, they are not worthie to hould and enjoy those places they have under me."

Justify themselves—but to whom? James drew back at this point. "My Lords," he wagged, "take my woords according to my meaning. Legalitie, how farre you of the upper howse may judge of, not of mens estates. You are a howse of Record, but how farre you may punish, what your priviledges be, is a question."

James continued:

> For though Sir Edward Coke be verie busie and be called the father of the Law and the Commons' howse have divers yonge lawyers in it, yet all is not law that they say, and I could wish, nay I have tould Sir Edward Coke, that he would bring presidents of good kings' tymes. . . . I scorne to be likened to the tymes of some Kings. H(enry) 6 was a sillie weake King. . . . I hope in his vouchinge presidents to compare my actions to usurpers or tyrants tymes you will punish him, for the Starr Chamber which is an inferior Court to this will punish *pro falso clamore*.
>
> I will give accompt to God and to my people declaratively, and he that will have all doon by parliament is an enemie to monarchie and a traitor to the King of England.

With James's commonsense refutation of the sophistries of precedent law, one can readily sympathize. He argued that the records nearest to his own time were the ones most pertinent to the interpretation of his reign. This was special pleading in a sense too; the precedents James called for are those of a strong Tudor kingship. But it was at least as arguable a bias as the common lawyer's. Coke, to prove that the Lords could try crimes against the Commonwealth, was wrenching medieval precedents out of their contexts to make them say what they had never said to anyone before.

Yet there was something plaintive in the King's protest; it was a plea against the rules of a fixed and inflexible game. His entire stance, indeed, was that of a man on the defensive. He warned Parliament not to go too far, but dared not check its proceedings. He all but accused Coke of treason; yet he could not touch him. As long as James was forced to appeal to Parliament for vindication, Coke's position would be unassailable.

At the end, perhaps secure in the fact that he had armed Buckingham sufficiently against attack, James shrewdly decided to humble his favorite a bit. If any should accuse him, said the King,

> I desire you not to looke of him as adorned with theise honours as Marquess of Buckingham, Admirall of England, Master of my Horse, Gentleman of my Bed Chamber, a Privie Counsellor and Knight of the Garter, but as he was when he came to me as pore George Villiers and if he prove not himselfe a white crow he shalbe called a black crow.[110]

Whereupon the favorite, on his knees before his fellow peers, submitted himself to the King's grace.

Bacon was then permitted to speak in his own behalf. He spoke briefly and simply. He was ready to submit his conduct to the censure of his peers, and asked only time to consult his papers. He was unafraid of judgment; and, he added, "may it please your Majestie, for all my Lord Coke hath said, I hope in futuer ages my acts and honestie shall well apeare before his, and my honesty over ballance and waigh his and be found hevier in that scale."

Treasurer Mandeville, and Buckingham again, spoke to exonerate themselves, and James then concluded. He warned Parliament to leave the legality and "convenience" of the patents to the ordinary courts of justice, to which they properly belonged. He repeated his plea for vindication: "I thinke you conceave you have a good Kinge. I beseech you, my Lords spirituall and temporall, soe to chalk out the way that my people may know my zeale to justice and my desire to free them from opression." And he reminded his auditors—and beyond them, his absent Commons—of the worsening crisis abroad: let justice be done, "but consume not millions of dayes in those thinges which have enterveyned since the Parliament began, and were not the cawses of calling of it."[111]

The King was once again impatient over supply. Although Convocation had just voted him a handsome three subsidies,[112] the Commons had not yet framed their grant into law. The presumptive difficulty was whether the passage of a subsidy bill would automatically terminate the session, thus interrupting Parliament in the midst of its work.[113] But the real fear of the House was that the King, his subsidies enacted, might dissolve Parliament rather than see the monopoly prosecutions carried to their conclusion.

Nonetheless, under pressure of their own promise to assess the first subsidy in March,[114] the Commons had brought a bill out of committee, and scheduled a final reading for the tenth. When James, who had just finished his speech in the Lords, heard that Coke had been admitted (over Bacon's objection) to request a second conference on the monopolies instead, he hastened back to the Upper House. The diarist of the "Lords' Debates" noted laconically, "The King taketh notice that this afternoone is appointed for reading the Subsidie and his highnes would not have that neglected."[115] Salvetti gives us more details. James entered the House in a fit of rage, volleying oaths. He gave order to forgo all other business until the subsidy bill had been passed by both houses, and told the Lords to inform the Lower House of his command at once. But the Lords demurred; they had already given their consent to the conference and could not now go back on the word of a joint resolution. They suggested that the King might send his order to the Commons by his own direct authority. James immediately dispatched his attorney, Thomas Coventry, with the message.[116]

The Commons were taken aback by the arrival of Coventry, as royal messages were normally delivered by the privy councillors of the House. Exactly what etiquette should be employed in receiving him? While William Hakewill and Sir Edward Montagu plied precedents, Coventry waited at the door. Coke, who knew that the King had spent all morning haranguing the Lords, and must have known at least the gist of it, quickly stepped forward:

The Attorney General being sent to the House in a message from the King, said Sir Edward Coke, let us do the messenger this respect and the King this honor as to be bare while he is here. And it was so ordered. Whereupon he coming up with three congees to the table, all were uncovered.[117]

The Commons replied that they would finish the subsidy bill that day if they sat until ten o'clock to do it. But it was no less their courtesy than their answer that mollified the royal tempest. Two days later Calvert presented a message from James thanking them not only for the final preparation of the subsidy bill but for

the singuler dutie and affection wherwith his Message, sent hither upon Saterday last by Mr. Atturney generall, was both receaved and answered, aswell in the manner as the matter. . . . there wanted not any due respect, and Ceremonie fitt for his Majesty's honour; not only at the delivery of the Message, but during the whole time of the Messengers stay in the house.[118]

As Coke seldom lost sight of his main objectives, so he was careful of those small but crucial arts by which they were won. This apparent mellowing of a famously violent temperament was noted by Chamberlain, who wrote that Coke "hath proceeded hitherto with a great deale of sinceritie, temper, and discretion more then usuall in him."[119] But Coke's newfound tact was less mellowness than the mien and judgment of a man in complete control of a situation constructed step by step by himself.

The second conference with the Lords was held on the afternoon of the tenth. Finch and Crew made good their previous omissions, and formally laid the names of the referees before the Upper House. Bacon thereupon came forward in his own defense. Whatever abuses had cropped up in the execution of the patents, he said, "was nothing to the Referres and that the thing might be lawful thowgh used unlawfully." Concerning the imprisonment of the men who had defied the thread patent, he said he had committed them for their contempt, and "so as not to discountenance the act of the generall attornye." He dismissed Yelverton's allegations with the remark, "the testimony of a discontented person is but poore." Mandeville followed Bacon with his apology.

Coke seized this moment with a shrewd and hawklike cunning. Did the statements of these lords, he asked, represent the consensus and vote of their House? The answer to this all but rhetorical question was a unanimous negative. Gardiner commented on this scene, "Not a voice was raised on behalf of the King's theory that the Commons had no right to interfere with the conduct of his ministers."[120] But did the question, as phrased, admit of any other answer? Legally speaking, this brief exchange meant nothing; dramatically and symbolically, everything. Though no formal charge had yet been placed against him, Bacon now stood isolated, the target of every shaft; and with every passing hour his role was being more surely shaped: the victim, the sacrifice, the scapegoat.

Buckingham was now alarmed by the proceedings in Parliament. He had been frightened and humiliated by the submission he had been forced to make in the Lords. He turned to his new political mentor, the dean of Westminster, John Williams, for advice. Should he not urge the King to dissolve Parliament before it wreaked havoc in the state?

Williams replied bluntly, "The former Parliament was very tart, if not undutifull; what then? Shall we be fearful to put our hands into cold water, because we have been scalded with hot? There's no colour to quarrel at this general assembly of the kingdom for tracing delinquents to their form: for it is their proper work."

His advice was attractively simple: "Swim with the tide, and you cannot be drowned." He continued:

> I have searched the Signet Office, and have collected almost forty [patents], which I have hung in one bracelet, and are fit for revocation; damn all these by one proclamation, that the world may see, that the King, who is the pilot that sits at the helm, is ready to play the pump, to eject such filth as grew noisome in the nostrils of his people.
>
> And your Lordship must needs partake in the applause, for though it is known that these vermin haunted your chamber, and is much whispered, that they set up trade with some little license from your Honour, yet when none shall

appear more forward than yourself to crush them, the discourse will come about, that these devices, which take ill,
were stolen from you by misrepresentation, when you were
but new-blossomed in Court, whose deformities being discovered, you love not your own mistakings, but are the most
forward to recall them.[121]

This was nothing but the advice Bacon had given Buckingham
four months before. Now it had the ring of genius. Buckingham hastened to James. The next day, March 13, he formally
announced at a joint conference of the houses that the King
would support them fully in their investigations, and that for
his own part, he would do nothing to defend his brothers if
they had done ill, for "he, that begot them, had begot One, that
would seek for their punishment."[122]

The general change in tone on the Crown's side was notable.
Coke complained before the Lords that he had been "taxed for
the Presidents he last brought them [on March 10] as the inven-
tions of his own head. . . . But my Lord Marquis told him if
any did so charge him they were like Him that acted the part
of Ignoramus the Lawyer in the play at Cambridge." On the
fifteenth, after Coke had presented a report to the Lords sum-
marizing the information imparted by the Commons at the previous two conferences, Prince Charles "said he was never wearie
with heareinge Cooke, he mingled mirth with busines to so
good purpose."[123] The threats of a few days before had turned
to praise. Coke had mastered the Court; he was at the crest of
his triumph.

The drama of patents and referees had almost wholly absorbed
the House of Commons for three weeks. When the committee
for courts of justice met on March 14, it was for the first time
since February 28. The chairman of the committee was Sir
Edward Sackville, the brother and heir of the childless Earl of
Dorset, a man of moderate views and eloquent address, close to
the Court and a known friend of Francis Bacon. He was a useful
figurehead for the committee; he summarized its proceedings
ably in the House without in the least grasping their import. He
had evidently no idea that his own attacks on the referees might
ever involve Bacon. As late as March 5 he declared vociferously
that "the questionynge of noe referee should bee spared, howe

great or in what place soever."[124] By the twelfth of March, however, it was clear that his committee had bared the knife for Bacon, and that its next meeting would be the stage for the decisive assault on the Chancellor's tottering position. Sackville, pleading illness, asked to be temporarily removed from his committee responsibilities, and the House appointed Sir Robert Phelips to sit in his place.[125]

Cranfield began at the meeting by moving the investigation of bills of conformity.[126] "The Business of Sir Giles Mompesson is but a Trifle compared to these Kinds of Injunctions, which strike at Men's whole Estates," he said. The King had never authorized these bills; indeed, when they had come to his attention, "he was so angry as I never saw him" and said he would not "endure" the officials responsible for such things about him. They were a prime cause of the decay of trade; for who would extend credit under such conditions? May and Heath, both government men, solemnly supported him.[127]

Was Cranfield merely carried away by his enmity for Bacon, and the irresistible pleasure of giving him the last push, or did his attack signify that the government had decided to throw Bacon to the wolves? His purpose cannot be certainly known; nor can we judge what the effect of the attack might have been, for the next order of business on the committee's docket was the petitions of Christopher Aubrey and Edward Egerton, and their sensational charges of bribery immediately swept all other accusations off the board.

The matter in both petitions was similar: it was alleged that Bacon had accepted money from the petitioners to expedite suits pending in Chancery. It was not clear with what understanding Bacon had accepted the money, nor what return, if any, he had given for it, but that he had taken payment from two suitors in his own court seemed beyond doubt: the relevant witnesses were all present.

Bacon had been forewarned about Aubrey and had attempted, unsuccessfully, to silence him.[128] Egerton's petition apparently caught him by surprise, because it was not until the morning of the fourteenth that he tried to persuade Egerton to withdraw it.[129] It was a hopeless gesture: those who had encouraged the two suitors to bring forward their accusations, those who had shielded them from Bacon while they waited for a cue to come onstage, those who had already arranged to have Bacon's go-betweens present at the committee to testify, had constructed a trap in which it was useless to struggle.[130]

Thomas Meautys, Bacon's secretary and a member of the committee, spoke up bitterly. He did not need to express his allegiance to the Chancellor; all who knew him knew it. In this proceeding against his lord, he said, he saw the intent of many more against others. The committee demanded that Meautys explain this remark. He replied that he merely referred to "the Order and Course that is held by this House, for the examining of the Abuses of the Courts of Justice."[131]

The committee agreed that, in view of the gravity of the charges and the eminence of the accused, the matter be reported to the House without delay. Noy added that, considering the testimony of the witnesses, he did not think it necessary "that the Complainant should be bound to stand to prove his Accusation, which is the Course in like Cases," but urged haste "for the clearing of so great a Magistrate."[132]

The next morning, Phelips made his report:

> I am commanded from the Committee for abuses in Courts of Justice to render an account of some abuses in courts of justice which have been presented unto us. In that which I shall deliver are three parts: 1, the person against whom it's alleged; 2, the matter alleged; 3, the opinion of the Committee with some desire of further direction. 1, The person is no less than the Lord Chancellor, a man so endued with all parts both of nature and art as that I will say no more of him because I am not able to say enough. 2, The matter alleged is corruption. . . .[133]

The committee thought the matter should be searched into as quickly as possible, "because a great man's honor is soiled with it." It proposed to meet again that afternoon, and submit the results of its investigation to the Lords, the procedure followed in the Mompesson case. The House gave its approval.[134]

Bacon was overwhelmed. At sixty years of age, the first statesman of his country and the foremost intellect of his time, he found himself ruined in a week. On the fourteenth he wrote to Buckingham:

Your Lordship spake of purgatory. I am now in it, but my mind is in a calm; for my fortune is not my felicity. I know I have clean hands and a clean heart; and I hope a clean house for friends or servants. But Job himself, or whosoever was the justest judge, by such hunting for matters against him as hath been used against me, may for a time seem foul, specially in a time when greatness is the mark and accusation is the game. And if this be to be a Chancellor, I think if the great seal lay upon Hounslow Heath, nobody would take it up.

His only fear, he said, was that his weak and ailing body might not stand the strain of events, "and then it will be thought feigning or fainting." But he hoped that "the King and your Lordship will . . . put an end to these miseries one way or other." Crossed out was the sentence, "I hope the King and your Lordship will keep me from oppression."[135]

After Phelips' report had been delivered, Coke went up to the Lords with his final summary of the case against Mompesson and the patents. Sir Edward outdid himself in denunciation of the vanished monopolist. The deeds of Dudley and Empson were as nothing by comparison: "Sir Giles Mompesson hath gone so far beyond them all as that a man had need of an astrolabe to take the height of it." But in all his speech there was barely a single allusion to the referees, whose omission had so exercised the House a week before. Parliament, Coke said, had taken care to observe a due respect for three things: the King's prerogative, his necessities, and his honor, "which done, by *mentioning* the Referrees [italics mine]."[136] That this course had had the approval of the leaders of the House is apparent from Coke's reception when he reported his speech back to the Commons: "Cooke thanked by MALARY, DIGS, and PHILLIPS, from his hart and soul, and after all the house."[137] The Lords, who that afternoon at last consented to act upon the Commons' presentation, made no mention of the referees in setting up their committees of investigation. Southampton, who led the debate, and had the closest liaison of any peer with the Commons' chiefs, conspicuously omitted any reference to the subject:

> SOUTHTON. To putt this buissines in a methode, and to expedite the same. Mocion. To begynn with the execucion of the Patents and to deale with the Patentees, and parties by them

used. There be 3 patents. To appoynt 3 Comittees of a fewe number, eache comittee to peruse each pattent, and to examyne the parties that executed the same.[138]

While the Lords were at work on this, the committee for courts of justice continued its examination of the two chief witnesses against Bacon, Sir George Hastings and Sir Richard Yonge. John Finch, loyal to his patron, attacked Hastings for his "ungratefull accusation," "hopeinge soe great a man showld not fall by the testimonie of one who had most reason to excuse himselfe for soe fowle a fact as the deliverye of a brybe." The truth, charged Finch, was that Hastings had taken money from Aubrey for himself, and was trying to clear himself by calumniating the Chancellor. The scene was stormy; the committee wanted to censure Finch, but remembered it lacked the power to do so.[139]

The report of the committee's hearing was delayed the next day by a sudden dispute between the two houses. The Lords sent down a message signifying their acceptance of the Mompesson case; but, "that the proof be without exception," they requested that those members of the Commons who had testified in the matter repeat their declarations under oath. The Commons were severely jolted. Perrot took it as a "disparagement" to the members cited, and Alford found it "preposterous." For "members of this house to be misdoubted of truth is very hard from the house," said Noy; should the Commons question the veracity of their lordships? "The Lower howse in respect of the Higher is to bee ressembled to a Graund-jurie," declared Brooke, "which after they have given a Verdict are not to be sworne that the Verdict is true."[140] The issue was a serious one; had Coke and the Commons raised the Lords' judicature from the dead only to see themselves treated as no different in kind from the petitioners who came to them? A recrudescence of aristocratic power independent of the Commons was not at all what they had had in mind.

But Sir Humphrey May pointed out that the case against the Lord Chancellor rested chiefly on the testimony of two MPs; what, then, was to be done if members of the House would not be sworn? Digges snapped that the two questions were totally dissimilar, and Solicitor Heath made an interesting distinction between cases "wherin wee have iudged" and "wherin wee only informe."[141] What he meant was that the patents sent up to the Lords had already been judged by the House in its official formula of condemnation, as "a grievance in creation and execution." This assertion by the King's officer was of course flatly counter to James's own argument that neither house, let alone the Commons, could judge the legality of patents.

May's objection was dismissed, but the question of the swearing remained, and, according to Pym, was "likely to be denyed."[142] At this point, Sir Edwin Sandys brought the House around to reason again, asserting, "The Question before us was of the Pattents and the Projects, which we have adjudged to be greivances both in the originall and the execution." But to judge without power of sentencing was not fully to judge. It was for that reason that the Commons had gone to the Upper House. And, they concurring, "The Question before the Lords is of the punishment, which may reache to life, and God forbid they showlde proceede upon an implicite faith of the examinacions taken by us without oathe. Noe man but knowes That the Condempnacion doth not ensue upon the Verdict of the Grand-jurie But that there is a further tryall. The Lords send not for these Gentlemen in any compulsary manner, which might breake our Priviledge, but by intreatie." The judges of assize and of oyer and terminer gave evidence on oath; so might parliament men. Sandys therefore suggested that the members called by the Lords might individually and voluntarily agree to take their oaths, thus satisfying the Lords while protecting the Commons' privileges.

The common sense of this suggestion was immediately convincing. The House adopted Sandys' resolution, and hurdled the crisis. It had cost but a day.[143]

The next morning, March 17, Phelips reported the committee's second hearing. It had further questioned Hastings and Yonge, and it recommended now that the House take the case "single" to the Lords. Two considerations urged this: "(1) Of Precedent, that in this Course we may followe the stepps of our Ancestours. (2) Of necessitye, which is dowble, (1) the respect of the person, being a Member of the Upper Howse, (2) our want of that Towchstone whereby truth may be bowlted out," that is, the Commons' lack of power to swear witnesses.[144]

Coke quickly seconded the motion, suggesting that Phelips set down his points in writing. He assured the House that "we must go to the Lords," according to all past precedent. But what precedent was there in fact? The last impeachment in the House of Lords had taken place in the middle of the fifteenth century.[145] William Noy, for one, lacked Coke's ready certainty that the authority of the Lords would suffice. Bacon's offense was against the King, "for as much as in him lyeth he hath broken the kings oathe. . . . Of necessitie we must goe to the Lords But there may be a question whether to them alone and without the Kinge; in one case this was demanded but refused." Noy recommended that "In Commendinge it to the Lords, not to deliver it as a thing certeyne, as wee did in Sir Gyles Mompessons case"—in other words, as an indictment—but rather as an "Informacion."[146]

Calvert took the point up. He doubted "whether so great a Man may be examined by the two Houses," and suggested that they petition the King to hear the case himself.[147] That, clearly, was the last possible move for Bacon: to deny the jurisdiction of Parliament to deal with so high a matter, and throw the case on the King himself.

The House was also uncomfortably conscious of the thinness of the evidence. Sackville, a most perplexed and conscience-stricken man, protested that he would bite off his tongue and throw it to the dogs before he would speak for the Lord Chancellor, if he proved guilty of the heinous crime of which he was accused. But he did not think Hastings and Yonge competent witnesses: "They spake to discharge themselves." Sir John Strangways pointed out that the only evidence that Bacon had ever received the money came from the two persons who were supposed to have brought it to him, but no third party. Bacon had reportedly told Hastings that he would deny the receipt of the money under oath: would it come, then, to his word against the Lord Chancellor's? Above all, the House was aware that for each charge the evidence against Bacon rested on the testimony of one man—Hastings for Aubrey's, Yonge for Egerton's. Could so great a man be properly accused of so grave a crime by the word of a single witness?

Coke rushed in to allay these fears. In Newarke's case, 37 Eliz. (actually 38; Coke slipped), concerning the ransom of rich men's sons pressed into the army, though in certain instances there was only a single witness for a particular act, the similarity of several cases taken together was held sufficient for conviction. "Therefore, albeit Sir George Hastings only prove the Delivery of the Hundred Pounds given by Abry, and Sir Richard Young only testifieth the Four Hundred Pounds given from Mr. Egerton, yet both of these Witnesses agreeing in *eodem tertio* (viz. of Corruption) are not to be held as *singularis testis*." As for the involvement of the witnesses themselves in the crime, "It wilbe impossible to prove Bribery if yow will not accept of those that carrie the brybe. *Participes Criminis* is often taken for two good witnesses." He that in accusing another incriminated himself was, far from being suspect, actually the best and most reliable kind of witness.[148]

This reasoning was perhaps not entirely straightforward, particularly as Coke admitted that Hastings and Yonge "came not to accuse, but were interrogated." But it pacified the House. Calvert's objection was dismissed by the equation of the pressers' case with Bacon's. In Coke's eyes there was no man too mighty for the common law.

The House thereupon resolved that the heads of the accusations against Bacon be drawn up in writing by Coke, Digges, Phelips, and Noy, and presented verbally to the Lords on Monday the nineteenth.[149] Actually, there was no dispute over going to the Lords per se,[150] and general agreement that it must be done quickly, for evidence taken without oath would soon degenerate to rumor. The question was how the Commons should present the evidence they had thus far gathered, timidly and tentatively, or with a prosecutor's assurance; and then, whether the Lords would prove a sufficient tribunal. Clearly, the manner of presentation would largely determine the Lords' reaction. If the Commons came before them in the manner of a grand jury, with firm proofs that merely required the formality of an oath-swearing, it would smooth the way for the Lords' assumption of judicature; but if the Lords themselves were asked to function as a grand jury first, the step to judicature would be a much longer one, and the King might well be able to intervene. Coke's victory was in that crucial intangible. He had convinced the Commons to present their case with confidence.

James faced his last decision. He saw, no doubt, that there was little that could be done for Bacon. The Chancellor's scalp was the price that would have to be paid for hurdling the scandal of the patents. But beyond Bacon was the larger question of the revival of judicial impeachment in the Lords and the ultimate issue of ministerial responsibility. If the King allowed Parliament to proceed alone now, he would forfeit all future power in such cases; for if a binding precedent did not yet exist, the Bacon case would forge it. Yet how was James to interpose himself without seeming to whitewash Bacon, and without alienating his two houses, on whom the success of his German policy depended?

Between Saturday afternoon the seventeenth and Monday morning the nineteenth, the King and his Council worked out a solution. It was unveiled with the utmost circumspection and care. First Edmondes thanked the House effusively on the King's behalf for throwing out a bill for commoning sheep in Waltham Forest; then Calvert praised it for passing the subsidy again. Finally Calvert brought forward the royal proposal. The King had taken notice of the action against the Lord Chancellor. "Noe Prince could answere for all the faults of his servants, yet he tooke Contentment in this, that his owne honour remayned cleare." To expedite justice the King was ready to empower a special commission consisting of twelve members of the Lower House and six of the Upper, to be chosen by themselves, to examine the Chancellor's proceedings on oath. If the Commons should agree to this, the proposal would be made to the Lords, and the commission might sit during the Easter recess.

The seeming reasonableness of this plan, the freedom to accept or reject it, and the flattery implicit both in the proportion of commoners to be named and the fact that the King had submitted his idea first to them, nearly swayed the Commons. Perrot and Alford, the first to respond, both approved it. Coke was appalled. He grasped immediately the significance of the King's plan. Instead of asserting its own right to try Bacon, Parliament would be taking a temporary power from the King, and that merely to investigate the case: the King would reserve the right of final judgment to himself. The presence of a majority of the Commons on the commission would merely emphasize its dependence on the royal grant of authority, for the Commons could not examine upon oath, whereas the Lords could. The temporary commission would strike a deadly blow at the as yet unfledged judicial power of the Lords, without which Coke's grandiose plan for the High Court of Parliament was a broken dream.

None of this dared be said: the King's honeyed offering precluded any direct criticism. Coke merely cautioned the House against forsaking its previous resolutions, "that this gracious Message taketh not away our parliamentary Proceeding." He suggested that Phelips deliver the charges against Bacon, as planned, and that the House wait for the Lords' opinion on the King's proposal and return a joint answer, as it was a matter equally concerning both of them.[151]

The Commons, waking from their trance, readily agreed. It was obvious that to send an answer without consulting the Lords was to invite a breach between the two houses. Sir Thomas Wentworth alone objected that the House should delay its proceedings against Bacon until the question had been settled. Coke leaped up briefly at this. "*Contra*," is all we have of his reply. The Commons requested the King to inform the Lords of his proposal as well and promised to make a joint answer.[152]

That was the end of the temporary commission. The government knew that the Lords would never accept a scheme so detrimental to their new authority. Its only hope had been in fact to try to slip the plan through a mesmerized House of Commons before the Lords had taken official cognizance of the case. This failing, there was no point in proceeding further. The King's proposal was never delivered to the Lords.[153] Had James insisted on his plan, Parliament would undoubtedly have had to accede to some kind of compromise, but he felt his doing so might jeopardize the entire outcome of the Parliament. The King had chosen to sacrifice the constitutional point for the short-run objectives of his continental policy and the clearing of his honor. He did not, of course, perceive it in quite this way. To James, his sacrifice of Bacon was the short ploy, and his credit and reputation at home and abroad, the longer view. The inalienable prerogative of the Crown could never, in the last analysis, be endangered by the pretensions of Parliament, which derived its authority from the King as (in the favorite simile of the time) the moon derived its light from the sun. Could Parliament assemble, deliberate, and make laws without being at every instant upheld by the consent of the sovereign will? In the final aspect of things, the paper triumphs of Parliament shrank to their true proportions. Or so it seemed to the King. With much hindsight, it may appear to us that the abandonment of the temporary commission was the most important single decision ever made by King James.

The Lords accepted Bacon's case from the Commons with alacrity, and immediately set up their investigative apparatus.[154] The great drama of the past two weeks was over. The choked and turbulent rush of events flowed into a calm channel as the Easter recess drew near. The Commons proceeded with their monopolies, the Lords with Bacon. The harmony between the two houses had never been greater, nor, apparently, had that between both and the King. "It is generally affirmed at London this week," wrote Dr. Mead, "that the king sends the parliament wonderful gracious messages . . . That he will continue the parliament till they are fully satisfied in all things; that they should ask nothing, but he would . . . incite and spur them forward."[155]

The immensity of Bacon's fall awed London. "Nothing like it has ever been seen in any other Parliament," reported Salvetti, "and, being so sudden, it is even more fearful." The dogs of malice were out; libels "not worth the repeating," said Chamberlain, were spread now against the Chancellor. When in Parliament Christopher Neville compared Bacon in Chancery to "a Minotaur in the Labyrinth of that Court, gormandizing and devouring all that comes before him," there was no one to check the slander; only Sir John Strangways remarked a little sadly that the Lord Chancellor was "a House that is falling." Bacon himself, meanwhile, had physically collapsed, as he had feared. He lay prostrate, "all swollen in his body," gave one report, "and suffering none to come at him. Some say, he desired his gentlemen not to take any notice of him, but altogether to forget him, and not hereafter to speak of him, or remember there was ever such a man in the world." But his spirit was not so far broken. "When I enter into myself," he wrote the King, "I find not the materials of such a tempest as is comen upon me. . . . I have been no avaricious oppressor of the people. I have been no haughty or intolerable or hateful man. . . . Whence should this be?"[156]

The answer to Bacon's question was a simple one. Viewed merely as a tactic to get the King to rescind the patents and to allow the Commons to frame an antimonopoly bill, the attack on the referees had been successful. It had struck so close to home as to compel James to support reform. But having broached the referees, and having cited them before the Lords, the question was how far and how high judgment would go. The situation was as embarrassing for Parliament as for the King, for to proceed against all the referees would virtually clear the King's entire legal staff right off their chairs. On the other hand, even if the Commons, having gotten their way on monopolies, had been inclined to drop the charges against the referees, it would have proved an awkward proceeding. The latter alternative would have been a tricky and unsatisfactory one, leaving the air unsettled; the former was a wholly intolerable proposition, for it would have involved the most far-reaching invasion of the King's prerogative. What the situation required was a scapegoat, a blind. The government had trotted out Mompesson and Yelverton, but they were too small. Bacon, his great eminence notwithstanding, had become the logical candidate. He was already under heavy fire not only for his role in the patents, but for the abuses in his court of Chancery. The problem was to find a charge to lay against him which would dramatically preempt attention and had no reference to the business of the referees, that is, which would implicate him alone. The discovery of Aubrey and Egerton provided the solution.

The Commons now sped toward the recess which, by the King's permission[157] they had set themselves for March 27. A coordinating committee was created to appoint interim committees for recusants, fees and impositions, courts of justice, free trade and decay of money, and the receipt of petitions, to function during recess.[158] On the twenty-sixth, James came again to the Lords. He wished to address his Parliament now for two reasons, "The first That we might conceive howe sencible he was of the dutie of beinge a Kinge," and of the faults of which his servants had been guilty, "The second, to Let us knowe That his comminge to Parliament showld never be to breake the Priviledges of a Parliament or to divert us out of any orderly or iust Courses"—a melancholy reflection on the result of his last appearance. James conceded misgovernment with a disarming frankness. "The State he compared to his owne Copices, the outside well growne and makeinge a good shewe But Inwardly eaten and spoyled. . . . His Government seemed to bee well fenced with Lawes, Judges and other Magistrates And yet his people, by secret Corruption, Proiecture, Bills of Conformitye and such like Courses, had been more greived and vexed then if they had given divers Subsedies." But he would prove his good intentions toward Parliament and his loving care for his people. For the former, he could give no better assurance than that "hee had sent his onely dearest Sonne to sitt amongst us." He did not know "what Bribes wee had given him," he added, with doubtful humor, but Parliament had no warmer advocate or sympathizer than the Prince. For the latter, the King took the occasion to announce a royal proclamation revoking the patents of inns, alehouses, and thread. And he wished and did not doubt that the present union of Crown, Commons, and Lords would make "the happyest Parliament that ever was."[159]

In the afternoon the Lords returned the call and found the King in a gay and gracious mood. Charles delivered their thanks, and James said he would return it double, averring that "He would carrye himself soe fairely That if a King were to be elected, he might hope to bee the Man."[160] Full of charm and ease and the cheerful grace of sovereignty, he was nonetheless conducting an arduous political campaign.

The next day was the Commons' turn. Speaker Richardson made their address, and James wore smiling airs again. He spoke, however, with some candor. "In former Parliaments there was noe true understanding betwixt my subiects and me. Wee were like the Builders of Babell, where one called for Morter, another for Stones. . . . But hereafter I hope all things wilbe soe cleare betwixt us That without any Orations our hearts shall speake for us." He held himself "much ashamed" to have appointed ministers "that have dealt so ill and vilely with me and so badly with the comune wealth," but he would now "concurre gladly with you in these your just proceedings." He admonished the House, however, to spend its remaining time wisely. "I knowe yow have a greate number of Pattents presented to yow. I advise yow to stand upon those That are of most importance, That when yow resort to me with your Greivances They may consist more in Weight then in Number And that the very name of a Pattent doe not become a Greivance." Finally, James asked his Commons to "present such a Mirrour of my heart to my Subiects That they maye know I hope for nothing more then to live long in the Contentment which I take in their ease and Prosperitie."

His speech done, James called Richardson forward. "Gentlemen," he said, "I meane to kill your Speaker in remembrance of this dayes work," and drawing a sword from the scabbard of a Scottish lord, he dubbed his long-suffering serjeant a knight.[161]

Dr. Mead gave an elaborate and joyful account of these proceedings. He described the panoply of bishops and peers who had come to present the thanks and homage of their House, the tears freely shed, and the King rejoicing that he had lived to find himself "inthronised in his people's hearts." "It is a day worthy to be kept holiday," said the Doctor. "Some say it shall, but I believe it not."

III

POPERY AND PREROGATIVE

King and Parliament had parted with a love feast; but the air still tingled with the shock of Bacon's fall, and no one knew on whom or what the Commons would light next. "Westminster Hall was never so made clene as it is like to be this year," wrote Thomas Locke to Dudley Carleton, " . . . [and] they may chance to find (if they looke well) as bad stuffe as any was cast about before."[1] The general excitement brought out the apprentice boys as well:

> On Easter daye Owld Don Diego went to see the Embassador of Pole in Fanchurch Street hee beinge in his Horsleeter; divers prentises & men dide come to his Leetter with stones in theyr hands and shaked them att hym, (but did not flinge any) & caled hym all to naught Dogg & Divell.[2]

The guilty youths were sentenced to be whipped through the city, but at Temple Bar a mob set them free "and beat the marshal's men sore." James, enraged, swept down to London (a hasty picture of Guildhall being hung with cloth of state), swore the city fathers blue, and threatened to garrison the town unless better order were kept. The apprentices were whipped again the next day under guard of a hundred halberdiers, and the day after "a terrible & strict" proclamation was read out. London sullenly obeyed. One of the whipped apprentices was dead.[3]

Bacon's fate was still the main topic of interest. Three committees sat taking evidence for his trial during the recess. When Parliament reassembled on April 17, the Lords began it promptly.

Bacon, having recovered from his initial shock, was resolved to make a defense. He still held the Great Seal. He felt no guilt. He had perhaps been careless in accepting gifts; but, he told the King, he had never taken a bribe.[4]

But when Bacon saw the arsenal of evidence being massed against him, he realized that any defense would be futile. Forty-one witnesses had testified to the Lords' committees; twenty-eight charges had been drawn.[5] Whatever their individual merit, the cumulative force of accusation was irresistible. Bacon thereupon offered his resignation to the Lords.[6]

He hoped that this would stop the trial, but the Lords were not so easily satisfied. Bacon was in effect sentencing himself, and his sentence, as the Earl of Suffolk declared, "is far short of that we expecte." Southampton added that Bacon's statement confessed no specific guilt. Indeed, it was so cunningly worded as to imply a near-vindication.[7] If the Lords did not see their case through now, they lay themselves open to a future charge of injustice.

Bacon had played his card. His only choice now was a full confession, or the protracted agony of the trial. On April 30, he sent his confession to the Lords.[8] A committee of twelve was deputed to visit his bedside to confirm the document. "My Lords," said Bacon wearily, "it is my Act, my Hand, my Heart."[9] The next day, he relinquished the Great Seal, and ceased to be Chancellor of England.[10]

There remained only the setting of his punishment, which quickly followed. On May 3, Bacon was sentenced to pay a fine of £40,000, and to imprisonment in the Tower at the King's pleasure. He was barred from holding any public office and from Parliament, and forbidden to come within the verge—twelve miles—of the Court.[11]

The sentence was much milder than it seemed. The first two items were merely token. For form's sake, the deposed Chancellor went to the Tower for a day or two at the end of the parliamentary session.[12] He was even permitted to make out his pardon and the remission of his fine. This latter he did by putting the sum in trust, thus freezing his assets up to £40,000 from creditors. John Williams, the new lord keeper, was highly disgusted at this. "His Lordship," he confessed, "was too cunning for me."[13]

The rest of the sentence was harder to shake. No sooner was Bacon out of the Tower than James was consulting him again, as of old, on Parliament.[14] But the twelve-mile prohibition remained. Not until the following March, in return for selling York House to Cranfield, did he regain formal access to the Court. It proved, however, a sterile bargain. Bacon never again served the state.[15]

Few historical figures have ever exerted such posthumous charm as Francis Bacon. If the live Bacon inspired remarkably little affection or loyalty among his contemporaries,[16] the dead one has lacked for neither. A devoted band of apologists has been working to rehabilitate him for more than a century. With great effort and ingenuity they have labored to disprove this or that article of the charge lodged against him by the Parliament of 1621. Their labors, however, are largely beside the point. The lords who investigated Bacon in 1621 were concerned with his conduct as Chancellor, a position he held in the last four years of a long career in government. But what of Bacon the attorney, say, or Bacon the solicitor? One need not dig very deeply to bear out Bacon's own admission that he was merely a man of his time.[17] His fall was the result of maneuverings as devious as any of his own, but it cannot of itself be called unjust.

While the Lords were preoccupied with Bacon himself, the Commons addressed themselves to the reform of the judicial system in general and the Court of Chancery in particular. The scandal of the Chancellor was only the last of a series of revelations about his court: excessive fees, forged orders, bills of conformity. It was Chancery that seemed to have corrupted Bacon, rather than vice versa. Sir Samuel Sandys voiced the general sentiment: "I wish we may not leave with the person, least we leave the place infectious for the next."[18]

During the recess, the committee for reformation of courts of justice was busily translating its mandate into action. It disgorged ten bills in the first week of the new sitting. Some of these struck at general abuses, and promised a healthy purge of the entire system. But the main thrust of the committee's work was directed at the Chancery. The result, however, could hardly be called reform. It was an attack on the very vitals of Chancery, a subversion of the entire principle of judicial equity.

Such an attack had been anticipated in the two preceding parliaments. In 1610, Chancellor Ellesmere complained that the

House of Commons had presumed "to examine in point of equity and conscience divers decrees made in the Chancery." A list of grievances drawn up by the Commons in that year included a demand that references to the masters of Chancery "be more sparingly given," and that the fees of the sinecure office of the six clerks be reduced. In the same list, significantly, was an item "Against restraint of prohibitions,"[19] which Coke on the Court of Common Pleas was throwing thick and fast in his personal campaign against Chancery. Nor was this the only matter on which Coke and the leaders of the Commons were in accord. Their strikingly parallel attitudes on the scope of royal proclamations and commissions foreshadowed the alliance that was to be consummated in 1621.

In 1614, a bill was introduced which would have prevented the reversal of any judgment at common law save by writ of error.[20] Yet the Commons were still a long way from ready to mount a serious attack against the Chancery when the Parliament of 1621 met. The measure of their residual timidity can best be gauged by the affair of Hall and Fuller. Hall and Fuller, two clergymen, had disputed a benefice. Hall found satisfaction in the Chancery and Fuller in the Court of Wards. A fierce battle for jurisdiction ensued, with the upshot that both parties were imprisoned by contrary injunctions from the two courts.[21]

The committee for courts was properly reluctant to become involved in this imbroglio, for jurisdictional disputes between courts were clearly outside its competence. It did so only at the insistence of Lionel Cranfield, the master of the wards.[22] A subcommittee was appointed; and, after sifting the evidence, it delicately concluded that "the Court of Wards had done very iustly and rightly and that the Chancery might graunt an iniunction. No injury to the Court of Wards in retaining the Cause. That neither Court did iniustice."[23]

This tactful solution did not satisfy Cranfield. "There must needs be iniustice in one of the Courts," he persisted, and demanded a further investigation. John Finch, the later "Blackrod" Speaker,[24] sprang to the defense of his master, Bacon: "Court of Chancery did nothing but iustly and honourably and what it hath done in a thousand causes besides." "The more the pitie," sneered Cranfield. "No pitie," returned Finch. It was "indisputable" that Chancery had done no wrong, but as for Wards . . .

Here Solicitor Heath stepped in disgustedly: "This private cause
not worthie the consideracion of this High Court."[25]

Two days later the quarrel broke out anew on the floor of the
House. Finch demanded a hearing and a judgment. "If this man
were worthy to Judge the Court of Wards," replied Cranfield,
"I would say somewhat to him for iudging it."[26] The case was
finally settled on March 16. It was resolved

> that both Courtes had done wronge, that both parties should
> be declared by the opinion of the parliament to be sett at
> libertie by both the iudges, that some course be taken for the
> reformation of abuses in both courtes, especiallie for writtes
> of assistance wherein in this cause both had offended.[27]

This sharp rebuke was a far cry from the committee's original
diffidence. Cranfield's spite had cost the Crown a damaging precedent.[28] Heretofore, the Commons had been content to follow the
rule of thumb laid down by Heath: only proof of corruption
could warrant interference in the decisions or competence of a
court.[29] After *Hall* vs. *Fuller,* they felt far less respectful of the
sanctity of judicial proceedings.

But it was the case of Bacon which finally emboldened the
Commons to undertake a thorough reform of the judiciary. With
public opinion at their back, the common lawyers set to work.
The result we must now examine.

There is no doubt that Chancery, no less than the rest of the
legal system, was badly in need of reform. Perhaps the most comprehensive critique of the court produced by the parliamentary
investigation was a paper drawn up privately by George Norbury,
a Chancery clerk, for the instruction of Bacon's successor, John
Williams. Norbury pulled no punches. The Chancery, he said,
had far exceeded its proper jurisdiction, which was confined to
matters of covin (fraud), trust, extremity, and casualty. It should
never deal with any case covered by the common law, or with
cases involving titles, wills, and marriages. Too often Chancery
admitted cases that would not have stood a chance at common
law, or that proceeded merely from malice or "turbulent humor."
Not more than three cases in ten presently before the court, Norbury estimated, had even a shadow of validity.

But good cause or bad, once admitted to pleading, all suits
mounted the same Ixionic treadmill of replication, rejoinder,

and reference. Lawyers, clerks, and masters, all paid by the page, had a common interest in the volubility of proceedings. "Alas how often have we seene ten or twelve order[s] in a cause and perhaps halfe as many reports before a heareinge," said Norbury, "and afterwards . . . all overturned or set aside as impertinent and the plaintiffe ordered to proceed to his prosses."[30] The sheer invention of orders for imaginary clients by the registrars of the Chancery, the first of the scandals which broke in 1621,[31] was only the logical end of the entire system.

Much of what the Commons did was no more than to legislate Norbury. One series of bills was aimed at cutting Chancery's business by discouraging frivolous suits and restricting it to its proper jurisdiction. A bill against "misproceedinges in Courtes of Equitye" was put in by Sir Peter Frecheville as early as March 6.[32] This bill was superseded by one "for avoiding vexation by process," which was reported to the House on April 17. It provided that no subpoena be issued from Chancery before the plaintiff's bill was filed.[33] Another bill "for avoiding insufficient jurors" was urged, not merely because the kingdom was "much scandalized" by the disinclination of people to serve on juries, but because "that it is which hath made the Court of Chancery swell so much with Business, and which hath increased that Court to so large an extent.[34] The committee for courts promised, but apparently never produced,[35] a bill that would have regulated the jurisdiction of the entire court system, common law and equity, temporal and ecclesiastical. Presumably, it would have followed the axioms so often enunciated by Coke[36] (and largely echoed by Norbury): that no cause determinable at the common law be tried by Chancery; that Chancery had no jurisdiction over land, and no power to fine, imprison, or grant writs of assistance.[37]

A final bill, introduced by Heath on May 4, propounded the simplest method of all for curtailing Chancery business. The Chancery was open all year. The common-law courts sat only twelve weeks, in sets of four. It was therefore proposed to limit hearings in Chancery to the four terms of the other courts, plus five days past each—about fourteen weeks in all.[38]

Extortionate fees were another major issue. The problem of fees cut right across the whole question of judicial reform. They were complained of in every court in the realm, and every litigant in the realm was a witness against them. Parliament considered fees the mainspring of all other judicial abuses, and no fewer than five bills to control them were introduced in 1621.[39]

Here again Chancery had pride of place, but this resulted as much from the court's own blundering as from the animus of the Commons. With the blithest effrontery, the twelve masters of Chancery petitioned the House on March 26 for confirmation of their new schedule of fees. There could not have been a worse subject to raise, nor a more inopportune time to raise it.

The masters claimed to have lost all their old fees, plus the church livings and diet allowances once available, and to have been reduced to a single stipend of £6.14s. for livery. Bacon had thereupon authorized a new schedule, after obtaining the King's consent and a ruling from his fellow justices that this did not contravene the statute 1 Jac. c. 10, which prohibited fee-taking for references.[40] The masters now craved the consent of Parliament as well, and an assurance that their new fees would be paid."[41]

It was scarcely to be believed. Not only had the masters the temerity to ask the Commons to confirm an act of Bacon's, but to overturn a parliamentary statute in doing it. Their petition was immediately remanded to the committee for grievances.[42] Witnesses were summoned. Thomas Ravenscroft, the clerk of the petty bag, testified that the masters not only took twenty shillings for a reference, as Bacon's patent allowed, but took them at every hearing, and of every litigant, plaintiff and defendant alike. Sir Eubule Thelwall, who had the unhappy task of representing his fellow masters, was asked how much they had paid Bacon for the patent. "Not a Penny," he snapped, but was forced to confess that, after it was sealed, eight of the masters had given him one hundred and fifty pounds apiece as a "gratuity." The distinction did not impress the committee. The patent was condemned, and a new count of bribery added to the charges against Bacon.[43]

This incident focused attention on the masters themselves. Originally, the masters had been legal assistants to the Chancellor. When a disputed point of civil or common law arose in a case, they produced an expert opinion or "reference" on it. From short answers on specific points, however, references had grown to whole tomes of research on every case, often down to a suggested verdict which the Chancellor had only to initial.[44] This raised the masters to something very close to associate justices. Coke vigorously denounced this practice. The Chancellor, he said, "hath noe power, nor any Judge whatsoever, to make a deputy. Nay, if the King seale a Patent to me being a Judge to make a deputy, it is void." The Commons moved to restrict the masters to their original functions, and Alford proposed to reduce their number from twelve to six, as fast as they died out.[45]

Up to this point, the Commons had taken reasonable action against real abuses. Indeed, they had done little more than re-state Bacon's own Orders of the Court. The Chancellor himself had laid down all the rules necessary to make his court a model of justice and efficiency. No injunction might be stayed or granted on any private petition (orders 21, 80). Suits already judged at the common law should be admitted only "after solemn and great deliberation," and with sureties from the plaintiff (33). No references might be made after the examination of witnesses, and no report admitted which exceeded the precise scope of the matter referred (47, 48). Bills and answers of "immoderate length" were to be penalized by fines (55). All documents copied out by Chancery clerks (who were paid by the page) were to contain a minimum number of lines to each sheet, "written orderly and unwastefully" (67).[46] These orders, like Norbury's treatise, show how freely recognized the abuses of the Chancery were, even within the court itself. They are also eloquent testimony to Bacon's tragic failure as an administrator.

But these merely procedural reforms did not go deep enough for the Commons. They could not be trusted to work without a thorough structural renovation of the Chancery. This was accomplished by two bills that wholly subordinated Chancery to the common law system and, in effect, legislated an independent equity out of English law.

The "Acte to establish two Judges Assistantes in the Court of Chancery," first moved by Alford,[47] was presented to the House on April 30.[48] It observed that the Chancery had only two regular judges—the chancellor and the master of the rolls—whereas each of the common-law courts had four. It was this deficiency, coupled with the staggering case load of the court, which had led the masters to encroach on its judicial functions. Merely to put the masters back in their proper place was not to solve the problem. "Be it therfore enacted," read the bill, " . . . that there shall two Judges, learned in the common lawes of this Realme, be added for *Continuall* assistantes to the saide Court of Chancery. And the same Court of Chancery shall hence forth *perpetualy* consist of fower principall Judges. . . . Namly the Lord Chancellor or Lord Keeper, the Maister of the Rolles, and two learned Judges of the Coyfe . . . [italics in text]."

These new judges were to have "equall power and voyce, in makeing of the Decrees and orders, and in all other the proceadinges of that Court." They were also to have, "for the tyme being," equal say with the chancellor in placing and displacing justices of the peace and of assize, and in choosing the masters of the Chancery. Henceforth all disputed points of law were to be referred to the new judges, and the masters to be reduced to mere clerks. No fee or gratuity was to be accepted for references, on pain of tenfold restitution.

But the final provision was the crucial one. It declared that all future decrees and orders of the court were to be made by a majority of the four judges, and that if they failed to reach agreement, "then the two Lord cheife Justices of the Kinges Bench and common pleas, and the cheife Baron of the Exchequer . . . shall ioyne with the other fower Judges of the Court . . . And this Decree or order made or confirmed by the most voyces of the saide Judges, shall stande firme and be fynall."[49]

In short, two common lawyers were empowered to block any writ, verdict, rule, or appointment in the Chancery, and in the event of a deadlock, three more common lawyers were to resolve the issue. Equity would henceforth merely supply lacunae in the common law, and civil law be banished forever from its precincts.

The *coup de grâce* for Chancery was delivered by the "Act for the Reversing of Decrees in Courts of Equity on Just Cause." It provided that any decree in Chancery might be challenged by a bill of review within a year of issue, and the case reheard with the three chief justices assisting.[50] Whether this bill presupposed the first one cannot say, but it was the logical and conclusive supplement to it. Should the new judges provided by the earlier act, good common lawyers though they were, begin to fraternize excessively with their equity associates, the ultimate check was still there.

Together, these two statutes gave the common-law courts an absolute veto over any decision in equity. Thus the whole intention of equity was repudiated. The Chancery, as Wolsey had conceived it, was to be an appellate court, in which the rigor or obsolescence of the written law could be mitigated. But Sir Edward Coke decreed otherwise. Equity was permanently relegated to inferior jurisdiction. While henceforth any verdict in Chancery would be reversible, "Noe cause to be entertayned in the Chancerie after Judgment at Common Lawe."[51]

Parliament did not of course confine its judicial inquisition to Chancery; but the faults of other courts, and particularly the common-law courts, were much less searchingly aired. There was good material for scandal, for example, in the Court of Exchequer. John Wilde of Droitwich, who practiced in the Exchequer, brought in a long bill of particulars:

> Newe Fees by the Clerkes of the Pipe, too much libertie to Informers by the Kinges Remembrancer, Exaction of Fees by the Treasurers Rembrancer uppon respite of Homage which should be but 2od. and is brought to 9s., Process to pleade Lycences of Alienations when they cannot be ignorant of the Lycences And the Plea costs twice as much as the first Lycence, Wronge chargeing men with Tenures, The Writt *Quo Titulo* against the heire that comes in by descent.[52]

It is true that many of these complaints—informers, alienations, intrusions—had been anticipated in Bacon's bills of grace, which to a certain extent blunted their impact. Nonetheless, the conspicuous absence of comment or reaction by the leaders of the House on this presentation was significant. They were not taking the bait. Another scandal like the Chancery could discredit the entire Bench, as that of the monopolies had threatened the integrity of the King's government. This was clearly not desirable. Thus, Chancery was to be the scapegoat among the courts, as Bacon had been among the referees. The choice of the first victim, indeed, had virtually determined the choice of the second. And, as Bacon's case had admirably served both public necessity and private revenge, so Chancery's served the private interest of the common lawyers.

These careful calculations, however, were all but overthrown by the case of Sir John Bennet. Bennet was judge of the Prerogative Court of Canterbury, and one of the most popular men in the legal profession. Coke, Digges, Mallory, and Sandys were among his personal friends.[53] Bennet was accused of gross malfeasance and corruption by Sir Richard Kilvert, a proctor in his court. Kilvert had been accumulating evidence for years. Given a hearing at last, he poured out his master's crimes with monotonous zeal. By April 20, when the committee for courts reported the case to the House, the charges against Bennet numbered twenty-nine, and Kilvert declared grimly that he was "but in the suburbs" of his tale.[54] Bennet's cause was hopeless. "Sir John Bennet," observed Locke, "hath made my Lord Chancellor an honest man."[55]

This new scandal raised gravely disturbing questions. How many more Bennets were the courts harboring? Where did corruption end, if crimes like his could escape so long? Thank heaven, Bennet had not been a common-law judge! But even common-law judges were not wholly free from aspersion. The masters of Chancery had implicated them in Bacon's patent for their fees. The Commons could not leave this stain on their honor.

The judges themselves were no less anxious to be cleared. Lord Mandeville, the now lord treasurer and then chief justice of the King's Bench, told Sir Robert Heath to inform the House that neither he nor any of his fellow judges had ever approved the masters' fees; indeed, they had categorically opposed them. "(I) Spake with Doddridge,"[56] Coke reported, "whereat he grieved that his name should be used, as to have given his Opinion, where none but a Parasite could ever do it." At last, Serjeant Davies set the record straight. Bacon had asked the judges' opinion of the patent. They were unanimously opposed. At this, Bacon rose, politely doffed his hat, "and sayd he reverenced their opinions, but would doe in his owne Court as he thought fitt."[57]

The Commons were overcome with gratitude at this voluntary testimony. "This is so worthy an act of thers that it deserves consideration and thanks," said Phelips.[58] Cross-examination, or even a formal deposition, would not be necessary. Sir Edwin Sandys explained, "We know the Judges have not of a good while ben complained of, which is an argument of ther integryty."[59] For the masters, however, justice had only begun. A special committee was appointed to frame an indictment against them for bribery and slander, for presentation to the Lords.[60]

Thus the good prevailed and the wicked were punished. A month later, Phelips was able to draw the satisfying moral of Parliament's great judicial inquiry: "That onelie the iudges of the Common Lawe have stoode untainted."[61] This conclusion was perhaps less dishonest than merely superficial. Only Coke approached a perception of the real source of the judicial malaise, when he remarked at a conference that those unwilling to use the perfectly available justice at home could not complain if it came high in London.[62] The system was abusive because it was abused. In the last analysis, it was an irresponsibly litigious public which insured judicial corruption. This in turn was part of the European-wide phenomenon by which the turbulence and civil disorder of an earlier age had been sublimated (at least partially) into judicial combat. In this sense, the evils of the system were ineradicable. But reformers might have taken comfort that, if things were bad at home, they were no better elsewhere. Justice Bennet would have been as much at his ease in Paris as Justice Bridlegoose in London.

"Our Parliament is mett againe," wrote Dudley Digges on the second day of the new sitting, "and goes on very mannerly with the King and Lovelingly with the Lords, unanimously among themselves, and constantly, though slowly, in examination, and reformation of things amiss."[63] But John Chamberlain, writing on the same day to the same correspondent, prophesied that if the House of Commons did not stop chasing scandal, it would never get anywhere.[64]

Two days later, April 20, the King called both houses to Whitehall to tell them the same thing. His office, he said, was that of Baron Tell-Clock,[65] to remind them that time was running. Parliament must be judicious in its choice of business. "Make not all patents odious, but onelie such as harme the multitude. Punishe so corrupt iudges that you dishonor not good Judges. Bee not greedie to snatch at accusations, serve not the passions of others . . ."[66]

But the Commons were in no frame of mind to accept the King's sober advice. "This greate Parliament," said John Pym, "is the greate watch of the Kingdom to find oute all faults."[67] Brooke called it "the grand jury for the whole Commonwealth,"[68] and in a score of other speeches, the theme of a general responsibility to the nation was sounded.[69] But what general responsibility implied in practice was unlimited obligation. James had warned the Commons not to strike down patents on a single man's complaint.[70] But was not one man's wrong the wrong of all? Where more fitting that every man's cause be heard than in the high court of all England?[71]

This attitude reflected the loss of confidence in the King's government which, despite the disclaimers both of King and Commons, was the inevitable result of the scandals of the past two months. Privy councillors no less than country squires shared the same dismay. "Abuses were growne to such a height of ill," Sir Thomas Edmondes admitted candidly, "as the kingdome had ben undone, yf wee had been much longer time without a parliament."[72]

That "responsibility to the nation" was also a convenient rationale for incursions into the domains of prerogative became apparent as the Commons moved from spectacular exposés to the more traditional grievances of local government. Digges offered a petition to "stint the number" of justices of the peace, with a long list of new qualifications for that office.[73] Coke's bill against informers, it was charged, gave sweeping new powers to the justices "to determyne all treasons, felonyes, and praemunire," abridging the power of Star Chamber and barring the action of the King's attorney.[74] Sir William Fleetwood's bill for purveyance[75] devolved responsibility for fixing rates and hearing complaints arising from the requisition of labor solely on the justices, thus abrogating the function of the royal commission set up for that purpose.[76] And not the least remarkable provision of that remarkable bill "For Judges Assistant in Chancery" would have shared among the proposed four judges the power to appoint justices of the peace which had hitherto been exercised by the Chancellor alone.[77] This provision was a clear usurpation of prerogative. The choosing of justices of the peace was an uncontested function of the Crown; and the Crown, in assigning this function to the Chancellor, was making a direct delegation of authority. To add common-law judges to this task by statute was to do what only the King had the right to do.

The explanation for all this was quite simple. The country gentlemen who comprised the bulk of the Commons, and from whose ranks justices of the peace were usually drawn, traditionally resented the poking hand of central government in their private bailiwicks, be it in the shape of purveyor, commissioner, or writ from the King's Bench. In the present discomfiture of the government, they were trying to gain full control of the office of justice, and to enhance its authority.

The interest of the gentry was also apparent in the attack on baronets. The baronets were a class of subpeerage, created by James in 1611 to translate the gentry's thirst for honor into a new source of royal revenue. After a brief pretense at maintaining armorial standards, the new title became the badge of the parvenu, readily available on the open market.[78] The gentry were appalled by the prospect that, as Withrington put it, "every skipp Jack shall precede both me and my posteryty."[79] The baronets had been attacked in 1614,[80] and perhaps only the King's violent anger at the Lords' recent petition against the sale of honor[81] had detained the subject as long as late April.

But no sooner had the Commons broached it than the King intervened. He wished the House to know, he said, that he was "hable to impart honor to whom he pleases and in what extent and no man to Question him."[82] The Commons, stirred by the issue, reacted strongly. "Matters of honour are proper to the kinge, yet wee maye speake of our greivances in pointe of honour or otherwise," asserted Poole. Rich complained that the secrecy of the Commons' debate had been violated, and Alford wished "To moove the King that ther may not be so many interpositions, which interrupt the business of the House very much."[83] The House instructed Greville to remonstrate with the King. But the old courtier demurred: "I am your servant and to be commaunded to doe yowr service, but I desyer that you will impose no difficultyes on me."[84] The Commons grudgingly gave way.

The gentry were not the only interest group in the Commons, however. The story of the Virginia Company is an almost textbook example of how a lobby functioned through Parliament, and brought it into conflict with the Crown. The Virginia Company was in dire straits. The colony's cash crop was tobacco, but its product was both inferior to that of the Spanish West Indies and higher in price. Only a public lottery kept it from bankruptcy, and when Lionel Cranfield, by some deft maneuvering, secured the repeal of this lottery in February, 1621,[85] the company had only one recourse. It had to lobby a protectionist bill against Spanish tobacco through Parliament, or face dissolution.

This job fell to Sir Edwin Sandys, the principal figure in the company.[86] He preached powerful sermons against Spanish tobacco in the House,[87] appealing crudely but effectively to anti-Spanish nationalism, and, by dint of hard labor, pushed the company's bill through.[88]

The government was extremely annoyed at this. First, as Cranfield and Calvert pointed out in the House, the bill violated the Treaty of London, which guaranteed free trade between England and Spain.[89] Secondly, Sandys' incitations against Spain were in direct opposition to Crown policy, and were causing it considerable embarrassment. Finally, Parliament had no jurisdiction over Virginia, and therefore any attempt to legislate for it at all was an invasion of prerogative. Calvert put this government view very clearly in the debate on another Sandys-sponsored measure, the bill "For Liberty of Fishing in America":[90]

> That if Regall Prerogative have power in any thinge it is in this, Newe Conquests are to be ordered by the Will of the Conqueror. Virginia is not anex't to the Crowne of England And therefore not subiect to the Lawes of this Howse.[91]

This claim was rebutted by Brooke. He pointed out that Parliament could legislate for Ireland, Jersey, and Guernsey. "The Seigniory is the Kings, but the Land is the Planters and the Trade is the Kingdomes."[92]

The most vocal lobby in Parliament was that of the Outports. Their trade, they claimed, had been strangled by the great London companies. Sandys again was their champion. Hoisting the banner of free trade, he assailed the commercial monopoly enjoyed by the seven companies of London, and suggested that if the House wanted to get to the bottom of the depression, it need only appoint seven committees to investigate them.[93]

Sandys' position was not as contradictory as it might appear. "Free trade," in the seventeenth century, meant not unrestricted competition, but a more equal apportionment of government favors. Unfortunately, the Outports, with their ruined quays and abandoned forts, had little to offer in return, while the London merchants were the government's chief source of credit.

But Sandys, as chairman of one of the two standing committees of the Commons on trade, was in a position to do considerable mischief. His prime target was the Merchant Adventurers, the oldest and most powerful of the trading companies. He denounced their charter, subpoenaed their records, and even succeeded, with the help of his friend Coke, in hauling them before the committee for grievances.[94]

At this point, James intervened on the Merchant Adventurers' behalf. "Theay are not like Mushrums and new Patentees start up yesterday," he told the Commons. "Now there have been diverse things between them and me not so fitt for yow to see and deale in. Medle not, with those things that belong to me and the state."[95]

James's statement brought from Alford the most challenging retort yet made to the doctrine of "matter of state":

> It was an ancient Order in both Houses of Parliament, that, whilst any Thing is in Debate in either of these Houses of Parliament, the King should not be acquainted with it, till the House had taken some Course in it:—That it is against the essential Part and Course of Parliament, that those Things which are here in Debate should, by the King, be taken out of our Hands. He must say thus much, although it may never so much displease the King.[96]

If the King could not halt any proceeding or debate in Parliament once begun, how were the Commons to be kept from dealing with matters of state? Since as soon as a matter had been raised, it was technically "under debate," the only way to proscribe a given subject was to prevent its ever being mentioned. But even if a timely rumor were to reach the King's ear, the Commons had only to deny it, and raise the cry of false informer. Thus the King was effectively precluded, on Alford's assumptions, from interfering with anything said or done in Parliament. From this position it was only a short step to assert that Parliament had the inherent right to discuss any subject it chose, and indeed the public obligation to do so. This step was precisely the one the House of Commons took in December.[97]

Thus the Commons, partly carried by the momentum of their triumphs, partly pulled by the hundred pressure groups that composed, or sought to compose them, were increasingly mired in controversy with the King, and in serious danger of failing to enact a legislative program at all. Debate begat debate, committee begat committee. The leaders of the House grew apprehensive. Their responsibility, as tradition defined it, was clear and limited. The country would expect redress for major grievances, and relief for trade. As matters stood, both were becoming less and less likely with each passing day. On April 26, Hakewill and Phelips moved to choke off the flood of petitions, and to audit the bills and business in hand.[98] But before anything could come of this, the House had gone over the brink.

Edward Floyd, a Catholic barrister formerly attached to Lord Ellesmere, had spent eighteen months in the Fleet for calumniating a now-dead Welsh judge. Confinement had not dampened his interest in politics, however. His sympathies lay with his coreligionists. Hearing news of the battle of White Mountain, he exulted that "Goodman Palsgrave and Goodwife Palsgrave had taken their Heels, and were run away," and "Bess must come home to her father."[99] This gallows chit-chat was reported by a chambermaid to the warden of the Fleet, who quite properly ignored it. There the matter would doubtless have rested to the end of time, had not the House of Commons, upon a petition from a number of prisoners in the Fleet, appointed a committee to investigate conditions in the prison.[100] It was this committee that turned up, along with hideous tales of squalor and corruption, the five-month-old remarks of Floyd. On April 30, when the committee reported to the House, the warden was reprimanded for his failure to punish Floyd's "contempt." Floyd himself was brought to the bar where, crossing himself, he denied the words imputed to him.[101]

Calvert immediately moved to take the matter to the King, but the House felt its chivalry offended. "The Ladie Elizabeth," said Sandys, though "unfortunate in the atcheivements of her husband," was "the bravest and most honorable Ladie in the world." Phelips was sorry the matter had ever come up, but now that it had, he thought the House was obliged to "do something." What that might be was not readily apparent. Floyd was the King's prisoner, and the House had no conceivable jurisdiction over him; but it was finally resolved that "if there were noe President Rather to make a president then to let the offence slipp out of their hands."[102]

On the next day, Tuesday, May 1, took place one of the most

extraordinary scenes in the history of the Parliament of England. The House listened with great gravity to "divers testimonyes" of Floyd's blasphemies. Sir Arthur Ingram and Sir Jerome Horsey, who had been deputed to search his effects, reported the discovery of beads, girdles, popish books, a crucifix, an *agnus dei*, a box of relics including "a peece of our Ladyes Peticoate, and of the Crosse," and, perhaps less surprisingly in a lawyer's kit, a libel against Sir Edward Coke.[103] This completed the presentation of evidence.

It was enough for Phelips. He jumped to his feet. Floyd's was a crime "without Limitation," and a just God demanded his punishment. Let him be ridden from Westminster to the Tower in disgrace, there to lie "in little Ease, with as much Pain as he shall be able to endure, without Loss or Danger of his Life." Roe and Digges suggested a whipping, but they did recall that the House had no power to inflict it, and suggested a conference with the Lords. But More and Seymour brushed this aside: if the House lacked power, it should "make Precedents" and acquire it. With this, what can only be described as mob fury swept over the House. Let Floyd have as many lashes as he had beads, said Seymour. Mr. Whitson, an alderman of Bristol, remembered the good old Spanish custom of dripping hot bacon fat into the wounds at every sixth stroke. Sir Francis Darcy was for boring through his tongue; let it be cut out, cried Horsey, "or slit at least." Sir Edward Cecil favored branding, though he could not decide which letter would be most appropriate. But Sir George Goring outbid them all: "Whippynge at 12 stages, swallowe a bead at each, an Asse tayle for bridle, nose and chops slitt and cut, and hanged at (the) tower and their is an end of him."[104]

Not until this bloodlust had partly abated could reason be heard. It was Sir Edwin Sandys who reminded the Commons that their actions would be watched and judged by the whole world. To punish Floyd for his religion, or with "his trinketts hanged upon him," would make him a martyr. Whip him they could not, for a gentleman could not be whipped, and the House had no power to degrade him. His punishment must fit his station, his act, and the dignity of the House. Sandys suggested the pillory, imprisonment "for some moderate Time," and a fine.

Cranfield and May seized this opportunity to plead for moderation. The former wondered aloud if the House should act, "pussled as it is by infinite doubts" about its jurisdiction. Montagu and Strode, as Roe and Digges before them, remembered that Floyd was still the King's prisoner. Most of the Commons were still closer to the messianic mood of Sir Francis Kynaston, who likened Parliament to "the high court of heaven, sitting as angells to iudge the world at the last day."[105] But they were nonetheless careful to send Floyd back to the Fleet rather than to their own prison, the Tower. That, after all, was where the King's Council had put him, and without their consent, he could not be discharged from it.[106] But the Commons failed to carry their logic to its obvious conclusion: if they could not move the King's prisoner, still less could they punish him. Floyd was ordered to spend the night in Bolton's Ward, the dankest and foulest dungeon in the Fleet. At nine the next morning, he was to be placed in the stocks outside Westminster, ridden "barehorse back-wards" to be exposed at the Exchange at eleven, and pilloried again the next day from ten to twelve at Cheapside. A placard in his cap was to proclaim his offense, and a fine of £1,000 to pay for it.[107]

James was speedily informed of these proceedings, and so was Count Gondomar, who accosted the King on his evening stroll in Hyde Park to lodge a protest.[108] The next day, the members of the Commons did not see Floyd in the stocks on their way to Westminster. Instead, Greville met them with a message from the King. James wryly thanked the House for its "zeal" for the welfare and honor of his children; but affection must have "fit limits," and with this in mind, he had two questions to propound: whether the House could punish those who were not members of it, and, if so, whether it could pass judgment without receiving sworn testimony on a man who denied his crime. Cranfield then produced, with some embarrassment, a record from the Roll of 1 H. 4, to the effect that the Commons had no power of judgment, except with the Lords, or upon special commission from the King.[109]

The debate that followed was somewhat abashed. The Commons' action, said Sandys, "was only *error amoris* to the young Princess . . . though I sayed not so yesterday, my opinion was first to have preferred it to the Lords and to have akquainted the King with it, being his prisoner." Noy and Hakewill were extremely dubious about finding precedents, and Coke, after a rambling and truculent disquisition on the powers of the House, suggested a conference with the Lords. But Phelips disagreed:

> Tis best to deale plainely and not to minse, vary or disguise that we did yesterday; it was a reall, possitive, and setled iudgement. . . . Presidents of this case I see are not easyly fownd out, that we have had Judicature; but that upon occasion w[e] might create a president, and if ever a time for that, now ther is. And for his majestie, he haveing received a large wittness of our dewtyfull affection, he may please to corroborate our power. If we proceede not in this, the honor of the house will be scandalized, particularly because he is a Papist and all Papists are our deadly enemyes; and so I hould all Papists in the world. I am not of opinion to goe to the Lords, for that were to play boe peepe, vzt., to give iudgment heear and then goe to them for an other iudgment.[110]

The House broke up for lunch without having decided what to do. Gloom had only settled the deeper by afternoon. "Tis better to acknowledg that we have trodd awrye then obstinately to persist," counseled Thomas Wentworth. Few, however, were ready to do so. "We want nothing but a president to make this Parliament the happyest that ever was," sighed Cecil. But if none existed, and the King would not permit the House to make one, then it could only petition him for permission to punish "the veryest villaine that ever was but Judas." This was the course agreed upon at last. A committee, led by Coke, was appointed to draw a petition, and Greville, Calvert, and Cranfield were instructed to request an audience.[111]

The next day, the third of May, Coke presented the draft petition. In petitioning the king, there were two alternatives. The Commons could ask him to carry out their sentence by his own authority, or to confirm the sentence and then permit them to execute it. The first was a dignified capitulation; the second would be victory. The petition used the intentionally ambiguous word "countenance": "Wherefore we humblye beseech yowr majestie that this iudgment of ours may not be reversed to the discorageing of your loveing subiects . . . but that [you] will please to countenance it to the suppressing of the greate insolency of those that usually doe defame your majesties children."[112]

Coke, in glossing this, did nothing to clarify the matter: "We desyr that he will ratyfy that which we have donn; it will be his act as well as ours."[113]

But in the full context of the petition, it is clear that a confirmation of the Commons' power was being aimed at. The petition itself explicitly denied any such intent, but it also repudiated the application of 1 H. 4 to the case in hand. What James had cited—showing that two could play the game of precedents—was the Commons' petition to be dissociated from the deposition of Richard II. This, the present Commons thought, "doth not so much impeach their authoritie as manifest their loyaltie."[114] For the King to accept such a fuzzily worded document which contained so evident a rejection of his own argument was to give the case to the Commons on a silver platter.

Certainly Calvert had no doubts about this. "We go about to justify our Power; which," he warned, "may draw a negative Answer from the King, and so bar us for ever." Cranfield read the petition the same way. "The forme of the draught is well cowcht, but it will amount to as much as the Confirmeing Judicature on uss in effect." Hakewill added that the draft implied that the House could produce precedents of its own where, in fact, he knew of none.[115] These admonishments produced not the slightest effect. "Some Exceptions," commented Pym, "were made against these instructions, but of noe such moment as did induce any alteracion."[116] The petition was approved.[117]

That afternoon, it was presented to the King at Whitehall. James was gracious but firm. He thanked the Commons again for their solicitude to his children; but judges should deliberate before acting, and they had acted in haste. "Many Lawyers of the Howse, I heare, were absent [i.e., on May 1].[118] Yet such as were present cannot be excused for not telling yow the Lymitts of your power." They had grounded their judgment on "reason and precedent."[119] To show precedents would be highly in order, "but for reason, that is so large a thing as that a man knows not where to pitch. . . . As I owght to love yow, soe I owe Justice to all my people And must not give away to any newe Power of Judicature which, being as it were Omnipotent, may stretch I knowe not howe farre." But, concluded the King, though he was obliged to deny the form of the petition, he was able to grant the substance. Floyd, in petitioning him for mercy, had confessed his guilt. Thus he could be punished, and would receive from the Crown at least as great a punishment as that recommended by the Commons.[120]

This solution might have given the Commons a graceful way out, but the next morning, the councillors were obliged to retract the King's promise. "The petition was a little mistaken by his majestie," confessed Calvert. It had actually come from Floyd's son, Richard. Floyd himself, examined by Heath and Coventry, the King's Attorney, persisted in his denial "with a greate deale of bouldness and impudence." Therefore, explanied Heath, the King had sent the case to the Lords. If the Commons could think of a better way to proceed, he would gladly assent to it, but he "would not have us condemn a denying Man without Witnesses upon Oath."[121]

Here was the crux of the question. The Commons could not give oath; therefore, they could not judge. "The house took it heavily," comments the B diarist.[122] "We be catcht in a Nett," said Sir Thomas Jermyn. But some still struggled. "An Oath not requisite in all Causes," Sir George More asserted. "The Matter not obscure, but plain." "Obscure" matters, presumably, required oath, but "plain" ones did not. Sir Samuel Sandys agreed. "The witnesses [against Floyd] did solemnly proffesse before God and as they were Christians; shall we thinke we should have more reason to beleive them yf they had been put to the formalitie of Sweareinge." What was an oath, anyway? "Wee are a Courte and I dare boldly say we were a Courte before there was any such Ceremonye."[123]

The lawyers of the House had remained conspicuously silent during this debate. "I think him not honest that can now helpe us and will not," said Sir Edward Giles, turning toward Coke. Coke replied in a rapid legal patter. The suit was immediately the King's, as it concerned his blood. Any man might stay his suit, and so the King might his. True, judgment had already been given; but where the suitor was the only party, he could remit its execution. This was of no concern to the court, however, for "staye of execution is no adnullinge of the iudgment."[124]

This reasoning was not exactly candid. For one thing, the "suitor" had never sued at all; and the question was not the judgment of the court, but its competence. No one was more painfully aware of this than Coke, of course. It was he who had turned the rhetorical Court of Parliament into a real one, and he who had persuaded a reluctant House of Lords to assume the judicature which the Commons could not exercise alone. This course was the one he had urged upon the House at the beginning of the Floyd affair. But the Commons, inflated with success, had decided to dispense with the Lords entirely. Nor was this decision a sudden development. Pym had argued, two weeks before, against sending Bennet's case up to the Lords except for the bare formality of a sentence.[125] The Commons' reaction to Floyd, minus the chauvinism and hysteria, was only to carry this argument to its logical conclusion. The Lords had been excluded pure and simple.

Coke realized that the Commons' legal position was hopeless. His only wish was to bury the whole issue as quickly as possible, and repair what he could of relations between the two houses. The aim of his speech had been to convince the Commons that the case was over, and they could do no more.

But the House was not satisfied with Coke's formulation. If a legal judgment had been made, said Seymour, then it must be formally entered in the Journal. "Why tis so allready," Coke replied with mock surprise. But what the Clerk had jotted down on May 1 was not a verdict but a series of resolutions for individual items of punishment, each separately voted and approved. Seymour wanted to put the whole in proper declarative form. Coke realized, and Heath warned,[126] that such a step would only further antagonize the King. The Commons took it nonetheless; a committee was chosen, and a new judgment penned. The King promptly acquired a copy.[127]

On the morning of the fifth, the House was debating the repair of a bridge at Tewkesbury and the passage of a bill to confirm Magna Carta, and business seemed back to normal. But Phelips had a premonition: "This the fatall hower that every day produces somm question that houlds us all the morn after in debate."[128] No sooner had he spoken, than Justices Dodderidge and Hutton entered the House with a message from the Lords.

The Lords had all this while been deeply immersed in problems of their own.[129] They came to the Floyd imbroglio with fresh and dispassionate eyes. It may reasonably be assumed that some of the cooler heads among the Commons had privately briefed the Lords, and assured them that there was no intent to usurp their privileges—Coke, no doubt, and Hakewill, Noy or Sandys.[130] The Lords were thus disposed to treat the whole affair in a generous and comradely fashion, as a junior colleague's youthful transgression.[131]

The Commons were vastly relieved to discover the Lords' leniency. They had made an agreement in March. Their House would indict, the Lords prosecute and judge, in all cases not involving members of Parliament itself. Neither house was to act without the other. The Commons had broken this pact, and if, in consequence, the Lords had taken the Floyd case from the King, they stood to lose the crux of their judicature, which was the unique power to initiate actions in the Upper House.[132] The King had made his first attempt on this power in the proposed commission for Bacon.[133] The Commons had now given him another prime opportunity. But the Lords merely requested a conference at three o'clock to accommodate the business of Floyd "without Prejudice to the Privileges of either House."[134]

The Commons' relief quickly soured, however. The prospect of forgiveness engendered embarrassment and stubborn pride. When they met the Lords, they attempted not an excuse but a defense of their actions. There had been no intention of encroaching on the Lords, began Sir Samuel Sandys,[135] "but, having such an Occasion offered, we thought we might without Offence or Prejudice, extend our Jurisdiction; which yet we have not done farther than, we conceive, Reason did lead us." As for the question of oaths, "All men say truth is trewth"—our diarist's witticism is no doubt unconscious—"and so we thought him so generally accused worthy of censure." The elder Sandys concluded with the pious hope that the Lords would not deny the Commons their "possessory right."

This drew a sharp retort from the Lords. "We desyr yow to descend to somm particulars wherin yow may shew this possessory right," said Mandeville. Their lordships had been of the opinion that it belonged to them.

Coke came next, trying to jest away his colleague's blunders. But his well-practiced charm failed to hide the thinness of his case. He proved the Commons to be a court of record with a great wealth of precedent, none of it, however, germane to the Floyd case. He showed at length that the Commons could give oaths, but failed to explain why they had not done so. At last he was

thrown back on the fanciful idea that the Commons could punish
Floyd because the King was a member of Parliament: *"Filia est
pars patris,* and the King is ever intended to be resident in our
House."

The Lords parsed these ingenuities coldly. Mandeville declared that he found the Commons' argument no further advanced. Sir Edwin Sandys, the last of the Commons' spokesmen,
lamely praised his House for its speed in avenging the King's
honor. "Delay had indeed ben a cold zeale," agreed the Lords;
but, asked Pembroke, would the Commons accept a similar defense from the Lords had they voted a subsidy "out of their Zeale
to the defence of the Palatinate?" So they might have, before 9
H. 4, sallied Coke; to which Pembroke retorted, "As power of
Judicature was to the Lords by the Ordinance of 1 H. 4." Coke
started to reply, but the conference was already breaking up.[136]

On Monday, the seventh, the Lords debated the results of the
conference. All agreed that the Commons' performance had been
wholly unsatisfactory. Another conference would have to be held.
The debate was between those who wanted to put the Lower
House in its place and those who wanted to patch things over as
quickly as possible. On the former side were Prince Charles, the
Earl of Arundel, and Lord Treasurer Mandeville. Mandeville
proposed that the new conference "handle this only, that they
have no power of judicature, nor coercion against any that are
not members of ther Howse." This was perhaps correct, but it
was hardly a formula for reconciliation. Southampton quickly
cut in, *"Ad idem,* to handle only this poynt of judicature, wherein they have wronged us," which seemed to say the same thing;
but between admitting a particular mistake and making a general renunciation of power, past, present, and future, there was
really a good deal of difference. Southampton further proposed
that, at the next day's general conference, each house appoint a
small committee "to consider and determine howe this may be
ended without wrong to us, and least touch to them." That was
all very well, said Lord Cambridge, but it was the Commons'
place to propose such a committee, not the Lords'. Southampton
and his allies—Sheffield, Walden, North—tried to convince their
fellow peers that they could take this marginal initiative without
loss of dignity. When they felt sure of a majority, they put the
matter to a vote—surely one of the most curiously worded ques-

tions ever to be put in Parliament: "Yf the Comittees of the Lower House at the Conference to-morrowe doe not desyre a Sub-comittee, then the LL. to propounde yt, yf neede be. Agreed, per pluries, the LL. to propounde yt yf need be."[137]

Southampton immediately cued Sir Edwin Sandys,[138] who proposed the subcommittee idea to the Commons the next morning. The House readily agreed.[139] It had been much chastened by the previous day's fiasco. A good deal of blame was portioned out, rather unfairly, to Coke, who had violated instructions by arguing from precedent.[140] But Sandys had to admit that the argument from "reason" had been scarcely better received. He proposed that the Commons now simply seek an accommodation, which he defined as "a yeildinge of both sides without preiudice to either."[141] Sandys' phrasing was strikingly similar to that of the Lords' original message; the Commons were ready to compromise.

Archbishop Abbot opened the new conference with almost comically elaborate courtesy: "We doe not rapp we do but gently knock at your doores and desyre yow but to leave us where yow found us in our power of iudging." Cranfield, who had been delegated sole spokesman for the Commons, replied that his House had likewise come for accommodation. This led to an exchange of civilities with Archbishop Mathew of York:

YORK: My Lords with a loving ear heard the word accomodation . . .

CRANFIELD: Seeing your Lordships have accepted the word of accomodation, we thinke it fitt to leave the way to your Lordships.

YORK: My Lords doe wonderfully well acqui[e]sce in that which yow say, and we relye so much on the ponderousness of your iudgment that as you have propounded an accomodation so we assuer ourselves yow have thought of a way.

CRANFIELD: We have had somm speech of a subcommittee . . . [142]

Cranfield reported back to the waiting Commons that the Lords had agreed to the subcommittee "and only were a little daynety of propounding it." A debate sprang up on the powers to be given the subcommittee, and the precise nature of the accommodation it was to seek. Coke and Sandys cut this discussion short, and relayed the message to the Lords confirming the appointment of the subcommittee.[143]

With these ceremonies performed, the two houses were ready for the "accommodation." The Commons agreed to leave the case of Floyd entirely and unreservedly to the Lords, and pledged to enter a protestation on their records that they would never use the now-annulled judgment as a precedent in any future case.[144] In short, the Commons capitulated, as the wiser heads in both houses had known would happen all along. But Sir Edward Coke, to whom the task of spokesman had been now assigned, added a *caveat* in parting. He formally "prayed them [the Lords] . . . to take the Cause into their Examination, Judgment, and Execution."[145] Coke's object was clear. The case was now wholly the Lords'; but Coke wanted them to take it, not from the King, but from the Commons.

Cranfield leaped up. The Master of the Wards, who fancied himself the true reconciler of the two houses, was burning with pique at Coke's selection as spokesman for this final conference. "We have no other commission but to leave the man and his cause to the Lords," he declared. Coke had no leave to "pray any thing." Sir Edward whirled round. Those who sowed confusion and sedition between the houses, he bristled, were not worthy of their heads.[146]

The two men took their quarrel back to the Commons. Here Coke, once again master of his temper, lightly outwitted his mulish colleague. He had not meant to signify the Master of the Wards by his comment, nor anyone else, he said blandly, "but spake it in general." Cranfield was like the gullible dandy in Burchin's Lane, who thought the ready-made doublet had been specially tailored for him.

Cranfield, doubly enraged, demanded vindication. The House tried to bury the matter, but again and yet again he raised his complaint, until members were shouting him down, and Coke cried in final exasperation, "I protest as I am a Christian I intended it not to him." He who pursued "this miserable difference," observed Phelips acidly, "deserves most blame."[147]

This victory must have been sweet for Coke. He had had little enough thanks for his efforts to put a decent face on the Commons' blunderings over Floyd. But there was more to the scene than that. The Commons' clearly expressed sympathy for Coke was a vote of confidence in his leadership at a moment of personal stress and embarrassment. Coke's son Clem, who sat for Dunwich Borough, Suffolk, had had a silly brawl with a fellow MP, Sir Charles Morrison. His father's son in obstinacy if nothing else, Clem refused to apologize as directed by the House, and was sent to the Tower. Coke was thereupon obliged to plead for him, and he was released in Coke's custody, "Out of the Respect the House hath to his Father."[148]

The vote of confidence in Coke was at the same time a final rejection of Cranfield. Cranfield had aggressively contested Coke's leadership from the beginning of Parliament, but especially since Easter. Finding that the guise of the reformer had worn thin, Cranfield changed his tack. Since unity was now the theme, he posed as the one man who could boast both the confidence of the Commons and the ear of the King.[149] When Coke failed to assert his leadership in the Floyd case, Cranfield bid hard for it. He was in the forefront of every debate, scurrying dramatically between Whitehall and Westminster. When Coke was chosen to conclude matters with the Lords after all, he could not contain himself. Thereafter Cranfield's role in Parliament was largely confined to acrimonious quarrels and blustering assertions of authority.

As for Floyd himself, he fared no better with the Lords. On May 26 his case was considered, guilt pronounced, and judgment delivered. The sentence of the Commons was taken as a mere starting point. The Lords added branding, flogging, "disgentillizinge," a fine of £5,000, and life imprisonment in Newgate.[150] These severities aroused great indignation in the large Catholic population of London, and Chamberlain reported "divers called in question for speaking so liberally against yt."[151] But many others recalled with equal bitterness the fate of the three apprentices. If good Protestants had been flogged for merely looking askance at the Spanish ambassador, what punishment would fit a papist who slandered the royal family?[152]

James immediately remitted the fine and flogging, and Floyd was released from prison in the general amnesty of July.[153] But the rest of the sentence was carried out. Floyd was branded with a *K* in Cheapside. Defiant as ever, he fleered at the crowd that he would give a thousand pounds to hang for his faith. The villain, at least, lived up to his role.[154]

IV

PRIVATE MEN AND
PUBLIC GOOD

While the Commons strove vainly after Floyd, a drama of far greater moment was being enacted in the Lords. A determined minority in both houses—principally Coke, Mallory, and Seymour in the Lower, Southampton, Sheffield, and Spencer in the Upper—had set their sights again on the Marquis of Buckingham. On no subject were the two houses so united as in detestation of Buckingham. The Lords loathed him as the debaser of the peerage, the Commons, as the evil genius of monopoly. To these grounds had been added, since March, the open secret of the Marquis's attempts to persuade James to dissolve Parliament.

Buckingham was a frightened man. He had weathered the monopoly scandal only by the sacrifice of Bacon. There was no surrogate available for the next attack. But for once, George was not to have his way with his James. The King could not dissolve Parliament at this juncture without patently suppressing reform. When Buckingham persisted, the King displayed his anger publicly. He spent his first Easter in many years without the favorite.[1]

The anti-Buckingham forces in Parliament rallied at these signs. They had the man they thought could bring Buckingham down, Sir Henry Yelverton. The former Attorney knew enough, and he was bitter past caring at the consequences.

Yelverton had made an enemy of Buckingham from his first days as attorney. On his appointment, he refused to offer the customary obeisances to the favorite, and, finding his patent of office blocked as a result, appealed directly to the King for confirmation. Later, he showed scruples over enforcing Mompesson's patents, and was threatened with immediate dismissal by the Marquis. At one point, he appears to have sought an ally in Bacon, but that canny gentleman would have none of a loser's cause.[2] At last, a suitable pretext arose. Yelverton, in drawing a new charter for London, had been overliberal with the city fathers. No one proved, or attempted to prove, that he had been bribed. His judgment alone was called into question. Yet he was not merely dismissed, but imprisoned at the King's pleasure and fined £4,000.[3]

The fallen Attorney was still in the Tower when the monopolies scandal broke in March. Phelips proposed to interrogate him; and he proved, as we have seen, a most willing witness.[4] The Court retaliated, seeking to discredit him. James, speaking to the Lords on March 1,

> iustified my Lord Ch[ancellor] as having staied 4 patents and remembered that Sir H. Yelverton being then my Attorney told of it, assuring that those patents were good. He was [a] rashe Attorney. I was forced to put him owt of my service.[5]

When Bacon fell, the King was determined to punish Yelverton for it. On March 26, he reminded the Lords that Yelverton had set his hand to a warrant dormant,[6] which was "as odious a Matter as any is before you." If the Lords had foregone questioning Yelverton out of respect to the Crown, whose prisoner Yelverton was, James now remitted jurisdiction to them.[7]

This move was virtually an order that the Lords summon Yelverton, which they did on the first day after the recess. A list of six charges was read out to him. Yelverton made provisional replies, and asked further time to consult his papers and organize a defense. His request was granted.[8]

Five of these charges concerned Yelverton's conduct in the patent of gold and silver thread, for which the warrant dormant had been issued. The sixth, however, had an extremely suspicious air. It dealt with the patent of inns, a subject the Crown had no desire to see revived. Yelverton had already done his worst in the thread patent, but he had never testified about inns. The charge itself, moreover, was so watery and qualified as to constitute little more than a covert invitation to such testimony.[9] Yelverton's reply was an acceptance of this invitation. He asserted "that, if he ever deserved well of His Majesty, it was in this," and added, "that the King and Subject were more abused by the Patent than by any other; and that he suffers at this Day for that Patent, as he takes it."[10] Off the record, the former Attorney was apparently even bolder. Chamberlain noted that "he seemes to speake bigge that he will spare none."[11]

Three days later in the House of Commons, on April 21, William Mallory "remembered" the House order of March 12 to proceed further against the patent of inns. Sir Francis Seymour followed with a long harangue against its referees.[12] The King saw clearly what was afoot. The next day he sternly warned the Commons against raking up dead coals, and two days later, he appeared in the Lords:

> His Majesty said, It seemed strange unto Him, that Sir Henry Yelverton should be examined here upon any Thing, save the Patent of Gold and Silver Thread; for that His Majesty did not conceive that any Matter was complained of against Sir Henry Yelverton, touching the Inns and Hosteries.[13]

But in his answer to this question, James continued, Yelverton had implied that his imprisonment was connected with this patent. This was a slander against the Crown, and the King directed the Lords to punish Yelverton for it.[14]

The King's new attack on Yelverton dimmed the hopes of the anti-Buckingham party.[15] It was clear that James had no intention of abandoning Buckingham, as he had Somerset, to judicial proceedings. Nonetheless, a second front was opened in the Commons against the favorite on April 26. Sir John Jephson, who had embarrassed James before,[16] denounced misgovernment in Ireland. Popery and monopoly, he charged, had brought it to the verge of revolt. Coke called for a full investigation, and a committee was appointed.[17]

This maneuver was transparently aimed at Buckingham, who had the Irish patronage.[18] James moved to counter it immediately. He was "neither [an] Idle nor sleepinge kinge," he told the House. Ireland had never been in better order; it had been "one of his master peices to reforme it." He therefore referred it "to the Judgment of the house whether they will . . . examyne any further his doyngs or rather returne him thanks for what he hath done."[19] Thus died the Irish question. There was some grumbling. "It's dangerous to give over a business upon the motion of the kinge," warned Alford. But James had not made the obvious mistake of forbidding the subject of Ireland: he had merely made his displeasure at it so plain that the uselessness of proceeding further was evident.[20]

The same, at this point, might have been said for the entire anti-Buckingham campaign. It had failed; and Sir Henry Yelverton, the star witness, was now just a man out on a limb. On April 30, the Lords heard his case. "Being justly compassed about with soe many terrours from his Majestie," as he himself put it, Yelverton might have been expected to plead guilty to the five remaining charges, and throw himself on the King's mercy. But the former Attorney did no such thing. After years of silence and frustration, and a secret trial that had been a mockery of justice, he had at last a public forum. He used it.

Yelverton dealt first with the patent for thread. He had testified originally to the Commons that he had been compelled to imprison the silkmen who resisted the patent by Mompesson and Sir Edward Villiers, the favorite's brother; but it was "not in a base feare" of those two that he had done it, he now said. "He knewe them to be but shadowes of a greater. . . . He feared the power of the L. of Buckingham, he whoe was ever present at his Majesties elbowe ready to hew him downe."

Buckingham himself, in his place as a peer, sat mute at this. Yelverton proceeded to the patent of inns. Once again, Sir Giles Mompesson had tried to force him to arrest those who opposed the patent; but Yelverton took his case to the King, "and tolld his Majestie yt would be an yll preparacion to a parlement." The King supported him. "His Majestie charged me not to streyne his prerogative against the auncyent right of his subjectes."

Here Yelverton paused dramatically. He begged to be excused from speaking further: "I had rather weepe alone then speake what I had to saye." At this, the whole House rose with cries of "Go! Go on!" And so the defendant did.

After his interview with the King, Mompesson came to him, "like an Herald at Arms," with a message from Buckingham. If he did not "conform" himself forthwith to his previous instructions, said the Marquis, he would not hold his place a month longer. "This staggered me," said Yelverton, "for if Sir G. M. sayd trewe in this message, . . . I was in a streyght whether to obey the Kinge or Buckingham."

Yelverton resolved to be, in his own words, "as stubborn as Mordechay." Not half the writs for arrest came from him; many he stopped. For this he soon suffered. The profits of his office were diverted "to one of my Lord's Worthies," and he retained little more of his office than its title. Rumor of the Marquis's disfavor ruined his private practice: "It became so fatal, and so penal, that it became almost the Loss of a Suit to come unto me." Yelverton wheeled finally on his adversary. "He honoured his Lordship's name, which he had from his father of all the gentlemen of England. He wyshed his Lordship had been pleased to have read the articles against Hugh Spencer[21] in this place, for taking upon him to place and displace officers."

Pandemonium broke out. The Prince rose whitely from his seat and demanded that Yelverton's testimony be stopped, as he could not permit his father's government to be "paralelled and scandalised" with the reign of Edward II. But Buckingham reacted superbly. "Let him proceede," said the Marquis, "and he that wyll seeke to stopp him, [is] more my enemy then his." The House subsided, and Yelverton plowed on to the end. He did not come before the Lords as a bitter man. He was glad to be quit of his office, which had become simply a burden to him under Buckingham's persecution. His life was now "easy and of repose," and he left it willingly in their lordships' hands.[22]

When Yelverton had finished, Buckingham demanded that he be sent to the Tower for reflecting on the King's honor, but the opposition peers were not so ready to see him whisked off the stage. Sheffield and Saye saw nothing disrespectful in Yelverton's testimony, and Southampton taxed the Marquis for "straining words." Thereupon James and Buckingham decided to act. They took Yelverton back into royal custody, and committed him to close prison in the Tower. James sent word that he would leave the accusations against Buckingham to the Lords, but that he would repair his own honor against Yelverton.[23]

James's action caused an explosion. The King had given Yelverton to the Lords to judge the very question of his honor. For him to remove Yelverton in midprocess was a breach of their privilege as a court, and worse, a slur on their loyalty to the

Crown. Sheffield moved that the Lords petition the King to return Yelverton to them.[24]

To general surprise, Buckingham calmly agreed to this proposal and the King soon after as readily.[25] Their strategem had worked. By seizing Yelverton, James had not only decided the question of whether his honor had been impugned by the Attorney's words, but had implicitly rebuked the Lords for not recognizing the fact themselves. By returning him, he placed the Lords squarely on the defensive, for how could they erase the "suspicion of our zeale to his honor" now cast on them, but by condemning Yelverton?[26] The charges made by Yelverton were thereby thrust into the background, and the principal issue was once again Yelverton himself.

Having gained the advantage, the Crown pressed for judgment. Coventry opened the case on May 8. No sooner had he finished than Charles demanded bluntly that the Lords clear Yelverton or condemn him. The opposition peers pleaded for delay. The Earl of Arundel brushed them aside. There was no time, he said, to pick the man's words apart. Lord Spencer asked that Yelverton be called to the bar to speak in his own defense. No, said Prince Charles, "for we have his wordes and are to judg uppon him." The debate grew steadily more heated. A motion of censure was formulated. Once again Spencer called to hear Yelverton. Arundel again opposed him. Spencer rose and said:

> The Lord which spake last might worsse speake against this motion than any man in this house, for that two honorable persons of his Auncestors the Duke of Norfolke and the Earle of Surrey were condemned heare in parliament uniustly without being heard.

Arundel, who had only regained his title on the accession of James, got up crimson. "My Lords," he said, "I doe acknowledge that my Auncestors have suffred, and it may be for doinge the King and Country good service, and in such time as perhapps the Lords Auncestors that spake last kept sheepe."[27]

An uproar followed. Everyone agreed that Arundel had violated the decorum of the House. His uncle, the Earl of Suffolk, moved to bring him to the bar.[28]

Here, in a single dramatic incident, all the skeins of conflict in the Upper House were laid bare: pro- and anti-Buckingham, new and old peerage, those in and those out of favor at Court. The Prince kept Arundel from censure that day;[29] But the Earl, persisting in his remarks and refusing to apologize to Spencer, finally obliged the Lords to send him to the Tower. He remained there, adamant and the center of great fuss and attention from the Court, until James procured his release at the end of the session.[30]

The Lords returned to Yelverton on May 14. He was much chastened. Permitted to make a statement, he denied any intent to slander or disparage the King's government. "Lett me never fynde mercy with God . . . yf I ment to compare my Lord of Buckingham with Spencer [i.e., le Despencer], or the King James with Edward 2," he said. He had raised the subject "only to saye, as yt were, remember Lott's wyfe."[31]

The next day Yelverton was judged. The Lords found him guilty of impugning the King's honor by unanimous vote. He was sentenced to the Tower during the King's pleasure, fined 10,000 marks, and required to make a submission. The sentence was not unanimous. "Some of the L.L."—we may guess who—walked out in disgust.[32]

On the sixteenth, Yelverton was called back to answer for his attack on Buckingham. He had produced no proof of his assertions, charged Coventry, and therefore was guilty of great slander. This was a cruel taunt. Yelverton had been a close prisoner in the Tower since April 20,[33] and had been denied all access to his papers. The Lords' own investigation of his charges had consisted in the examination of one witness.[34]

Yelverton replied with cynical resignation. "I fynd," he said, "that there is noe daunger in sylence, much in speeche." But if the court wished proof, he could readily provide it.

Sheffield, Dorset, and Suffolk moved that Yelverton be permitted to call witnesses, but their motion was defeated. A motion was quickly produced to censure the former Attorney "for false and scandalous wordes spoaken by him in this House against the L. Admyrall." A protest was raised at the word "false," but the majority upheld it. Did those, asked the Speaker,[35] who dissented from the word, dissent from the charge? No one replied. The censure was carried unanimously.[36] Yelverton was ordered to pay Buckingham 5,000 marks, and required to make a submission to him.[37]

As usual, John Chamberlain had the last word.

Thus we see that great men weakly opposed, thereby become the stronger, and yt is no small comfort to him and his (as he professes) that he is found parlement proofe.[38]

Buckingham's boast was accurate, but premature. The *putsch* of 1621 was only the first of four parliamentary attempts to dislodge him from power. All of them failed, and all for the same reason: Buckingham was protected by the King, James in 1621, Charles in 1625, 1626, and 1628.[39]

But the four campaigns, or rather cabals, against Buckingham, succeeded in something far more important than their immediate objective. They kept alive a more or less continuous opposition in the House of Lords in the 1620s, something no other issue could have done. The Lords' interest was with the monarchy. They were its social and political elite; they reaped its honors and filled its offices.[40] Their chief rivals, the class immediately below them, were the gentry who comprised the House of Commons. Yet, throughout the crucial decade of the twenties, the Lords made common cause with the Lower House against the Crown. The reason for their doing so was primarily Buckingham's monopolization of power.

The term "opposition" must be used very loosely, for it sometimes describes no more than a series of personal quarrels between Buckingham and individual peers. It should not therefore surprise us to find this "opposition" exhibiting great variation in number, cohesiveness, and personnel. In 1626, the year of Buckingham's impeachment, his chief opponents in the Lords were Abbot, Williams, Arundel, Bristol (Digby), and Pembroke. All of them had been his friends in 1621. There were, it is true, a handful of habitual malcontents in the Lords—men like Southampton, Dorset, Sheffield, Saye and Sele, Spencer, Essex, and Warwick—whose opposition, whether based on personal grievance or class desertion, was independent of the Buckingham issue. Without that issue, however, they would have had little impact.

The effect of Buckingham's status on the nobility was thus less to produce an opposition than a general disaffection from the Crown. This was a serious blow. In a faithful House of Lords the king had a potent lever against the Commons. By rejecting its bills, by refusing its indictments, the Lords could have hamstrung the activity of the Lower House considerably. Such support, of

course, could not have been had for nothing. It might have required substantial concessions of power. But even the prospect of
an "aristocratic resurgence" would have been less dangerous to
the Crown than the position into which it ultimately maneu-
vered itself. The King was better off playing both ends against
the middle than a losing game at one end. Not until 1639, however, were such concessions even considered.[41] The Commons, on
the other hand, offered the Lords a revival of their ancient judicature as early as 1621. The Lords took it up, as we have seen, with
hardly a thought of how they would use it, or how they might be
used by it.[42]

The Yelverton debacle, however, was the end of all serious
resistance in the Lords for 1621. If it demonstrated anything, it
was the weakness of the Upper House as a staging ground for
parliamentary opposition. The number of peers was much
smaller than the number of the Commons—ninety-two lay lords
in 1621, and twenty-six docile[43] bishops—and the proportion of
Crown councillors, much higher. Most daunting of all, however,
was the presence of Prince Charles in the House. It took a great
deal of courage to favor something once he had opposed it, or to
oppose what he favored.[44]

The two houses thus emerged from their respective adventures
—Floyd the Lower's, Yelverton the Upper's—with sails sharply
trimmed. The Crown had checked, at least temporarily, the
parliamentary invasion of prerogative, and regained the initiative in the duel of wits which the Parliament of 1621 had increasingly become.

The House of Commons was badly demoralized. Its leadership
had faltered after Easter, and collapsed over Floyd. But it had
divided most deeply on the issue of Buckingham. From the first,
voices of warning had been raised against the plot to overthrow
the favorite;[45] and when, on May 2, an attempt was made to bar
Sir Edward Villiers from entering the House, there was open
conflict. Villiers, Buckingham's half-brother and the instru-
mental figure in the patent of gold and silver thread, had returned from an embassy abroad[46] and without undue delay
prepared to take the seat he held in the Commons.[47] He waited,
however, until Yelverton had shot his bolt in the Lords, so
that his appearance in the Commons was particularly galling

to the failed conspirators, a viceroy's triumphal entry into a conquered province. Coke, Mallory, and Edward Spencer promptly challenged Villiers' right to take his seat.[48] This brought a sharp rejoinder. "We are diverted by motions rather springing from passion then iudgment," said Samuel Sandys, and Sir Thomas Wentworth warned the House sternly against turning from bills to "musketts and shott." "We have had bones cast emong us," said Giles; "Lett us not rayse them our selves."[49]

The battle over Villiers' seat had shown how close the Commons were to a split between moderate and radical leadership. Men like Wentworth and Sandys were becoming convinced that the Crown had been pushed as far as it would go. The impregnability of Buckingham was an established fact. To challenge it further could only invite the dissolution that the Marquis—and the Spanish—had worked so hard to procure.

A dissolution was, indeed, freely rumored. John Dickenson, a diplomatic emissary just back from the Continent, picked up the scent quickly. Within a week of his arrival he had begun "to doubte the continuance of the Parliament." Lando reported James loud in his complaints of the "four hundred kings" in Parliament.[50] In any event, the present session could not have far to go. The King dropped a broad hint on May 3 when he complained that while his councillors were tied up in Parliament, "the busynes of my State lyes a bleeding."[51] "Our parlament waxeth olde," wrote Calvert in midmonth, "and how long it will continue I can not tell, but I beleeve this first session will not be many dayes longer."[52]

With these omens on the wind, the Commons strove at last to organize what time remained. They found themselves in a desperate tangle. Their attempt to reconduct the entire course of government business over the past seven years had hopelessly overloaded their resources of time, manpower, and organization. With new matters indiscriminately heaped on it every day, the committee system broke down. The pileup of meetings and assignments became so ludicrous that on the climactic day of May 9, Sir George More found himself listed as a member of no fewer than four committees, Coke and Carvile, of three. All these committees had themselves been postponed from a previous date at least once.

Despite afternoon sittings and evening conferences, it seemed

impossible to unsnarl the mess and establish priorities. With
lobbying rather than leadership in control, minor legislation
slipped through while important bills and even whole programs
languished. Court reform was still unenacted,[53] the trade problem scarcely dented.[54] "What is the Bill of Saboth, swearinge and
certioraries to a man in want," Sir Edwin Sandys lamented.
"What is the bills of welch Butter."[55]

Sobered at last by the imminence of adjournment, if not dissolution, the Commons pressed forward with two major bills. The
first of these was the Act against Monopoly.

A general bill against monopoly was first suggested by Sir John
Walter in the debate of March 5.[56] A committee was appointed,
and a draft produced within a week. It was largely the work of
Coke,[57] who chaired the committee, and from the first domi-
nated the project. The King appeared to encourage the bill. "I
am contented," he said on March 10, " . . . there should be a lawe
made against theis thinges."[58]

A satisfactory bill could not, of course, be devised on so complex a subject as monopolies in a mere seven days; and after a
second reading on March 14, the draft was committed again for
serious reworking.[59] The House watched its progress closely. On
March 20 and 26, new versions were debated on the floor. Salt-
peter and ordnance were excepted from the bill as defense industries, and wine because, almost alone among the monopolies, it
actually brought the Crown a significant revenue; but the essential alterations were two.

In the original draft, monopolies were declared illegal by virtue of James's "Book of Bounty," the royal proclamation of 1610
against patents of monopoly and dispensation.[60] The text of this
draft read: "Forasmuche as your most excellent Matie, in your
royall judgment, hathe of your blessed disposicion to the weale
and quiet of your subjectes, published in prynte, to the whole
realme, and to all posteritye, that all graunts of monopolyes, and
of the benefitt of any penall lawes, or of power to dispence with
the lawe, or to compound with the forfeiture, are contrary to your
Maties lawes." To this sentence was now added: "which your
Maties declaracion is truly consonant and agreable to the ancient
and fundamentall lawes of this your realme."[61] The additional
clause changed the "Book of Bounty" from a direct declaration
of law to a mere commentary on it.

The danger of the original wording was obvious. By citing the "Book of Bounty" as the authority for the statute, the authors of the original draft implicitly accepted Bacon's old notion that the king was *lex loquens,* that a royal statement *about* law was a promulgation *of* law. If this were true, then the King's word alone could overturn courts and statutes. This notion was precisely the one Coke had fought all his life. Hence the additional clause which reduced the citation of the "Book of Bounty" to a courtesy.

But if the "King's Book" was not to be the authority for the statute, what was? There were a number of good legal precedents against monopoly to choose from, as Coke himself was well aware.[62] Yet none of them was cited in the bill. Instead, the appeal was to "the ancient and fundamental laws" of the realm— as loose and dangerous a formulation as could be.

Why did Coke omit the precedents? The reason may be inferred from a comparison between what he meant by monopoly and what the courts had held before him. The most recent and sweeping decision against monopolies, the case of *Darcy* vs. *Allen* (1603)—a case in which Coke, incidentally, as attorney general, had argued for the defendant—laid down three criteria for determining monopoly: that the price of the product in question had risen, that its quality had declined, and that its former artisans had lost work.[63] In place of this earlier interpretation Coke proposed the flat and simple dictum that "The sole buying and selling of anything . . . is a monopoly.[64] It was this latter definition that went into the bill.[65]

The difference between Coke's formulation and the court's is clear. The court required the plaintiff to prove specific injury. Injury was therefore the crucial factor in determining monopoly, rather than the patent itself. The court thus avoided the imputation of judging the legality or illegality of royal grants; it merely offered the subject redress against those that had injurious consequences. Coke, on the other hand, deliberately sought to define certain patents as illegal, and so to restrict the King's power to grant them. Such a position was not merely unsupported by *Darcy* vs. *Allen;* it was implicitly contradicted by it.

In his most extended discussion of monopolies, in the third book of the *Institutes,* Coke based his definition on the famous Article 29 of the Magna Carta: "No freeman shall be . . . deprived of his freehold or liberties, or free customs . . . but by the lawful judgment of his peers or by the law of the land." Coke argued from this that "all monopolies are against this great charter, because they are against the liberty and freedom of the subject, and against the law of the land."[66] He prudently refrained from putting this not very skillful example of *petitio principii* into the bill, contenting himself with the still vaguer generalization of "ancient and fundamental laws," and even more prudently refrained from divulging his definition at all to the Lords. Speaking in the Upper House on March 15—the only formal brief Coke made against the lawfulness of monopoly—he hewed strictly to the letter of recognized precedent, and there was nothing in his remarks to indicate that he went beyond *Darcy* vs. *Allen* in any way.

The second major alteration in the bill concerned the adjudication of future cases of monopoly. "Where the words were 'to be tryed by the Common Lawe'," reported Glanville, "Nowe is added to except the Chancery, for there is a Chancery by Common Lawe for Chancery matters and a Counsel Table for Counsel Table matters. That this tryall shalbe by the Ordinary Courtes of Comon Lawe."[67] What this meant, simply, was that all jurisdiction over patents was to be withdrawn from the Privy Council, for that was the body that habitually exercised it. To emphasize this point more fully, it was further declared that "all proclamacions, inhibicions, restreintes, and warrantes of assistance of, for, or concernying [monopolies] . . . are and shalbe utterly voyd."[68] Thus, in addition to the limits placed on the royal power to create patents by the bill's definition of monopoly, the power of proclamation was also abridged.

There had never been any finally settled procedure for hearing complaints against monopoly. Elizabeth in 1597 and James in 1606 had promised to allow suits against patents in the common-law courts;[69] but both sovereigns were well aware that if such action were ever permitted in fact, the whole system would soon be litigated to death. *Darcy* vs. *Allen* was the sole exception, and after this case James kept jurisdiction in his own hands by the device of appointing councillors and Crown lawyers as referees to certify all patents before they passed the royal seal.

The clause for trial at common law was really then the teeth of the bill. As long as the Crown determined suits against its own patents, monopoly would continue, no matter what the statutes said. But on the other hand, for the Crown to lose a competence it had exercised *de facto* for fifty years would be a serious blow to its authority and prestige. And to vest that competence by statute in the courts of common law was an open invitation to other raids on the provinces of executive government in the future.

Thus amended, the monopoly bill was committed on March 26 for engrossing.[70] Because the session was still young, there was no hurry to put it to the last formalities of a third reading. Moreover, new monopolies were still being "beaten upon the Anvile every Day"[71] in the committee for grievances, and might perhaps suggest some last-minute improvements. This they did, but not to the original authors. On May 8, Sir Edwin Sandys reported that two clauses had been inserted into the text, "no Man knows how . . . which do clean overthrow that Bill." The first clause stated that the Act was to expire immediately upon the first meeting of the next Parliament; the second, that any royal *non obstante* granted against the Act would render it void.[72] The committee for the bill was sent out to investigate the matter, and repair the text. It accomplished the latter, and reported the bill "ready to pass, if it please the house."[73] But the secret scrivener was never found.[74]

Four days later, the bill went up to the Lords with a special recommendation for dispatch,[75] but it did not come to a vote in the Upper House until December 1. By that time it was not very difficult for the Crown to quash an offensive bill in the Lords; but, as this was a bill originally sponsored by the King, and much anticipated by the country, it was necessary to do it with some show of regret.

As the bill arrived in the Lords, it was clearly unacceptable without major alteration; therefore, the best strategy for securing its total rejection was not to alter it at all. This was precisely what happened. Archbishop Abbot, the chairman of the Lords' committee on the bill, steered it to the floor for a third reading without either debate, amendment, or conference. Asked if the committee thought the bill ready, Abbot replied that the "major parte" did. The bill was thereupon read. No sooner was the reading finished than Arundel attacked it violently. Abbot admitted that the bill, though "very benefyciall to the Subject" in general, might have been phrased "more myldly, & c." He moved to recommit it; but Arundel immediately "reminded" him that the bill had already been read, and "All Bylles after the 3 readinge must be put to the Question, and either be passed or rejected." The councillors then did the bill gently to death. It was a good bill in substance and intent, but its wording trenched upon prerogative.[76] Since it could not be committed again, let it be rejected and a new one drawn. A strong minority moved for recommitment "by special order," but it was rearguard action. The Crown had the tactical advantage of procedure, the moral advantage of sweet reason. The bill was forced to the vote, and defeated. A committee was appointed to draw a new bill, but this was mere ballet. The Lords knew that the Commons would never accept the insult of a bill rejected without consultation, and replaced without agreement. Such was the case. The Commons indignantly spurned the substitute,[77] and monopolies legislation was terminated for 1621.[78] But three years later, Parliament enacted a bill on the subject that was, in its key passages, almost word for word the text of the one rejected by the Lords.[79] That Charles had little trouble evading it in the twenties and thirties— the exception for "new manufacturers" rendered the bill virtually inoperative—does not diminish its constitutional significance. It remains, as Professor McIlwain called it, "the first statutory invasion of the royal prerogative."[80]

The Commons' other priority bill laid no claims to new power. It expounded, not "fundamental law," but a very concrete and specific one, the statute *tertio Jacobi* "For the Better Discovering and Repressing of Popish Recusants."

This bill was only the forward prong of a general attack on recusancy. What Parliament had failed to obtain by petition— namely, James's voluntary revocation of the policy of Catholic toleration—it was determined to get by statute.

The temper of the Commons on the subject of popery differed little from that of the London streets, as the case of Floyd had shown. Each, indeed, inflamed the other. As the presence of Parliament had emboldened the mob to jeer at Catholic ambassadors,[81] so country MPs, newly come to Sodom, listened solemnly as Phelips described them as surrounded by 40,000 seditious papists.[82] There were few who, like Sir Edwin Sandys, the humane and enlightened author of *Europae Speculum*,[83] were capable of drawing a distinction between Catholics by "con-science" and Catholics by "faction."[84] To the average member, every papist was an active or potential recruit to an international conspiracy, and the cruder forms of religious, national, and ethnic hatred combined to endow him with the most sinister aims and the most superhuman capacities for accomplishing them. There was, of course, a strong Puritan element in the Commons; but doctrinaire Protestantism was as little the cause of the anti-Catholic hysteria as a passionate commitment to the ideals of democracy was in the rabid anti-Communism of American Congresses of the postwar period.

Laws were not lacking on the subject of recusancy. What stymied Parliament was James's refusal to enforce them. True, James could as well ignore a new law as an old one, and his response to the Commons' petition in February[85] was clear notice of his intention to do just that if presented with one; but the mere passage of recusant legislation at this, the most critical diplomatic moment of the reign, might have a more significant effect on Catholicism in England than a dozen laws implemented with the utmost vigor, in an ordinary time. Lord Digby, James's ambassador extraordinary, was on the point of departure for negotiations in Vienna and Madrid which would decisively affect the future of Germany and Europe, and the succession of the English throne. The key to these negotiations was the support of Spain. New recusancy laws might well make this support impossible, and perhaps sabotage the entire Anglo-Spanish alliance. But this in turn would remove the chief impediment to those laws themselves, which was Spain's opposition to them. Thus at one stroke Parliament might both free England from her servile and humiliating dependence on Madrid, and enable her to deal with the Catholic menace at home.

A revival of the statute of 3 Jac. was an excellent means to this double end. This statute, enacted in the wake of the Gunpowder Plot, was itself largely a reenactment of the Elizabethan law of 1581, the peak of anti-Catholic hysteria in its generation. It was straightforwardly designed to bankrupt wealthy Catholics, and hence to destroy the financial base of Romanism in England. It declared that all convicted recusants who failed to take the Anglican communion within a year of their conviction would be liable to a fine of twenty pounds per month, "except in such Cases, where the King shall and may by force of this Acte refuse the same, and take two parts [i.e., thirds] of the Lands, Hereditaments, Leases and Farms of such Offendour, till the sayd Party . . . shall conforme himselfe and come to Church, according to the meaning of the Statute."[86] In short, even if the recusant could afford to pay two hundred and forty pounds per year for his sinning, the King could seize his lands at discretion.

This law, confessed the legislators of 1621, "hath not wrought that good as was expected." Wily papists had balked its "true intent" by putting their lands in trusts assigned to their own use. Thus held, the King could not get at them. This practice was now declared illegal. Such was the burden of the new act, which passed both houses on May 15.[87]

The new provision itself could not be called especially belligerent or repressive, but the restatement of the bitter language of 1606 left no doubt of the feeling of Parliament. Short of actually saying so, the two houses could not have made it clearer that they would never accept a Spanish alliance and a Spanish marriage.

In addition, the Commons had in committee another and far broader bill which aimed to summarize the entire field of recusant legislation since 1 Eliz. It redefined recusancy, stipulated the legal processes for its discovery and punishment, and laid down strict terms for readmission into the Anglican church.[88] Special attention was also given to the education of wealthy recusant minors in continental seminaries. This portion of the bill was aimed particularly at Gondomar, through whom many such children were sent abroad.[89]

Though this bill was only in the formative stage, it was confused in the public mind with the Act of 3 Jac. which had just passed both houses. Lando reported that

> Parliament has passed a law through both Houses that the king shall take possession for ever of all the goods of the Catholics . . . and if anyone wishes to save his goods he must conform to the Anglican religion, go publicly to the Protestant church, abjure the Roman Catholic faith and receive the communion after the manner of the country four times a year. Moreover, his Majesty is to place the children of rich Catholics in colleges to be brought up as Protestants,

the parents to pay the cost. Nothing is lacking for the execution of this most rigorous law except the King's signature.[90]

This reaction was typical, at least among Catholic observers. Salvetti called the new laws the severest to pass an English Parliament since the Reformation.[91]

Gondomar, of course, protested immediately. He came to Court in high dudgeon and announced that, in the light of Parliament's behavior, Digby's mission was now "superfluous." It was pointless to discuss a marriage treaty or the restitution of the Palatinate when England was about to embark on a persecution of Catholics. His own continued presence in England, he added, seemed equally pointless.

James closeted himself with the irate ambassador. His reply must have been satisfactory, for, as Salvetti noted, Gondomar "looked very well pleased when he came out, and Lord Digby is to leave in three days' time for Vienna."[92]

The recusant crisis brought the King's disputes with Parliament to a head. The Commons' legislation posed a serious dilemma. It "could neither be well graunted nor well denied," as Chamberlain observed.[93] In the first instance, James would lose the Spanish. In the second, he might very well lose his subjects. A month before, Sir Benjamin Rudyard had astutely predicted that the King's great problem would be to carry Parliament and the Spanish match "soe neare together without iustling."[94] The attempt had failed. One or the other would have to go.

Parliament had served its purpose, at least for the present. The threat of war which it invoked had produced negotiations for peace. Its further sitting, however, now placed those negotiations in jeopardy. The sword James had drawn had begun to rattle of its own volition; it was time to sheathe it.[95]

On May 28, Calvert announced to the Commons that Parliament would be adjourned in seven days. The House was stunned.[96] Despite the recurrent rumors of dissolution, and despite the King's own warnings, it had hoped for another few weeks of life. In no lesser time could it have hoped to sort out the legislative mess.

In their first shock, the Commons were confused but submissive. They were prepared to bow to the King's will. Sir Edwin

Sandys, as so often, expressed the general sentiment with pith and eloquence:

> As it was our greate care that ther might be a perfect union between both houses and between us and the King, we showld desyer this still, and that it may appear. The eyes and cryes of all the land are upon us. The Hope deferred is the fainting of the hart; but sith it must, lett us consider how we may spend our little time left for the session well, lett all bills be brought in, lett us debate how we may best report in the Country our imploiments heear, and that most of ther content and the Kings honor.[97]

But by afternoon, the House had hardened. The King's message was the greatest grievance of all, said Giles.[98] The Commons decided to approach the Lords, and jointly petition for more time.[99]

James was not long in responding to their action. On the morning of the twenty-ninth, the Commons were called unexpectedly to the Lords, where Treasurer Mandeville told them that it was the King's "Determinate purpose not to alter the daie allreadie set downe, And therefore [he] commanded noe such Petition . . . be made unto him."[100] At this, the Commons' messengers bolted from the conference chamber, crying wildly, "To the House! To the House!"[101]

The excited messengers threw the Commons into pandemonium. Heath tried to speak, but was shouted down with cries of "no, no, rise, rise."[102] It seemed that the House might do so on the spot, but cooler heads prevailed. Nothing more could be accomplished, however, than to inform the Lords "that the Committee is returned with great Grief to the House, and is now unfit to send an Answer." But so long were the Commons in their state of agitation in phrasing even this brief reply, that the Lords had already left for the day by the time they delivered it, "and so the House rose in a great Passion and Confusion."[103]

The next day was no better. Phelips delivered a funeral oration for the session. Religion abroad was endangered, reform at home diverted. He rose to an impassioned climax: "I beseech God in heaven, that chose this corner of the earth to plant his trewth on, to preserve it."[104] Barnabe Gooch pointed boldly at "that Man of Rome and his Son of Spain." "I have seene a greate quaileing since Easter," said Alford. "I pray god there be not more respect of private men than of the publuick good." Sir Robert Crane brushed aside official explanations. "There are reasons of weather alleged to make us break up. But God sends us such weather as if he did invite us to sit still."[105]

The Crown tried to steer debate into more constructive channels. "We all greive one greife, that we can not doe so much good as we would," said Heath, "but shall we therfor refuse all that we may doe." But the Solicitor was unable to give the Commons the one assurance without which all further effort was clearly futile: that Parliament would be reconvened, that the adjournment was not merely a prologue to dissolution. This was the unspoken question that hung over the House. Heath could only offer "an expectation of our meeting againe." This sorry evasion deepened the gloom. Sirs Wm. Spencer and Wm. Herbert moved to adjourn the House immediately and conduct no further business.[106] Crane bitterly expressed the Commons' sense of betrayal: " . . . we have graunted all that the King hath desyred, and we have nothing that we desyred graunted unto: for the matter of popery we were denyed, for ordnance denyed, For the Counsell obiected, theay may be spared[[107]] . . . we have given Two Free Subsidies; and they are like to prove a Free Gift indeed."[108]

Thus the Commons floundered toward adjournment in irresolution and dismay. James saw that something must be done. To send Parliament home in its present frame of mind would unsettle the whole country. On Saturday, June 2, the last day of meeting, he came to the Lords. He praised the nobility for their obedience to his commands. They had not questioned his will or quibbled over their powers. They, then, would make the choice he had decided to offer Parliament: the adjournment as prescribed, or another ten days to pass bills and have a session.[109]

The King withdrew to wait for an answer, and the Lords hastily sent messengers to the Commons. This move was both tactful and wise. It referred the decision to those it logically belonged to, and repaired the rather bad grace of James's offer.

The proposal itself was obviously infeasible. The Commons preferred to pass no bills rather than just a few, and an offer of ten days was little better than the week's notice they had previously been put on. But the act of concession was more important than the thing conceded. Confidence in the King was restored. The House could opt for adjournment without fear.

Coke and Digges returned the Commons' answer to the Lords. "'Tis a ioyfull thing," said Sir Dudley, " . . . that we have now 6 windy dayes turned into a faire evening." A committee of twelve peers and twenty-four commoners was chosen to present "most humble and lowly thanks" to the King.[110]

James received this delegation the next day at Greenwich. He was still testy with the Commons. They complained of lacking time for bills, yet refused to use the time they had; and when more time was offered, they refused that too. But, he said finally, "we made choice of what we liked best, and he was contented."[111]

One more rub remained. The King had announced his intention to adjourn Parliament by commission, a method employed only once before, by Elizabeth in 1585. That Parliament had objected to the innovation and this one felt even more strongly about it. "'Tis dangerous to adiourne by commission except in a prorogation," said Hakewill.[112] In fact, such a step very nearly amounted to prorogation. The significance of this was that during an adjournment, members of Parliament kept their immunity from arrest, while in a prorogation they did not. If the King adjourned Parliament by his own authority, he might claim the power to punish those who had incurred his displeasure. Sir Edwin Sandys thought so. His advocacy of the Cinque Port merchants and the Virginia Company had made him powerful enemies, and he had bitterly clashed with Cranfield only two days before.[113] He asked the House to clear his conduct.[114] It did so by acclamation; but, as John Smyth noted ominously, with none of the councillors present.[115]

The question of adjournment was unresolved as Parliament met for its last day, Monday, June 4, but the Commons were still in Saturday's euphoria. They had been ready to go home gulled and ridiculous, with nothing to show for sixteen weeks' work.[116] Now they could face their neighbors without shame. Yet the Commons did not want to end merely on a reprieve. They felt the need to make some positive gesture of their own.

It was Sir James Perrot who found it. The maintenance of true religion had been the first care of the House, he said, and it should be the last. He recalled the straits of religion at home and abroad, the grief and exile of the King's children, and his "princely and pious Protestation" to restore them by all necessary means to their rightful inheritance. Parliament too had a role to play in these great affairs. He therefore "humbly beseeched" the House to make, before its departure, "a public Protestation and Declaration, That, if Religion and Right may not be restored by Treaty and peaceable Means, that then, upon our Return to Parliament (being thereto required by his Majesty) we would be ready to adventure the Lives and Estates of all that belong unto us, or wherein we have Interest, for the Maintenance of the Cause of God, and of his Majesty's Royal Issue."[117]

Perrot's motion was received "with much Joy and a general Consent of the whole House, and sounded forth with the Voices of them all." Cecil exclaimed that "this Declaration is come from Heaven," and was worth ten thousand soldiers on the march. Towerson, the London merchant, vowed to give ten subsidies to support the declaration, and "if ten Subsidies will not serve, twenty shall; if twenty will not, thirty shall." Only Alford grumbled that it was "too greate an Engagement." The Speaker put it to the question, and the Commons cheered in reply, "withal lifting up their Hats in their Hands, as high as they could hold them, as a visible Testimony of their unanimous Consent, in such Sort, that the like had scarce ever been seen in Parliament."[118]

A committee was appointed to put the declaration into writing. A few minutes later it returned with a draft, which was read to renewed acclamation. The clerk was ordered to inscribe the declaration, and close his Journal.[119]

Soon after, the lord chief baron, Lawrence Tanfield, came down from the Lords with a delegation of fellow justices and Crown officials, to read the commission for adjournment. Tanfield informed the House that the Lords had already been adjourned by authority of the commission until November 14. Phelips answered for the Commons. The reading of such a document, he said, was against precedent. The messengers were asked to withdraw. The House thereupon voted to adjourn itself, and signified so to Tanfield, handing him back the commission unread.[120]

Sir Edward Coke then rose with tears in his eyes to read the closing prayer for the King and his children from the Book of Common Prayer. "*And defend them from their cruel Enemies* [italics in Nicholas]," he added at the end, sitting down and shutting his book. Speaker Richardson stood up, and pronounced Parliament adjourned "till the 14th of November next, . . . at Nine of the Clock."[121]

"So the House arose, every man taking his leave until the next meeting."[122]

In the first few weeks after Parliament's adjournment, the Privy Council got more work done than it had in years. Some of it—for example, instructions to circuit judges to keep an eye out for unscrupulous informers and exorbitant fees—was merely administrative tightening. Some of it—like the new regulations for the export of ordnance, or the investigation of grievances in Ireland—was only tokenism. But in at least two major areas, the Council undertook serious and sustained reform.

The first of these was the state of trade. Whereas the Council's previous efforts to cope with the depression had been sporadic and superficial, a standing commission was now established. Prominent merchants and expert opinion were consulted, and, for the first time, Outport spokesmen were invited to participate as well. In the spring of 1622 this commission issued the most comprehensive report on the clothing industry ever compiled.[123]

The second subject of reform was monopoly. The Council made an exhaustive review of patents, not merely those condemned or complained of in Parliament, but all of which the Crown had cognizance.[124] On July 10, twenty of them were revoked by royal proclamation. Seventeen more were disowned; that is, the Crown announced that it would stand aside in any court action brought against them. Still others were earmarked for further examination.[125]

In short, the greater part of the parliamentary program was now being carried out by executive order. But it was Parliament, of course, that had made all the difference. Its revelations of corruption and incompetence had at last put the government on its mettle. If James did not want to "have all doon by parliament,"[126] he and his ministers would have to do a great deal more themselves. The King was particularly irked by the implication that his subjects could get no redress for their grievances except through Parliament. In early 1623, more than a year after the dissolution of Parliament, he announced that, to further evince his royal care, "which is not confined unto times and meetings in

Parliament, but at all seasons and upon all occasions watcheth over the public weal of his kingdoms," he would establish a standing commission of five—Buckingham, Arundel, Pembroke, Andrewes, and Laud—to sit at least once a week in Whitehall to receive petitions and complaints "for any notable oppression," especially "where the quality of the offence, or eminence of the person . . . may require an extraordinary proceeding."[127] It sounded like nothing so much as the committee for petitions and grievances of the House of Commons.

But the hand that lifted also let fall. On June 16, twelve days after Parliament's rising, the King arrested Sir Edwin Sandys, the Earl of Southampton, and John Selden, the brilliant young lawyer who, though not a member of Parliament, had been a legal consultant to both houses.[128]

The arrest of Southampton was a foregone conclusion. The Earl said staunchly to his captors that "If there had bene unkindnes betweene him & any neere the King, that concerned not his Majestie." This was a mild enough description of his attempt to overthrow Buckingham. But there were other charges. He was accused of plotting with the leaders of the Commons to frustrate the King's ends and abridge his prerogative. Did he not, he was asked, "wishe that the house of Commons had power of Judicature?" Had he not urged the investigation of Ireland? Did he not advise the Commons to pass no bills at the adjournment?

Even more serious were charges of conspiring with a foreign power. Southampton was a known confidant of Baron Dohna, Frederick's ambassador, and had numerous contacts in Holland, where Frederick and Elizabeth had made their court of exile. He was said to be behind an attempt to bring the deposed rulers to England, and to even have "practiced" to send the Commons' subsidies directly to the King and Queen of Bohemia "without comminge att all into the Exchequer."[129]

At first Southampton stood on his parliamentary privilege, and refused to answer questions; then he demanded to be personally interrogated by the King.[130] But he soon realized the gravity of his position. He was threatened with the loss of his pensions, worth £3000 per year. At that, he agreed to retire quietly to his estates for the remainder of the Parliament.[131] The ease with which the leader of opposition in the Lords could be disposed of was in sharp contrast with the untouchability of Coke. There

was perhaps no more telling illustration in the Parliament of
1621 of the difference between the two houses vis-à-vis the Crown.

Selden's arrest in a sense symbolized the unexecuted warrants
against Coke, Hakewill, and Noy. The King had singled him out
precisely because he was not a member of Parliament. His case
could not be cited as a breach of privilege, but his offense was
that of his fellow lawyers in the House of Commons, the resur-
rection of the High Court of Parliament.

The King, moreover, knew his man. Selden was not the stuff
of which martyrs were made. James knew his quality too. He
was the finest legal mind of his generation. Such a man could do
great things in the Crown's service. He had already, on royal
commission, written his *Mare Liberum* in answer to Grotius'
famous tract. At the suggestion of John Williams, James offered
Selden a sinecure at four hundred pounds per year.[132]

Sandys was indubitably an MP. The government, anticipating
a reaction, took pains to assure the public that he had been committed for nonparliamentary reasons.[133] Its efforts did not alter
the technical breach of privilege, and convinced no one. It was
generally assumed that Sandys had suffered for his close connection with Southampton, if indeed the reverse were not true. "I
did ever assure my selfe that that mans busy head would never
be the author of any good to that Lord," remarked Sir Robert
Mansell on the two arrests.[134] It was also obvious that the enmity
of Cranfield had played its part. He and Sandys had clashed as
violently in the Commons as Southampton and Buckingham in
the Lords. As it was usually Cranfield, morever, who reported
the day's events in Parliament to the King, Sandys' conduct in
the Commons doubtless appeared in the most lurid colors.

Actually, the government did have plausible reason for acting
against Sandys. Sir Edwin's dealings in the Virginia Company
well justified an official investigation.[135] But imprisoning him
at this time was a grave mistake. Sandys may have been a nuisance
on economic matters, but on almost every important political
issue of the session he was the most valuable moderate in the
House. On popery, on Floyd, on adjournment, and in innum-
erable minor crises as well, his was the voice of reason, of compromise, of adjustment. And as one of the most respected and
venerable figures in the House, his voice often prevailed in situa-
tions where no councillor's could. The arrest of Southampton

was a daring and successful stroke, but that of Sandys was a disaster.

Within a month, the arrests had served their purpose. The three prisoners had been brought to contrition, and the monitory effect of their imprisonment had presumably been felt in the right quarters. They were released.[136] But Williams, the newly designated lord keeper,[137] and the man closest at the moment to the ear of the King, proposed a much grander gesture. The King had just issued, in the proclamation against monopolies, perhaps the most popular declaration of his reign. Why not follow it up with something even more popular, a general amnesty? Whatever bad taste might remain from the three arrests would surely be washed away in the generosity of such an act.

James assented, and on July 18, 1621, the gates opened to virtually every political prisoner in the realm. Sir Robert Naunton, the suspended secretary, and Sir Thomas Lake, his predecessor, were set free. Roger North, imprisoned on his return from Guiana, came out; and so did Yelverton, and even Floyd. But the biggest stir of all was created by the release of Henry Percy, ninth Earl of Northumberland, who had spent fifteen years in the Tower for his alleged part in the Gunpowder Plot.[138] Gondomar made it a point to call on England's most famous Catholic. The Earl then rode away in a coach and eight, never again to appear in public life.

James, too, sought his peace and quiet in the annual tour of his country estates. On his way, perhaps having second thoughts about the effect of the amnesty, he issued a new proclamation against "licentious speech." It seemed to have little effect,[139] however, except on the King's own entourage. A "profound silence"[140] on all public affairs descended upon the Court. But there was no real rest for the weary King. Half a continent away, the final chapter of his reign had begun.

V

THE DISSOLUTION

As Parliament recessed for the summer, James's ablest advisor and diplomat, Sir John Digby, was on his way to negotiate the restitution of the Lower Palatinate in Vienna. The foreign situation had deteriorated considerably since the previous autumn. In January, Ferdinand had put Frederick under the Ban of the Empire, thereby declaring him—and any who rendered him assistance thereafter—proscribed of life, lands, and titles. The Emperor could not by law declare a ban without the consent of a Diet; his doing so in defiance of tradition was a grim indication of how far the Imperial party was now prepared to go. The Princes of the Evangelical Union, meeting at Heilbronn, denounced the ban promptly;[1] but their resolve melted away at the prospect of being subjected to its provisions. They broke ranks, and by the Treaty of Mentz (April 2, 1621), agreed to withdraw their troops from the Palatinate within thirty-two days. This deadline coincided with the expiration of the charter of the Union itself, so that the treaty was in effect the death warrant of the only organized Protestant resistance in Germany.[2]

Only the tiny English garrison under Sir Horace Vere now remained to face Spinola's army. But, by exerting pressure on Madrid, James was able to arrange a general cease-fire during the Princes' withdrawal, and for subsequent six-week extensions, pending the outcome of negotiations in Vienna.[3] The Palatinate hung by a thread, but it was not one Spain would lightly snap while she feared the wrath of England.

But Digby's reception in Vienna was cold.[4] He found that Spanish influence in the Emperor's Court was far from what the facile assurances of Madrid had led him to expect, and without it, his cards were pitifully few. It appeared, moreover, that Ferdinand himself was so heavily mortgaged to his principal ally, Maximilian of Bavaria, that he could make no move without him, and Maximilian openly coveted both Frederick's lands and his titles. But it might still have been at least faintly possible to negotiate a settlement had James at last been able to hold his son-in-law in line. Ferdinand had little enthusiasm at the prospect of the already-powerful Maximilian engorging another state as large as his own. Had England been able to produce a promise of submission from Frederick, and to enforce a cease-fire on his side, the weight of German public opinion might have produced sufficient pressure to force an accommodation. Certainly it would have been more difficult to justify a war being fought solely to indemnify Maximilian than one to quell an unprovoked rebellion against Imperial authority.[5]

But England could guarantee neither the Palatine nor his armies. The latter, unpaid and desperate, were obliged to go wherever forage offered; they simply could not sit indefinitely in defensive positions. And Frederick, though in the grim hour after the Princes' desertion he had placed himself unreservedly in James's hands,[6] was still inwardly pursuing his fantastic dreams. He sent his own envoy to Vienna, who promptly denounced every engagement Digby had undertaken on the Palatine's behalf.[7] Under these circumstances, the war resumed. The Upper Palatinate fell into Maximilian's hands at once, and the Lower was saved only by a timely infusion of Dutch gold.[8]

Digby had meanwhile left Vienna. His only hope seemed in direct negotiations with Spain, and he pointed at once for Madrid. The Spanish warmly encouraged him, though less from any relish at confronting their angry ally than from fear of risking a new fiasco at the Austrian Court. But James recalled his envoy in midjourney. The mission to Madrid was postponed indefinitely.[9]

In his final dispatches, Digby gave vent at last to his anger. "I know not what I may be held in England," he wrote, "but I am sure I shall hardly ever be held Spanish hereafter"; and as for the Emperor, he wished to "conjure him upp such a storme, as shall make him wish he had better requited his Majestyes most syncere and worthy proceeding towards him." But his bitterness was no less directed at his client. "I will tell you freely," he wrote to

Calvert, "and desire you humbly to represent to the King, that if hee thinke to overcome this Businesse, hee must first reduce it to such a conformity that that which his faithfull ministers have established in one part, bee not overthrown by the malice or artifice of the attempts of others in other parts."[10]

Digby arrived in London on the last day of October, and was closeted with the King that evening. The next day, he made his formal relation to the Council. He urged war. English arms must uphold the Palatinate, or what remained of it; the results of failing to control the military situation had been seen. Frederick must be forced to submit once and for all to the King's dictation. To this James fully assented.[11]

The year had circled, and James's resolution to go to war had circled with it. Both stood again pretty much as they had before. And once again, the same policy dictated the same strategy: a Parliament.

Rumors had flown at the end of summer that the King would postpone the scheduled meeting of Parliament in November.[12] They were correct; in early October, Parliament was prorogued until the eighth of February.[13] James did not express his reasons, but they were obvious enough. Parliament had already been a considerable embarrassment to him in his relations with Spain; grave misgivings were voiced in Madrid over the attempt to revive the Gunpowder statute.[14] To risk having it in session while Digby was in Spain, negotiating not only for the Palatinate but for the match, was merely to court trouble.

But all that had now changed. Digby had been recalled, his journey postponed, and the King resolved to put ten thousand English soldiers into the Lower Palatinate by spring.[15] The government's urgency was reflected in the speed of its decisions. On November 2, a day after Digby's relation, Parliament was ordered back to session on the twentieth of the month.[16] The next day, Thomas Locke went to the government printing house and plucked a copy of the new proclamation out of the press for his friend Dudley Carleton. "There is great reioiceing here upon this newes," he told him.[17] It was a year to the day since the first summoning of Parliament.

James was not present when Parliament met on November 20.[18] He had gone to Newmarket, as was his wont in autumn, and was not expected back until Christmas.[19] In his stead, his three chief councillors—Wiliams, Digby, and Cranfield, now a baron and new lord treasurer[20]—addressed Parliament.

Williams, opening, launched into a résumé of reforms achieved during Parliament's recess. Thirty-seven patents had been annulled by proclamation. Ireland was again secure.[21] Trade, he reported, "hath ben much debated and is conveniently established."[22] Cranfield followed in the same vein. Land had risen a third since the King's accession, corn forty percent, wool more than fifty.[23] The depression, according to Cranfield, was not merely over; it had never existed.[24]

The forced optimism was soon explained. Parliament had been recalled, said Williams, to vote emergency funds for the Palatinate. It would be adjourned at Christmas, and meet again as previously planned on February 8, to complete the work of the session. In February, the King had promised, "we may sit as long as we will." He would not object to bestowing on bills "such howers as may well be spared" from the crisis abroad in the present sitting. But its first and chief work must be "the mayntenance of a Warr."[25]

To soften the bad news, Cranfield emphasized that though the King's own wants were "the Misery of the State," he asked not a penny for himself. If Parliament would lay aside grievances, he would shelve supply. He asked money only to defend the Palatinate.[26]

The exposition of the crisis fell to Digby. He discussed his mission frankly. Ferdinand he had found "inclyned" to peace, but "much beholding" to the Duke of Bavaria. When Bavaria rejected a truce, the Emperor was forced to follow suit. Spain was helpful, but her influence indecisive. Hostilities resumed; the Upper Palatinate had fallen; the Lower was in peril. Diplomacy had failed, "and the Kinge for a Peace could descend noe Lower but must resolve either to abandon his children or prepare for a Warr." This meant, immediately, the defense of the Lower Palatinate. A mercenary army had saved it for the moment, but that army must be paid and maintained. This was Parliament's task.[27]

The Commons reacted with little enthusiasm. It was a fancier menu, but the same bill of fare: subsidy now, grievances later. Sir Thomas Wentworth grieved that Parliament would go home again with nothing but "plumes and hopes." Alford asked how

Parliament was to proceed. Two proclamations enjoined the Commons from matters of state, and three councillors urged them on. Calvert replied acerbically that the proclamations referred to loose talk in taverns and alehouses, "but I hope this is neither alehouse nor tavern."[28]

The House decided, on the motion of Phelips, to defer its debate to the following Monday, when it should be fuller in number and wiser in counsel.[29] The government also made preparations. Caesar, who was presiding in the Court of Requests, was ordered to attend the debate.[30] Monday promised to be a stormy day.

Phelips was the first important speaker that morning. He reduced all the complexities of power to a simple equation of good and evil. Catholics stood on one side, Protestants on the other. The aim of all Catholic states was the extinction of all Protestants. Spain was the greatest Catholic state, and therefore commander of the Catholic crusade. Phelips scoffed at Digby's analysis of German politics. The Duke of Bavaria was "but a petit Prince." Spain and Spain alone directed the affairs of Germany.

The situation there was serious, but not irretrievable. All depended on England. The Princes of the Union had fallen away through England's inaction; the Dutch neglected her in their "forgetful Pride." Her own sufferings were a retribution. "God is angry with us for not keeping the Crown of Bohemia," declared Phelips. It was the trust He had given the English nation. But there was still time to make amends. England must make a real war, not just a diversion, against her real enemy, not just his instruments.

The present moment, however, was not propitious. The country was weak. Trade was worse than ever, and—so much for Williams and Cranfield—"the Letters and Remedies administered by the Council have wrought no good Effects at all." Parliament's job now was to hearten the country with good laws. February was time enough to consider supply for a "thorough War."[31]

Phelips' speech, however it may have represented his own opinion, was the perfect expression of the Country view: eschatological history, hatred of Spain, and bedrock isolationism. The Country wanted the war of 'eighty-eight. Spain was the aggressor, now as then. Why should she not pay in the same coin, the coin of the Indies?[32]

Calvert replied. If God's cause suffered by English inaction, what sense was there in further delay? The crisis would not wait until February; it was now. "This Diversion worse, than the diverting War good." Digges, who had some experience of diplomacy, tried to shade in Phelips' crude sketch. "It is not onelie a quarrell of religion, t'is mixt. Some princes of the Union are Romane catholiques."[33]

But Crew backed Phelips, as he was to do on every important occasion in the ensuing month.[34] If Frederick's army wanted money, the London merchants could put it up. But before Parliament embarked on a major war, "He desiered the King would let us knowe the Enemy we must fight against."[35] Crew spelled it out: "If we might have some assurance from his Majesty that we might see the Prince matched to one of the same religion, how glad it would make us and willing to give."[36] In other words, the King must not merely declare Spain an enemy, he must make her one. He must break off the match. Only then would Parliament support the war.

There were murmurs of approval. "I see it is the voice of the howse to knowe the enemie," Digges conceded.[37] With that the day's debate ended.

John Wilde of Droitwich resumed it promptly at nine the next morning with a passionate attack against Spain. "Spain is Hanniball *ad portas*," he cried. "Let this Carthage be distroyed." The King was "deluded"; and Wilde moved "that if the kinge will not declare the enemie, he would give us Leave to declare him."[38]

This was too much, and the House shouted him down. Edmondes stepped in quickly. The time was not ripe for these great questions. Spain had not yet responded to the failure of Digby's mission, and no decision could be made until that response was known. The need now was supply for the Palatinate. The Commons had solemnly bound themselves to defend it by their declaration. Did they now demur, or impose conditions, or plead poverty upon the plain text of their oath?[39]

This argument threw the Commons badly off balance. If it did not oblige them to defend the Palatinate, then what did the declaration mean?

It was Pym who rose to answer this question and lay their consciences at rest. The declaration, he argued, had merely affirmed the common duty of every English subject to support and defend the King and his blood royal in the preservation of their lands, titles, and dignities. It bound the Commons to no specific course of action; they had never been asked to endorse one. In June, the Palatinate was presumed secure, and the King had placed his whole reliance on negotiation. That policy had failed, and Parliament was now asked to support a mercenary army. This proposition was entirely new. It could in no way be construed as a retroactive obligation on the Commons by the terms of their declaration. It was something to be examined on its own merits alone. Otherwise, what the Commons had given James was an open warrant on the lands and goods of his subjects for any policy whatever.

What were the merits of the government's proposal? England was to fight her enemy in his strongest position, Germany, with her weakest weapon, money. It was an unwise strategy and an unfair burden. The subject was "called to hazard and expence and debarred from the hope of profitt." And meanwhile England's navy, which promised to win both victory for the King and treasure for the kingdom, was locked up in her harbors. "Upon which premisses his opinion was not to agree to any contribucion for the support of that Warre uppon this Proposicion."[40]

The Commons listened attentively. They saw a choice of wars, one paltering, fruitless, and debilitating, the other certain, glorious, and profitable. Instead of a war which drained the kingdom still further, they saw money pumped into dead industries, moribund ports coming to life, dangerous rural hordes put to work, and, above all, the blissful expectation of Spanish spoil.

Spoil was not merely a special incentive to warfare. As redress of grievances was offered for domestic supply, spoil was the *quid pro quo* of military subvention. War, like finance, was the sovereign's responsibility. If, for either, he came to his subjects for aid, it was only fair that he offer something in return.

To understand this line of reasoning, we must consider the seventeenth-century Englishman's attitude toward his sovereign's wars. Pym expressed it very well when he likened the quarrels of kings to those of private persons. The latter, he observed, were settled by litigation; the former by warfare. And as the goods of a defendant were liable at law, so were those of an aggressor in battle. Thus, if a prince wanted his subjects to share the expense of his "litigation," he must offer them a share in his gains. This is what Pym meant when he spoke of being "called to hazard and expense and debarred from the hope of profit."

In an age of dynastic warfare, this attitude made sense. Some wars were hardly more than personal quarrels or bids for status within the little circle of Europe's crowned heads. Frederick's seizure of Bohemia was the perfect example of such a war, and James's defense of Frederick was itself, by his own admission, a dynastic obligation.

But even a purely dynastic war could never be wholly a matter of indifference. A king's prestige was part of the nation's, and a nation's prestige is part of its interest. Certainly, England's prestige would have been disastrously diminished if James had ignored Frederick's plight.

Parliament recognized this fact. That was the true meaning of the declaration. It was an affirmation of identity between the King's interest and his people's. But this was precisely the source of Parliament's embarrassment. Having endorsed the King's war in principle, it found itself in total disagreement with him on how—and against whom—it should be waged.

This was not simply a disagreement about how to conduct the war. It was about the nature and purpose of the war itself. James's primary aim was, perforce, the restoration of Frederick; but this, in James's view, was possible only as part of a general German settlement. Diplomacy alone could bring it about. War's only function would be to coerce unwilling diplomats to work. It was still a ploy for peace, not a solution in itself.

Such a policy was incomprehensible to Pym and his fellow gentry. They could conceive of the war as a defense of national interest, as a religious crusade, as legalized piracy; but war as a measured makeweight in a complex balance of forces, to be applied or withdrawn as the occasion might demand, was beyond their ken. It could only seem wavering and inept. The people, said one member, preferred a "plain war" to a "dissembled peace."[41] Such were the terms in which the majority of the Commons viewed the European crisis.

These attitudes were irreconcilable. In their conception of modern warfare, in their whole notion of the relations between national states, the King and the Commons were as far apart as Clausewitz and Canute. Neither could understand, neither convince the other.

Parliament had two choices in this situation. It could bow, against its own judgment, to the King's absolute prerogative in the conduct of foreign affairs. Or it could try to wrest control of the war from him by withholding supply until he fought the war it wanted.

No one, of course, wished to face these alternatives. Nor did this brief interim sitting seem the time to do so. Parliament would temporize: Pym, for all the rigor of his analysis, moved finally that, so "things might be kept upright for the present . . . somewhat might be added to our former free guift . . . without anie mencion of the Warr."[42]

Crown officials now believed the worst was past. Sir George Goring, Buckingham's personal agent in the Commons,[43] filed a highly optimistic report that evening:

> The howse is now in much better order and temper than yaesterday it was and I doubt not but havinge disported themselves they will every day more and more let his Majesty see that it was nothinge but theyr zeale that first transported them and a desire that his Majesty might knowe the streame of theyre affections which is as greate as ever was to any Kinge, and no way to crosse uppon his prerogative or direct him in his councells.[44]

But to "direct the King in his counsels" was the only way to avoid crossing his prerogative. Only by persuading the King from his policy could the Commons escape the dilemma of submission or resistance. Even "persuasion," however, might be construed as a breach of prerogative. Could the Commons give the King advice when he did not wish to receive it? The Commons might consider it a duty, but the King would call it presumption.

Pym's solution to this was a new recusant petition. Spanish Jesuits at home and Spanish armies abroad were two ends of the same stick: if the Commons could not grasp the farther end, let them seize the nearer one. True, James had rejected a recusant petition in February; but he had not quarreled with the premises of the petition, only with its timing. He did not want to imperil his negotiations with the Emperor. Now that the negotiations had failed, the objection was removed.

By accepting the petition, the King would assure both his own personal safety and the internal security of the country. But he would also be weaning himself away from the Spanish. Once they saw that there was no further hope of subverting England, they would show their true face to him. "Match" and "alliance" would vanish into thin air. If the King would but take this first step, everything that the Commons desired would follow.[45]

The House ordered a committee to draw the petition.[46] It also decided to ask the King for a session. The Commons could not go home empty-handed again. "Adiornement upon adiornement, subsidie upon subsidie, and nothinge done will make us ridiculous," said Sir Thomas Wentworth. "We come not only here to give money," grumbled Mallory.[47]

It was in this spirit that the Commons voted a single subsidy to the King at the end of their three-day debate. The councillors were wisely silent about the sum, for which Rich commended them. A double levy against papists was written into the bill. The two petitions were to go with it, and the Commons expected at least the session as their quittance. As Wentworth said bluntly, "if he thought we should not have a Sessions nowe he would never give his voyse for this subsidy."[48]

With the passage of the subsidy, it seemed, the Commons' great debate on foreign policy was ended. On Thursday, November 29, the House slipped back into the harness of domestic business. But as it was preparing to rise for the day, Sir George Goring made a sudden motion:

> that seeinge his Majesty hath taken all courses beseeminge a iust and prudent prince for the restoringe of his children to theyre auncient patrimony, and among other hath lately written (as I had understood) to the Kinge of Spayne, eyther to procure presently a generall cesation of Armes from the Emperour in the Pallatinat, or to withdraw his forces from him in case he refuse, and neyther to assist him directly nor indirectly the howse would ioyne in makinge a petition to his Majesty, that in case the King of Spayne shall not condescende to eyther of these soe iust and reasonable de-

maundes, his Majesty will be pleased to declare unto them, that he will not spare to denounce warre as well against the kinge of Spayne and any other prince or state that shall oppose or assist against his children, or against the Emperour or any other that shall goe about to dispossesse them of theyre ancient inheritance.[49]

The motion was "wonderfully well" received in itself, Goring reported. But there was great skepticism about its source. Goring's connection was notorious. It was thought "eyther . . . that I have undonn my selfe at Court, or else that I had some underhand advise to doe that I did." The second surmise was correct. The motion came straight from Buckingham.[50]

What was the favorite's aim? On the face of it, he had adopted Parliament's policy and was trying to bring about a break with Spain. This is in fact what he was to do in the spring of 1624; but it is the least likely explanation of his behavior in November, 1621. It assumes that Buckingham, who had never acted independently on foreign policy before, was suddenly prepared to undercut James's whole Continental strategy, and in the most unlikely manner imaginable—by a parliamentary petition.

Far more convincing is the converse: that the break Buckingham aimed at was between James and the Commons. Certainly there was no lack of motivation for doing so. Parliament had already tried to overthrow Buckingham, and Buckingham, Parliament. The Commons were ready to attack grievances again, and it was clear that once the Spanish interlude was over, fresh assaults on Buckingham's patronage empire were to be expected, if not on Buckingham himself.

This conclusion was the one drawn by Spain. After the breakup of Parliament, Gondomar reported that Buckingham had had "a great part" in its undoing and deserved "great thanks."[51] Parliament was of the same opinion as well.

Yet there is a third possibility. The Marquis may simply have been hedging his bets. The King was still committed to the Spanish alliance. But he was also committed to an intervention against Spanish forces in the Palatinate. If the alliance fell through, Buckingham could claim his share of credit for it with Parliament. On the other hand, if Parliament fell through, he would earn the gratitude of Spain, which is what happened.

Buckingham could not have assumed that his petition would prove decisive in either contingency. He could not have known that Parliament would ever adopt it. He could not even have foretold that an occasion would arise for presenting it. The petition was an improvisation on immediate circumstances. Buckingham, with Goring's report on the foreign policy debate in his hand, must have seen the opportunity for such a tactic, and given it a try. The result was beyond all expectation.

The petition was referred to the subcommittee that had been created to draft the petitions for a session and the enforcement of the recusant laws. On Saturday afternoon, December 1, the subcommittee wrote it up. It was incorporated into the text of the recusant petition, to show how closely related, in Parliament's opinion, the foreign and domestic menaces were.[52]

How had the Commons passed from the caution of Pym and the evident suspicion of Goring to the bold, almost exuberant step of not merely embracing Goring's motion but coupling it with the recusant petition? Had they continued to regard it as either a plot or an apostasy, they would hardly have proceeded with such confidence. Evidently, they expected a welcome reception. They had concluded, that is, that Goring's motion had the King's blessing.

The Commons had only one clue about what the motion meant: the behavior of the privy councillors. If the councillors attacked it, it would prove the motion tainted; but if they did not, if tacitly or openly they encouraged it, what could it signify but royal approval? The councillors were silent, and their silence was taken for consent.

In reality, the King's ministers knew as little as the rest of the Commons. Their silence indicated not consent, but perplexity and embarrassment. They had only the most general instructions for handling the whole foreign policy debate, and none at all for Goring's proposal. Did the extraordinary permissiveness of the debate, the sudden attack on Spain by a dependable courtier, the King's very absence from London, foreshadow a major policy shift? It was a brave man who would undertake to decide such questions for himself. But the councillors themselves secretly hoped so. They were only human, and their personal sympathies lay with their fellow MPs. As Calvert later testified,

wee . . . made such descant in the Lower house, after the
King was gone to Newmarket, and had left us to our selves,
as wee neither spared the king of Spaine, nor the match, nor
any thing that might concerne that Nation, but for a fort-
night together did so course them, as being not all that while
controlled from Newmarket, wee thought wee had done
well.[53]

The subcommittee finished its work on the petitions at three
o'clock on the first, and Coke, its chairman, wanted to ratify
them immediately in the House. He was forestalled, however,
by May. This was the highest matter that had ever come within
the walls of the House, said the Chancellor of the Duchy. Surely
it was worth a day's reflection.

May was playing for time, hoping to receive instructions. Coke
perhaps realized it. But so reasonable a request could hardly be
denied, and consideration of the new double petition was put
off until Monday.[54]

By then, the King must have learned what was going on,[55] for
on Monday the government suddenly presented a united front
against the petition. No sooner had Coke read it to the Commons than Sackville, now wholly again the courtier,[56] rose to
denounce it. Was the House, having so prudently respected the
royal prerogative throughout the sitting of this Parliament,
now to recklessly invade it, and in its very essence—war, alliance,
marriage? What honest man would propose something that could
only be rejected? The King would, he must, reject it. "Therefore
. . . let me entreat this House not to take into their hands, like
Phaeton, their father's chariot, whereupon a general incendiary
followed."[57]

Sackville was barely able to finish. He sat down in an angry
clamor.[58] A debate ensued, in which Crown spokesmen strove
to isolate the marriage clause from the rest of the petition. All
this was a very rude shock to the Commons. Brooke confessed
that when he left the House on Saturday, he "expected no Opposition against this Petition, but Matter of Form."[59]

As a result, the House closed ranks behind Coke and the subcommittee. The more the Crown attacked the marriage clause,
the more the House insisted that it was integral to the whole
text of the petition. If a division of religion could ruin a private
family, asked Perrot—himself the husband of a papist—what

would division in the royal family do to the state? The marriage of a prince was the concern of every subject, claimed Crew; and in the Spanish match, said Phelips, was "neither honor, profit nor safety." Thomas Wentworth, son of the fiery Peter, was afire himself. "I heard it demanded, did ever these walls hear such things proposed. *Tertio Jacobi* there is a relation of the Gunpowder Treason; I wish it may be read, for these walls (methinks) do yet shake at it. And I would know whether those 36 barrels of gunpowder under these walls do not require this?"[60]

Wentworth's image went to the heart of the Catholic obsession. The fuse was made in Rome, lit by Spain, carried by Jesuits, and planted by recusants—under the walls of Parliament. To preach God's word in the pulpit, to repress recusants, to contain Spain, was merely to defuse the same explosive at different points. It was useless for the sardonic Noy to treat Spain as an ordinary political entity, and ask how the assistance Spain rendered the Emperor differed from that given Frederick by England.[61] Spain was not a state; recusants were not Englishmen; Roman Catholicism was not a religion.

Yet the very vehemence of the Commons betrayed their embarrassment. The petition was the logical conclusion of their debate, a conclusion they had drawn but would never have dared to declare, did they not believe it had the approbation of the King. Now, too late, they had discovered it did not. They were committed to the petition. What sort of councillors would they be if, having discovered the deepest danger to the commonwealth, they withheld it from the King for fear of displeasing him? The Commons could not turn back now, said Heneage Finch, recorder of London, without becoming "neuters."[62]

At the same time, they *would* displease the King, and so they tried to soften the implications of what they said, if not the thing itself. They denied any invasion of prerogative. "We do not prescribe anything to the King," said Brooke. "We only present a humble petition desiring his Majesty to think of the fittest course, less than which we cannot do." The petition could not bind the King in any way, observed Coke. "He may give it life if he please and quash it at his pleasure." Wentworth and Phelips suggested that the House present it as simple advice, without asking any answer.[63] Before passage, a few words were added to insure against misinterpretation:

This is the sum and effect of our humble declaration which (no way intending to press upon your Majesty's most undoubted and regal prerogative) we do with the fullness of all duty and obedience humbly submit to your most princely consideration.[64]

The petition passed unanimously.[65] A committee of twelve was appointed to bring it to Newmarket the next day. All twelve were courtiers: Goring, Weston, Mildmay, Murray, Lords Clifford and St. John, Francis Fane, Harry Vane, Chaworth, May, Miles Fleetwood, and John Brooke.[66]

The petition was copied overnight and delivered in the House next morning to Sir Richard Weston, who was to present it to the King.[67] It had not yet left the House when Secretary Calvert brought James's answer, dated the previous evening. The King had heard, to his "great grief," that "some fiery and popular spirits" in the House of Commons, emboldened by his absence, had begun to debate "matters far beyond their reach or capacity, and so tending to our high dishonor, and to the trenching upon our Prerogative Royal." He therefore commanded the Speaker to inform the House that he would not permit further discussion of Spain or the match, and would not "deign the hearing" of any petition concerned with these matters. James added that though he had not imprisoned anyone for Parliament business this session, "we think ourself very free and able to punish any man's misdemeanor in Parliament, as well during their sitting, as after." He reproved the whole House for its abuse of Spain. No subject might speak of any anointed king with such disrespect, be he the last of England's enemies, let alone the closest of her friends.

At the end, to temper the harshness of his letter, James granted the Commons their session. But even here, his tone was monitory. If good laws were ready by Christmastime, he would be happy to sign them; if not, the House would know whom to blame.[68]

The House was stunned by the King's letter. It could do nothing but recall its messengers, listen dully to a second reading of the letter, and adjourn in confusion at eleven o'clock.[69]

It was clear that someone had betrayed the counsels of the House to the King, and had put the worst possible construction on them. Once again the specter of secret informers reared itself. Wentworth had spoken prophetically the day before: "There are some amongst us who act the devil's part by making dissension between his Majesty and this House and laugh at it when it is done."[70]

Overnight, the whole atmosphere of the session changed. A few days before, everything pointed to harmony. The King's lenity was permission, his absence, encouragement. Now all the signs read backward. The free debate was an illusion, the petition, a trap. Portents that, disturbing in themselves, had previously been discounted, now appeared in a far more sinister light.

Chief among these was the discovery of a plot against Sir Edward Coke. Its author was one John Lepton, who held a patent to draw bills, letters, and process in the Court of the King's Council in the North. The patent was a typical case of a courtier foisted on an already top-heavy bureaucracy, with the attendant rise in fees and decline in efficiency, and had been routinely condemned by Coke's committee of grievances in May.[71] Ironically enough—though presumably the humor was lost on Lepton—it was Coke who had originally drawn the patent, as King's attorney in 1606.[72]

But Lepton had friends at Court, and was able to save his patent. It escaped the list of those annulled by the Proclamation of July 10.[73] Lepton then sought revenge on his tormentor, Coke. Allying himself with another quashed patentee, Henry Goldsmith, he filed a suit against Coke in Star Chamber that was virtually an indictment of his entire career.[74] Lady Hatton, Coke's ex-wife, added a separate allegation of fraud for good measure. By this time, the plot was promising enough to attract important sponsors. It was even spoken of as "the King's service." James dropped another plan to send Coke to Ireland in favor of it.[75]

The plot was revealed to the Commons by Phelips on November 24. An immediate investigation was ordered.[76] An attack on Coke for his work as chairman of the committee of grievances was an attack on Parliament itself.

The House discovered, to its disgust, that its own Speaker was to be the chief counsel against Coke, and, to its dismay, that Lepton was at Newmarket, under the King's protection.[77] Goldsmith, however, was within reach, and the House jailed him. James thereupon demanded his release. It was no privilege of Parliament's, he said, to disturb the proceedings of an ordinary court of law.[78] This royal act confirmed the worst fears of the Commons: the King was in the hands of those who wished to strike down, not merely Coke, but Parliament itself.

The case of Coke revived that of Sandys. Sir Edwin, after his release from prison, remained on his estate in Kent. He pleaded illness as an excuse for his absence from Parliament. The House had accepted this, and refrained from raising the issue of his imprisonment.[79] But on December 1, after two days of debate on Coke, an inquiry on Sandys was ordered. Two members, William Mallory and Sir Peter Heyman, were sent to interview him. The plea of his brother Samuel to leave well enough alone only aroused further suspicion. Calvert's assurance that Sandys had not been committed for any act in Parliament was brushed aside by Spencer: "Mr. Secretary is a party and therefore no fit person to give satisfaction."[80]

It was against this background that the King declared himself "very free and able to punish any man's misdemeanour in Parliament," and rejected the Commons' petition as the work of "fiery and turbulent spirits."

The day after this message, December 5, the House convened in silence.[81] Finally John Delbridge arose, and began to talk about the state of trade in the West Country. But his voice suddenly broke, and, stammering passionately that he would as willingly "hang under the Gallows as fry over a Faggot," he urged the House to bring its petition again and again until it was heard. Phelips cried out at "this Soul-killing Letter," and Seymour moved to purge the House of those "who misreport all" to the King.[82]

The House then went into committee, which was no simple matter. Suddenly everyone had found voice, and no one would take the chair. At last Noy was shoved forward, asking bitterly "what Penance he had deserved, that the House should impose that office on him."[83]

Coke began the debate. He asserted "that we have done nothing but in the Duty of the most dutiful Subjects." The petition had passed unanimously. He wished that those opposed to it had said so openly at the time. Pym picked up this point. The words "fiery," "popular," and "turbulent" were laid on the whole House, for the whole House had agreed on the petition.[84]

Calvert tried to preach realism. The King disliked the petition; present it again and he would only dislike it the more. The

House had angered the King, and must needs explain itself. It could either attempt to justify its action, or excuse it. Of these, excuse was both the wiser and the safer course.[85]

Sir Thomas Wentworth supported Calvert. Always the practical bureaucrat, he foresaw a long, fruitless deadlock, such as Floyd's case had produced. He called on the House to return to work and to appoint a select committee to prune the petition of its offensive passages and defend the rest with precedents.[86]

But the House was not about to bury the issue in a committee. To present an excuse, said Phelips, "presupposeth an Error," which he for one would "not readily confess." "I think we did well and are not faulty," said Christopher Brooke. "Frustratinge of penall lawes no point of prerogative," growled Crew. Alford summed up the feeling of the majority. "Lett us not meddle other busines," he said, "till wee be a free parliament."[87] A select committee was appointed "to prepare a Declaration . . . of the Manner of the Proceedings of this House, in the Petition, . . . and also concerning the Privileges of the House, and all Things incident thereto." This committee promptly chose a subcommittee of twelve to do the actual work.[88]

On the morning of the sixth, the House sat idle waiting for the subcommittee's draft. It came at last after lunch. The Commons, it said, were "full of grief, and unspeakable sorrow" at the King's displeasure, and beseeched him not to judge them "by the mis-information of partial and uncertain Reports," but in the "clearness of your own Judgment." A résumé of the petition followed. In that petition, James was assured, "we did not assume to ourselves any power to determine of any part thereof, nor intent to incroach or intrude upon the Sacred Bounds of your Royal Authority, to whom [sic], and to whom only, we acknowledge it doth belong to resolve of Peace and War," but simply to inform him "of our cares and fears . . . without any expectation of any other Answer . . . then what at your good pleasure, and in your own time should be held fit."

The Commons feared, however, that the "largeness" and "generality" of the King's answer "doth seem to abridge us of the ancient Liberty of Parliament for freedom of Speech, Jurisdiction, and Just Censure[89] . . . the same being *our ancient and undoubted Right, and an Inheritance received from our Ancestors* [italics mine]; without which we cannot freely debate nor clearly discern of things in question before us, nor truly inform your Majesty."[90]

With this declaration, the whole focus of debate shifted. What the Commons' petition said was less important than whether it might be drawn at all. The point at issue was no longer the Spanish match or the survival of the Protestant religion. It was the liberty of Parliament.

The question turned on whether the King would read the petition. To read it was to recognize it. Whether he then accepted or rejected the advice it contained, he had tacitly acknowledged the right of the House to offer such advice on its own initiative. If the House could do that on war and marriage, it could advise James on anything. And the right to offer advice on anything implied the right to unrestricted debate. This was precisely as men like Phelips, Alford, and Crew felt it should be. They understood quite clearly what the petition implied. So did James. That was why he refused to read it.

Yet it was apparent from James's answer that he had read the petition, or rather a smuggled copy of it. That copy had come, obviously, from one of the councillors at the Saturday subcommittee. The councillors were in a very difficult and unhappy position. As MPs, they took part in the confidential business of the House; as councillors, they were duty-bound to report what they heard. This situation, of course, was nothing new; it was the normal state of affairs. The Commons disliked it intensely, but there was nothing they could do about it. It was what the councillors were there for.

There were times, however, when the situation seemed intolerable to the House. Such a time had been late April, when timely reports of the debates on Ireland and justices of the peace had resulted in sharp checks to Parliamentary strategy. The House had been so vexed that two members moved to send the Speaker to the King to tell him the "truth."[91]

But the betrayal of the petition was a far more serious incident. The Commons believed that the councillors had deliberately misled them. Henceforth they were regarded, not with suspicion, but confirmed contempt. Their position was roughly analogous to a contingent of blacklegs at a labor conference. They were enemies within the walls.

Poor Calvert was singled out for special derision. He was not merely the handiest target, but a known papist. His treatment varied. Sometimes the House would bait him, sometimes it sent him to Coventry. On the seventh, for example, he tried to deliver the King's order to release Goldsmith, an order he had been carrying about for three days. The House simply ignored him. Once again, with the aid of the Speaker, Calvert repeated the order. Loud buzzing ("private Speech") drowned him out. Finally a few members remarked offhandedly that they needed more time to think about it.[92] A few days later, Calvert's altercation with Alford about free speech[93] was brought up. Was the Secretary now satisfied that Alford had spoken nothing "unfitting or misbeseeming," a member asked tauntingly. Calvert replied with dignity that since the House had not seen fit to reprimand Alford at the time, his personal satisfaction was immaterial.[94]

Lesser courtiers and officials, upon whom the government normally relied, took pains to proclaim their independence of the Court. "My gown and knighting shall not carry me against my conscience," Serjeant Ashley declared ostentatiously.[95] Calvert counted but three men in the House who would "stand up for the King," Sackville, May, and Harry Vane. "I doubt not but there are many other well affected Men," he sighed, "but they are no Speakers for the most part."[96]

The isolation of the councillors was of serious consequence. The councillors were the normal channel of communication between King and Parliament. They absorbed the shock of any conflict between Crown and Commons. Merely by diverting frustration with royal policy to hostility toward themselves, they served a useful function in the House. But their usefulness was now at an end. The Commons would trust no intermediaries. They would hear no words but the King's own. Thus the King was forced to confront the Commons directly. In such a confrontation, as Heath put it, every word that fell fixed. There was no way to soften a stand or make a concession except by visible retreat.

On December 7, the Commons gave final approval to the draft of their reply to the King. They read and passed it section by section, scrutinizing the language with great care. The words "some of" were added, and "hitherto" cut out. Calvert and May, reduced to utter futility, joined a debate on whether the House had been "taxed" or "burdened" with the King's charges. But there were no changes of substance, and no changes at all in the offending petition itself.[97]

With the declaration ready for dispatch, the Commons faced another question. What should they do while waiting for the King's reply? Alford had argued that they could do nothing until they were a "free Parliament"—until, that is, the King had accepted their petition. Phelips vigorously expounded this idea. The very essence, the definition of a Parliament, was in its privileges. Without them, it could not properly be said to exist at all. How then could Parliament function, when its privileges were threatened? Samuel Sandys put the issue in slightly more practical terms. The House claimed in its declaration that it could not proceed in its present condition; how then was it to proceed without contradicting itself? Withrington considered it a closed case. "It was ordered, that all Proceedings should cease, till an Answer from his Majesty. If the Clerk have not entered it, to have it now ordered."[98]

But there was considerable sentiment for going back to bills. Digges, Giles, and Chaworth urged it, and Pym, whose recent speeches had given him great authority, challenged Phelips' argument about the nature of Parliament. The function of the House was not to maintain its privileges but to pass laws: "Bills are the End of a Parliament." There was no reason, therefore, why a question of privilege, which did not affect the legislative process, should hinder the passage of laws. The King had granted a session; the country expected one. If the Commons failed to have it, the onus would be theirs.[99]

These two views were profoundly opposed. To Phelips, Parliament was its capacity to function; to Pym, Parliament was the functioning itself. But this was not merely an argument *in abstractu*. What Phelips proposed was, in effect, a sitdown strike. If the King would not read the petition, the Commons would not work on bills. It was a dangerous game. A sitdown might embarrass James, but it could easily backfire on the House. In either event, Parliament might be dissolved. But, for Phelips, the Commons had no other choice. Deadlock was their only tactic. The King could ignore petitions, and petitions to read petitions, but he could not ignore silence.

Most of the House sided with Phelips, if only because they were too disheartened to work, but they refused to make a direct order. To do so would commit them irrevocably, and they were not prepared to be so committed.[100]

This solution satisfied no one. Those of Phelips' persuasion were not content with it, and those of Pym's opposed it. Thus both extremes contended for the wavering majority. The next day, December 8, an order to suspend business was moved again —by whom we do not know—"but the House would not have any such Order entered."[101] There were still a few details to dispatch on this day concerning the declaration, and finally the twelve deputies were sent off.[102] But on Monday, the tenth, the House again convened in silence. A strong attempt was then made to get business going again. Berkeley,[103] More, Mallett, Spiller, and Sackville spoke in succession for resuming bills. No sooner had they finished than a whole sheaf of them arrived from the Lords. In particular, the Lords requested a conference for the monopoly bill, which they had wholly rewritten.[104] So eager were they that they had already appointed their committee, and even suggested a time and place of meeting, which was usually the prerogative of the house of whom the conference was sought.[105]

Relations between the two houses had deteriorated.[106] Without Southampton who, like Sandys, stayed at home, opposition in the Lords fell apart. Baron Cranfield, the pose of popular reformer now shed, wrote smugly that "his Majesty will receive no discontentment in our house."[107] The Commons knew they could expect no sympathy in their struggle from the Upper House.

They were, moreover, highly resentful of the treatment of their monopoly bill. The Lords had shown a great "Disrespect" to the House, said Coke. Instead of conferring on the original bill, they had thrown it away. The bill they presented was their own. This compounded discourtesy with a serious breach of privilege, for the initiation of public bills belonged to the House of Commons alone. It was also a personal insult to Coke, who was the author of the Commons' bill. It was easy for the Lords to dismiss the bill, he said bitterly, "since Monopolies do touch or concern very little the Lords, or their Liberties, but only the poor People."[108] The House agreed. The conference was "mannerly refused."[109]

Calvert bowed to this, but still urged that work go on. Heath appealed to have at least a bill for continuance and repeal of statutes prepared, so "that we be not taken unprovided if it

[Parliament] should be broken up suddenly"—an ominous enough remark.[110] But the House frittered away another hour and rose for the day.

The morning of the eleventh was spent on Lepton's case, and the House thus avoided the work issue. The next day, however, there was silence again. After a few moments, Calvert rose with a message. The King, having granted a session at the Commons' request, and "taking now notice that the House forbears to proceed with any bills," commanded them to resume work. "His Majesty," Calvert concluded, "hopes they will not take upon them to make a recess in effect, though not in shew, without his warrant."[111] Sir William Fleetwood immediately followed with a motion to send the bill for Magna Carta up to the Lords.[112]

The plea of a councillor was one thing, the King's command, another. It was a decisive moment, but Phelips and his party were prepared for it. Sir Robert made the first reply. Let us, he began, "consider how we have walked these Eight Days, and how our Purpose of Silence hath been grounded." It was the silence, not of factious or frivolous men, but of troubled minds and hearts. It was not the Commons who had laid down their work, but others who had interrupted it. It was not in the House, but in the King, to end the deadlock. If the Commons obeyed this command, "we endanger all our Liberties; for then we shall never hereafter proceed but in such and such Businesses, and in such a Manner, as the King shall still command." Phelips moved for a committee—the eternal resort of delay—to seek precedents for an answer both respectful to the King, and consistent with the principles of the House.[113]

Crew and Glanville followed him. They denied that the House had been idle. Its time was consumed in answering the King's messages, and defending its members against threats and conspiracies. The House had not begun the present quarrel; its time had been wasted by it; and now it was taxed with that waste.[114]

But Calvert reminded the House that it had not been given a message to debate, but a command to obey. "It is not in the power of the howse to impose silence on our selves," warned Heath. Digges and More fell in behind. If the House was as busy as it claimed to be, remarked the latter slyly, then the King's order merely told it to do what it was already doing.[115]

The body of the Commons was as perplexed and undecided

as before. Sir Edward Giles's confusion was typical. Giles had previously supported a resumption of business. But this cruel command shocked him. How could the goodwill of honest men be so mistaken by their sovereign? There was only one explanation: that the order came not from the King, but from "the Man of Sin"—Gondomar.[116] This was the surreptitious opinion of many. Crew hinted of "evill spiritts" behind the scenes, "backt with authoritie."[117] But if such were true, what was to be done? The Commons could think of nothing—except to appoint a committee.[118]

This committee never met. The next day was wholly devoted to Lepton again,[119] and on Friday, December 14, James's answer to the Commons' declaration at last arrived.

The twelve deputies had reached Newmarket late on the night of the ninth. James gave them access the next afternoon. The King was in sardonic humor. "Bring stools for the ambassadors!" he cried, as the twelve knelt before him.[120] "It is thought," he said to them, "I am not rightly informed." He produced a copy of the Commons' petition, and bade the deputies compare it with their own. "The copie was sent me by the prince," James added triumphantly, "who complained that his marriage was continually prostituted in the howse." The deputies found that the King's copy lacked the final clause "wherein wee professed not to press upon his prerogative." They urged him to read the petition itself. James refused. He had refused in his written answer to the Commons, and he hoped the deputies would not "perswade me to give my selfe the lye."[121]

The King's new reply to the House was dated December 11. Probably the deputies started back for London Wednesday morning, and arrived the next day at nightfall. On Friday morning they appeared in the House. Sir Richard Weston related their audience, and then the Speaker read the King's letter.

The Commons had declared James misinformed. "We wish you to remember," he replied, "that we are an old and experienc'd King, needing no such Lessons, being in our Conscience freest of any King alive, from hearing or trusting idle Reports." This the councillors of the House could attest, "if you would give as good an Ear to them, as you do to some Tribunitial Orators among you."

The Commons had denied a breach of prerogative. But the

whole petition was nothing but that, for between a presumptuous introduction and a hypocritical conclusion, "what have you left unattempted in the highest points of Sovereignty, in that Petition of yours, except the striking of Coin? . . . it contains the violation of Leagues, the particular way how to govern a War, and the Marriage of our dearest Son."

These, said James, were no matters for a Parliament to handle, "except your King should require it of you." The Commons claimed the speeches of Cranfield, Digby, and Williams as their warrant; but these speeches dealt solely with the specific and immediate defense of the Palatinate. "Now, what inference can be made upon this, that therefore we must presently denounce War against the King of Spain, break our dearest Son's Match, and match him to one of our Religion, let the World judge: The difference is no greater than if we would tell a Merchant, that we had need to borrow Money from him for raising an Army; that thereupon it would follow, that we were bound to follow his advice in the direction of the War." But not content with this, the Commons then declared a general responsibility for the honor of the Crown, the welfare of religion, and the safety of the kingdom, "So as this Plenipotency of your invests you in all power upon Earth, lacking none but the Popes to have the Keys also both of Heaven and Purgatory."

Since, however, the Commons were so apparently convinced that the cause of Protestantism and the cause of the Palatinate were one, James would "a little unfold your eyes herein." The "miserable war" in Germany had nothing to do with religion. It was the consequence of Frederick's seizure of Bohemia, an act that not even Frederick had ever sought to justify as religious. It had, indeed, afforded the Jesuits an all too ample pretext for suppressing all Protestants within their control. But none of the powers of Europe wished to see a political conflict degenerate into an ideological one. For this reason, James rejected the "hot persecution of our Recusants" once again urged on him by the Commons. Its only effect could be to fan a war in which the future of the Protestant faith might well be placed in jeopardy.

But the concluding passages of the letter were much gentler in tone. Although, James said,

we cannot allow of the style calling it, *Your ancient and un-*

doubted Right and Inheritance [italics in Rushworth]; but
could rather have wished, that ye had said, That your Privileges were derived from the grace and permission of our
Ancestors and Us . . . Yet we are pleased to give you our
Royal assurance, that as long as you contain your selves within the limits of your Duty, we will be as careful to maintain
and preserve your lawful Liberties and Priviledges, as ever
any of our Predecessors were, nay, as to preserve our own
Royal Prerogative.[122]

Weston added a few more palliatives by word of mouth. Parliament would rise on December 22, and, in expectation of a session, the traditional pardon was being prepared by Cranfield
and himself. Goldsmith, whose release had been demanded
earlier by the King, was now remanded to the House. He and
Lepton had outlived their usefulness.[123]

The King's letter nearly swayed the House. Its very harshness
made the final concession, couched in handsome and generous
words, seem an act of great magnanimity. An angry king chastened his subjects, but lovingly forgave them. It must have seemed
to many that the only conclusion to such a letter would be a
pronouncement of dissolution. Instead, there was a confirmation
of their privileges. The immediate reaction was relief and gratitude. Christopher Brooke was the first to speak. He declared himself satisfied. James had dealt sternly with his Commons, but like
a true father. "In some Things [he] reprehendeth us; in other
Things argueth with us; but, in the End, concludeth, in effect, as
much as we desire." He moved "To read a Bill, and go to our
Business." Thomas Wentworth promptly seconded him.[124]

Phelips alone had his wits about him. The King's letter
changed nothing. He still claimed final control of the Commons'
privileges. If they acceded to this, everything they had fought for
would be lost. At least, Phelips pleaded, the House must keep
"the Constancy of its Proceeding," and send a formal reply to
the King.[125]

But the House refused to listen. It was weary of this battle of
words, weary of a dull standstill that went against everybody's
grain. The Christmas recess was a week away. The Commons had
given two subsidies, and now a third. After a year's work, and a
decade's interregnum, what would they bring home to their
people? "We have passed no laws. We have redressed no griev-

ances. But we have preserved our liberties." What would workers without hire, farmers without markets, tradesmen crushed by patents, say to that?

In February, at the very beginning of Parliament, the House had faced the same issue, the same dilemma. For a week, the question of free speech blocked all business. But the grievances of the Commonwealth were too pressing. The King offered a formula that was not quite satisfactory, but vague enough to do no harm. The Commons had accepted it. Now their instinct was again to see the same way out in James's new guarantee of their liberties.

The King's letter was read again, at the request of Henry Sherfield.[126] It produced no discernible effect. The House remained as before. The oftener we read the letter, the better we shall be satisfied, declared Heath. But Shervile's request had served one purpose. The morning was now far spent, and there was no question of initiating new business. Moreover, after two weeks of legislative inactivity, it was impossible to proceed without reorganizing. The clerk was ordered to list "the true State of all the Bills of the House." Calvert called on the Speaker to come early in the morning. The House rose, resolved to begin work the next day.[127]

What took place in the minds and consciences of several score Englishmen between twelve noon on December 14 and nine o'clock the next morning is perhaps more a matter for the novelist's imagination than the historian's. But when the House met again, everything had changed. The Speaker rapped twice for business. The only response was an angry buzz. Mallory asked for an order to silence Richardson, "that we might not be troubled this day with the Speaker." Amid laughter and shouts of "aye," Richardson sat down, baffled.[128]

Sir George More, one of the most outspoken opponents of the Commons' ten-day strike, began the debate. The liberties of the House were its freehold, he said. They were in danger; and once lost, they would never be recovered. He moved that a collection be made of all the documents in the controversy, "that it may appear to posterity how far we have gone and what we have done."[129] Mallory and Seymour expressed themselves in the same terms. The state of religion and the state of the realm *were* matters proper to Parliament, and Parliament must so declare it. Of what importance were a few bills beside this?[130]

The councillors, wholly unprepared for this sudden turn, counterattacked in confusion. They dared not defend the King's actual position. At most they could excuse his tone. "Equality of Language not to be expected by People from a King," blustered Weston. Let the House beware of contumacy. The King's words were perhaps strong, conceded Edmondes, but nowhere did he "directly impeach our Liberties." As Brooke remarked helpfully, it was "no matter how we have them so we have them." The councillors concluded with hackneyed appeals for unity, and a return to bills.[131]

Phelips, silent until now, rose in the mildest mien. He readily agreed that kings "should speak in other Language, than Subjects." He took "great Comfort" in James's vigilance for religion, and opined that if the House had known how far the match had gone, it would never have "touched that String." On these matters, the House might rest. Only the question of privilege remained. The King said that the House enjoyed its privileges from him. He had said the same in 1604, at his first Parliament. That House of Commons had replied, by written declaration, that its privileges were inherent. This one should do neither more nor less.

It was too late now, Phelips judged, for a session. But this was merely a detail. It would not hinder the subsidy, and after Christmas, the House could pass its bills, "with a greater Demonstration of our Duty to the King, in Supply, than [we] can now do."[132]

From this pleasant perspective, the whole affair was to be written off with a few words of polite reservation. The Commons would then vote money for a policy that seemed to them a sheer disaster, and pack up for good by Easter.

Phelips was hardly that ingenuous. What he really wanted was to pare away all circumstantial issues from the basic one: parliamentary right. His purpose thereby was not, however, to dramatize it. Quite the contrary. The last thing he wanted was to present privilege in terms of a grand and final confrontation between the King and the Commons. There would be few if any takers for such a battle. Instead, he treated it as a minor obstacle which a few well-chosen words would safely dispose of. Parlia-

ment had only to fall back on clear precedent. It need merely repeat a statement the King had never disavowed. In this could
surely be no harm.

Within this comforting framework, others felt free to sally.
The very walls of the House would speak out,[133] said Crew, if the
Commons did not defend their privilege. Coke, who since the
Lepton affair lived in fear, made a ringing and famous pro-
nouncement:

> I will not dispute with my Maister for his words, but when
> the kinge sayes he can not allowe our liberties of right, this
> strikes at the roote. Wee serve here for thousands and tenn
> thowsands.[134]

Such rhetoric might have seemed menacing and dangerous by
itself; but within the context of Phelips' proposal for a brief and
inoffensive protestation, modeled on that of 1604, it could pass
for letting off steam. Even Sackville and Heath endorsed the
protestation. As for the session, said Heath, "a short Acte of vi
lynes might passe to preserve all statutes as they nowe stand."[135]
Such was the end of what had seemed but an hour before the
certainty of a session by Christmas.

The Commons were now committed to a new statement in
defense of their liberties. It was their silent hope that the matter
would rest there. They did not demand that the King accept or
acknowledge their claims. Of course they wished it. But they
were willing to settle for the old tacit stalemate. Noy moved that
the protestation be entered in the Journal without any presentation to the King, lest it draw "another Censure" and begin a new
round of controversy.[136] The Commons were content to mutter
an *"eppur si muove,"* and leave the resolution of the problem—
if there had to be one—to posterity. But speak they must. The
Commons conceived of themselves as the guardians of a sacred
trust. On December 14, they tried to persuade themselves that
the King's message had not endangered that trust. On December
15, they reluctantly admitted that it had.

James, on his way back to London for Christmas, was now at
Royston, thirty-eight miles away.[137] Here he received, through
Buckingham, a letter from Lord Keeper Williams.[138] It was Williams who had bluntly counseled Buckingham to leave Parliament to its "proper work" in March. The problem now, how-

ever, was just the reverse. Parliament was doing no work at all. Nor, admitted Williams, did it seem likely to before Christmas. In this situation the King could do one of two things. He could dissolve Parliament and lay his case beore the country, or ignore the Commons' insubordination and prorogue the session till February 8, as originally planned. "This Course is fittest for further advice," he commented, "but the other to express a just Indignation." Whether James wanted to express his "just indignation" or have a successful Parliament was not for the Bishop to say: "I dare advise nothing in so high a Point." But in either event, the King could win public opinion by qualifying his position with "some mild and noble Exposition" on the question of privilege. If the Commons still persisted in their obstinacy, the onus of whatever followed would lie on them.

Williams was really hopeful that a few more gracious lines from James would do the trick. The House had nearly been won over by his last message. The Bishop was an essentially sanguine and pragmatic man. He did not think the quarrel really serious. After all, it was merely a matter of words. The King maintained (rightly, of course) that the privileges of Parliament were "but Graces and Favors of former Kings." The Commons claimed that they were an inalienable birthright. "Both these Assertions (if Men were peaceably disposed, and affected the Dispatch of the Common Businesses) might be easily reconciled."

Such a view inevitably presupposed a plot thesis. If the issue were a mere quibble, then why were men not "peaceably disposed" to settle it? Either the Commons as a body were simply insubordinate, or a passive majority had been willfully misled by an insubordinate few. If the former were true, then dissolution was the only alternative. Hence Williams fell back on "turbulent spirits"—men who, for their own dark purposes, had roiled up "that noble House of Commons." This was the exact reasoning the Commons had applied to the King's messages. James had been willfully misinformed. "Turbulent spirits" in Parliament were the precise counterpart of "false reporters" to the King.

But James had very firmly grasped the real nature of the situation. The Commons' claims usurped his authority. For the rights of power—and the "rights" of unrestricted debate, mandatory counsel, and absolute immunity were such—to be vested in-

herently in any place or person but the Crown was to create a
dual sovereignty in the state, to divide God's scepter, to destroy
monarchy. It was to put the subject on a par with his king. What
more monstrous, unnatural, indeed absurd proposition could
there be than that?

But James desperately needed this Parliament. He accepted
Williams's advice. He would make one final effort to placate the
Commons.

On Monday, the seventeenth, Calvert read the new message.
James was "sorry" to see that the Commons continued to waste
their time. To remove any doubts about his former messages,
and all further obstruction to the session, he would clarify the
point of privilege:

> Whereas in our said answer we told them that we could
> not allow of the style, calling it their ancient and undoubted
> right and inheritance, the plain truth is that we cannot with
> patience endure our subjects to use such antimonarchical
> words concerning their liberties except they had subjoined
> that they were granted unto them by the grace and favor
> of our predecessors. But as for our intention herein, God
> knows we never meant to deny any lawful privileges that
> ever any House injoyed [sic] in our predecessors' time and
> we expected our said answer should have sufficiently cleared
> them; *neither in justice what they have any undoubted right
> to,* nor in grace whatever our predecessors or we have gra-
> ciously permitted unto them. And therefore we made that
> distinction of the most part, for whatsoever privileges or
> liberties they enjoy by *any law or statute* shall be ever in-
> violably preserved by us and we hope our posterity will imi-
> tate our footsteps therein. And whatsoever privileges they
> enjoy by long custom and *uncontrolled and lawful prece-
> dents* we will likewise be as careful to preserve them and
> transmit the care thereof to our posterity. Neither was it
> any way in our mind to think of any particular point where-
> in we meant to disallow of their liberties. So in justice we
> confess ourselves to be bound to maintain them in their
> rights and in grace we are rather minded to increase than in-
> fringe any of them, if they shall so deserve at our hands
> [italics mine].

In conclusion, James admonished the Commons to finish its
work, "rejecting the curious wrangling of lawyers upon words

and syllables."[139] The world, he warned, would judge their duty by their performance.[140]

The King appeared to concede a good deal in his letter. He distinguished two kinds of privilege, one enjoyed by grace and the other by "undoubted right." That is to say, he was prepared to admit, at least in theory, the existence of privileges he could not lawfully retract. He actually said less than he seemed to, however. These privileges were restricted to those granted by "law or statute." But as James specifically exempted custom and precedent from this category, he virtually eliminated any kind of law but statute. The reason for his doing so is not far to seek. One statute could only be abrogated by another. In that sense it conferred rights that were fixed and inalterable. But statutes required the consent of the Crown to become law. Hence they might be construed as issuing in essence from the "grace and favor"—that is, the power—of the king. This argument preserved intact the principle that all privileges, whether permanent or permissive, derived ultimately from the power of the Crown. If custom could confer them, however, the locus of power would be Parliament itself, an idea James emphatically rejected. There could be no squatters' rights to sovereignty.

The Commons' reception of this message was in marked contrast to their hasty welcome of James's last letter. The House decomposed it as carefully as it had been put together. It contained, observed Coke, "an Allowance of our Privileges, which indeed are ours by Law, by Custom, by Precedent, and by Act of Parliament." By custom or by statute, equally *ours:* thus the old lawyer shrewdly erased the distinction so deliberately drawn by James. Seymour put the issue more bluntly. The King had not specified a single privilege guaranteed by statute or "uncontrolled precedent." There were very few precedents, he thought, which had not been controlled by previous kings. Coke suggested that the Commons present a list of their privileges to the King, backed by precedents, for his ratification; but Heneage Finch pointed out that if the Commons omitted any privileges from such a list by inadvertence, they would be lost forever, "for the King will say, if we had any more Privileges, we would have claimed and expressed it in that Writing."[141]

A much stronger position was taken by Hakewill. The King, he said, had nothing to do with privilege. "The privileges of this howse are the principall parte of the Lawe of the land . . . and therfore we hould them not by grace but by Lawe and right." They were the "inseparable incidents of a Parliament." The custom of "requesting" privilege from the King at the beginning of Parliament was unfortunate, "for that makes the King conceive, we hold it by the Grace and Permission of Princes, and not as our Inheritance."[142] By inference, Coke's plan for ratifying privilege was equally misleading.

Hakewill's stand was an unqualified assertion of parliamentary power. It rejected all compromise. But not everyone wanted to go this far. A tone of caution still generally prevailed. "The kings letter is a very gratious but a very wise and wary letter," observed Glanville. Phelips was "much comforted" by it, but not yet fully satisfied—though he did not specify what he was unsatisfied about. More professed "full Satisfaction," except for the command to go on with bills. Was this not an interference with the Commons' freedom of procedure? "Bills, Greavances, Judicature; Wee are not Commanded to goe on with those but bills," said Glanville.[143] It was bad enough for the Commons to be told what they could *not* do, without being told what they *had* to do.

This question was settled by a compromise of sorts. The House returned to work, but not to bills. The committee for grievances met in the afternoon to review the state of patents.[144] Thus the session was no further advanced. Nor was the question of privilege. The consensus was that the King's letter left the House just where it stood before.[145]

The Commons fell back on their protestation; but what they were to put in it, and what was to be done with it, was still undecided. Should it be a catalogue of privileges, or simply an assertion of their inalienability? Should it be presented to the King, or merely entered in the record? The Commons reached back for the precedent of 1604. But no one remembered what had actually been done at that time. Coke, who had been a member of that Parliament, asserted that the Commons had presented their statement to the King, which was not true. Pym asked whether it had ever been formally entered in the records of the House, which no one knew.[146] Obviously, there was a good deal of homework to be done. The Commons decided to start all over again next morning.[147]

But things had not merely been delayed by a day. Another

message had been rejected. The Commons had refused James's formula for privilege, and failed to obey his command for a session. On the morning of the eighteenth, he greeted them with a new note. The intent of his last message, he said, was to clear away all doubts about privilege, so that the House might "spend this short Time in preparing Things most necessary for a Sessions." As it had not had the "wished Effect," he would repeat himself more clearly. "We have an earnest Desire to make this a Sessions, to the End that Our good and loving Subjects may have some Taste . . . of Our Grace and Goodness towards them." The essential steps to the session were the pardon, the subsidy, and the continuation of statutes. If, however, in the short time remaining, the passing of the subsidy could not "conveniently be done, . . . We will not make that any Way an Impediment to the Good, which we desire Our People should feel by making this a Session."

> Thus much We thought good to give them to understand; and withal to assure them, that, if they shall not apply themselves *instantly* to prepare the aforesaid Things, for our Royal Assent, against Saturday next, We will, without expecting any farther Answer from them, construe, by their Slackness, that they desire not a Sessions; *and in such Case We must give a larger Time, for their returning homeward,* to such of both Houses, as are to go into their Countries, to keep Hospitality among their Neighbours in this Time of Recess.[148]

James suddenly appeared to want a session so badly he was even willing to forgo the subsidy for it. This seemed a strange about-face indeed. A month earlier his purpose in calling Parliament had been specifically the voting of supply, with bills to receive only "such howers as may well be spared from this Forreigne occasion."[149] Parliament had petitioned for a session. The King had granted it, as a favor; now he demanded it, as an order. Yet, as matters stood, neither bills nor supply would pass. The session would consist only of such bills as had passed in the spring. If the King had thought in June that these bills could wait until November, and in October postponed them again until February, what made their passage such a dire emergency now?

Actually, what James wanted was not a session but the time-killing mechanics of one. If the Commons were occupied in

examining the pardon and preparing the bill for repeal and continuance of statutes, they would have no time to make their Protestation. To block that Protestation was the sole aim of his letter.
James did not care whether Parliament accepted or rejected the
formula for privilege which he had offered the day before. He
did not need to have his sovereignty ratified by Parliament in
order to rule. But he had made his final statement. If the Commons openly defied it, he would have no choice but to dissolve
Parliament.

The threat of this, thinly veiled by sarcasm, was discernible
in the new message. Pym, without referring to it, remarked
obliquely that he could not "without a great deale of horrar
looke upon the dissolution of this parliament." If others felt
as he did, however, they did not say so. Giles chided Pym for
his indiscretion: "His good neighbor is more iealous of some
things then hee needs."[150]

Discussion centered instead on whether a session was still possible. Mallett had the bill for continuance and repeal in his own
hands, and begged leave to "goe fetch" it. "It hath bin soe well
discussed amongst them who have taken paynes in it," he said, "as
it will neede noe further great labour." Crew disagreed: "it will
ask a Day's Labour for two good Scriveners to engross it, and it
will ask here some Debate before it pass." Heath offered an
abridged version of the regular bill, but his suggestion was ignored. Noy agreed with Crew, and observed that the pardon
would also require some work.[151]

This debate was mere camouflage. If the Commons were to sit
til Saturday, the session was certainly feasible. But having quickly
dismissed the question, the House hurried into committee to
consider the Protestation, conscious that its time for this matter
would be far more limited.[152]

At this, several members began to leave the House. We do not
know who they were, but we may easily guess. They were the
men whom James had ordered to immediately report the result
of his message. The House evidently thought so, for their passage
was blocked. Amid angry cries, the sergeant-at-arms brought the
keys of the chamber forward. Sir Humphrey May—one of those
detained?—protested hotly that "Tis a fundamentall liberty of
the house that att a committee every man may goe out of the
house that will." His complaint was disallowed. A subcommittee,

which included Heath and May, was appointed to pen a reply to the King's message. This assignment kept them indoors, and out of debate.[153]

The House now realized the full urgency of its task. There was no time for elaborate argument or long lists of precedents. Let us be brief in statement, said Noy, for "long arguing argues a Doubt, and we are out of Doubt of the Right of our Privileges."[154]

Five points were affirmed as the basis of the Protestation: freedom of speech and subject matter, personal immunity, the innateness of privilege, and the confidential nature of debate. A subcommittee was appointed to draft it, and the Speaker ordered to return at four so that it might be ratified, "because otherwise it may be, the King will command the House to be adjourned, before such Protestation be made."[155]

A very shrunken House—not more than a third of the original, as James later claimed[156]—returned at four. Candles were lit in the darkened chamber, and men sat in their cloaks. The draft of the Protestation was brought in, read, briefly debated, passed, and entered in the Journal of the House. The entire process took something more than an hour.[157]

The Commons also dispatched a "petition of thanks and excuse" to the King, declaring the session infeasible.[158] His reply came the next morning, December 19. The House would be adjourned this day, at its request, to the eighth of February.[159] Sir Humphrey May, who brought the letter, added "that the King seemed well pleased, and said, that our Petition was a mannerly and well-penned Petition."[160]

The House then put its business in order against the recess. The Speaker was ordered to keep the Journal at his home, and Sir Peter Heyman was ordered to burn a document in his possession concerning the imprisonment of Sandys.[161] The Commons were hearing the story of a Monmouthshire preacher who had been assaulted by two recusants, when Justices Winch and Jones brought down the commission for adjournment from the Lords. The Commons took "notice" of this and, as in June, adjourned themselves.[162] Then they rose, and began their journeys home. They might or might not meet again, but their duty was done.

That duty was the production of the document which the

Commons called their "Protestation." In accordance with Noy's injunction, it was brief. It is only 260 words long:

The Commons now assembled in Parliament, being just-ly occasioned thereunto, concerning sundry Liberties, Fran-chises, and Priviledges of Parliament, amongst others here mentioned, do make this Protestation following, That the Liberties, Franchises, Priviledges, and Jurisdictions of Parliament, are the ancient and undoubted Birthright and Inheritance of the Subjects of England; And that the ardu-ous and urgent affairs concerning the King, State and De-fence of the Realm, and of the Church of England, and the maintenance and making of Laws, and redress of mischiefs and grievances which daily happen within this Realm, are proper Subjects and matters of Counsel and Debate in Parliament; and that in the handling and proceeding of those businesses, every Member of the House of Parliament hath, and of right, ought to have freedom of speech, to pro-pound, treat, reason, and bring to conclusion the same; And that the Commons in Parliament have like liberty and free-dom to treat of these matters in such order, as in their Judg-ments shall seem fittest; And that every Member of the said House hath like freedom from all Impeachment, Imprison-ment, and Molestation (other than by Censure of the House it self) for or concerning any speaking, reasoning, or declar-ing of any matter or matters touching the Parliament, or Parliament-business; And that if any of the said Members be complained of, and questioned for any thing said or done in Parliament, the same is to be shewed to the King by the advice and assent of all the Commons assembled in Parlia-ment, before the King give credence to any private Infor-mation.[163]

The Commons had avowedly based their Protestation on the Apology and Satisfaction of 1604.[164] The difference between the two can best be appreciated by the difference in title. The dic-tionary defines an apology as a "defense or justification of what appears to others to be wrong, or of what may be liable to disap-probation." A protestation, on the other hand, is "an act of . . . solemnly declaring true, . . . a public avowal." The Apology of 1604 is as circumspect and discursive as the Protestation is lean and concise. It is hedged about with explanations, qualifications, and professions of loyalty. Even so, its hard kernel of assertion was too daring for most of the Commons of its day. It was never formally adopted, and remained a mere committee draft.[165] Yet its unofficial character did not embarrass the Commons of 1621, who treated the daring assertions as established principle. But if the Commons so completely assumed the doctrine of inherent rights that it was not once challenged in the entire course of the December debates, it did so in great part because the Apology of 1604 had stated

> That our privileges and liberties are our right and due inheritance, no less than our very lands and goods.
> That they cannot be withheld from us, denied, or impaired, but with apparent wrong to the whole state of the realm.
> . . . That our making of request in the entrance of Parliament to enjoy our privilege is an act only of manners, and doth weaken our right no more than our suing to the King for our lands by petition . . . [166]

That the House of Commons had once before uttered this doctrine—even *sotto voce*—did not merely nerve the House to say it again. It represented a position already staked out, which, once abandoned, was unlikely to be recovered. In these circumstances, the best defense seemed a good offense. The "apology" became a "protestation."

Yet the defensive intent of the Protestation needs to be emphasized. James regarded it as a determined aggression against the foundations of monarchy; and later generations, who saw the Commons marching firmly to the historic goal of revolution, took a basically similar view. But the Commons regarded themselves as last-ditch conservatives, desperately defending embattled freedoms. As the Apology expressed it, in a passage Phelips always liked to quote, "The prerogatives of princes . . . do daily grow; the privileges of the subject are for the most part at an everlasting stand."[167] And in truth, they had a case, though it was not the one they were obliged to argue. The medieval curbs on monarchy were still very much a part of England's political heritage, but the practical means of enforcing them—the reciprocities of feudalism, the weakness of royal administration, the quasi-anarchy of the overmighty subject—had largely disappeared. A vacuum of power was thereby created in the *dominium politicum,* which Parliament was the only logical candidate to fill. Its problem was to prove its historical legitimacy in the new balance of power being struck. As that legitimacy was unfortunately nonexistent, the Commons were obliged to invent it. Hence the agreeable legends about Magna Carta, Arthurian parliaments, and "fundamental law,"[168] and the gross inflation of obscure and minor legal precedents, with which the Commons made up their case. In fact, the medieval system was dead, as any system is dead when its operative structure has ceased to function. The new balance of power Parliament was attempting to create was a new system. It might well have worked, as it did after 1688, if the Commons had not been compelled to deny that any change was taking place at all. They were so compelled, in part because the act of acquiring power, being one of the most embarrassing functions known to nature, has always required the fig leaf of traditional legality to clothe it, and in part because an exaggerated horror of "innovation" was one of the conventions of Tudor-Stuart culture, as it usually is of cultures marked by rapid social and political change. The most the Commons would concede was that they were "restoring" the old constitution. But restoring something is frequently as complicated a piece of change as replacing it. Hence the Commons posited a static past, long ages of constitutional harmony in which nothing much had happened and nothing new evolved. Thus it followed that the institutions of the present were substantially those of the past; or specifically, that seventeenth-century parliaments were little different from fourteenth-century ones. The Commons came gradually to inhabit this fictive world naturally, and anachronism became their second nature.

The nice thing about this world was that it greatly simplified the problem of proof. One had only to demonstrate that a given right, power, or privilege had existed at some historical moment; and, since all historical moments of a static past are equal, it followed that the particular attribute had always existed. Conversely, its existence could never be disproved by lack of evidence, for such evidence might always turn up.

Furthermore, as in all systems of faith, no single proof was necessarily decisive. If one should be discredited or prove defective, the matter argued suffered no discredit itself. It had only to find a better proof. For this reason, the Commons could afford to be casual and even sloppy in their recollections of the Apology. Whether it was a committee report or a full-fledged resolution of the House made no difference to its value as a proof. If the rights it claimed already existed, a formal ratification could not make them exist any more; and if they did not, no word or deed of the House of Commons could create them. Indeed, the Commons did not turn to the Apology for "proof" at all. As Noy had said, "we are out of Doubt of the Right of our Privileges."[169] The privileges asserted in the Apology were so notorious as to need no proof at all. Its sole interest was as a precedent for protest. Here was what another House of Commons had done on a similar occasion; could the present one do less?

The Protestation, therefore, was not a claim to privilege in the eyes of its authors, but a defense of privilege already possessed. No one, indeed, would have been more scandalized by the charge of claiming privileges—that is, asserting new ones—than they. If the Protestation was somewhat ampler or more categorical about some privileges than the Apology had been, this reflected only the different circumstances that inspired the former. The Apology was a response to the abridgement of free elections, and had a good deal to say on the subject. In 1621 free elections were not at issue, and consequently no mention of them was necessary. The occasion of the Protestation was an abridgement of free speech, and it was only logical to expect it to elaborate on this privilege, since what had been said in 1604 had failed to secure it. This did not mean, to the Commons, that anything new was being said. They were sure that, faced with the same situation, the Parliament of 1604 would have given the same answer.

From James's point of view, however, and from ours, the Protestation was not as innocent as its authors thought. Its assertions are not self-evident, and its variation from the Apology is highly significant. To this variation, in two key points, we must now turn.

On the questions of free speech and parliamentary immunity, the Apology states:

That the persons chosen [for Parliament], during the time of the Parliament as also of their access and recess, be free from restraint, arrest or imprisonment.

That in Parliament they may speak freely their consciences without check and controlment . . . [170]

The first statement is thoroughly, and perhaps intentionally, ambiguous. It might be construed as a blanket immunity from punishment for any act (except high treason) an MP might commit during his period of service, or it might simply refer to the customary immunity from imprisonment for debt, felony, and the like, about which no controversy existed whatever. But being so ambiguously framed, it posed no immediate threat to the King's claim to chastise errant MPs at discretion.

The second statement is similarly guarded. What it claims is merely the right of individual members to speak their minds on the range of subjects suitable to parliamentary discussion. It says nothing specific about what such subjects are, and thus at least implicitly leaves their determination to the King.

These two claims, though dangerously vague, are not prima facie incompatible with royal sovereignty. They entail tactical defeats to the Crown, perhaps, in the managing of Parliament. But they do not encroach on prerogative as such. They do not enlarge the scope or function of Parliament.

The language of the Protestation is much more sweeping. It claims that all subjects concerning the Commonwealth—the "arduous and urgent affairs" of church and state, war and peace —are "proper Subjects . . . of Counsel and Debate in Parliament." The King could neither command nor forbid the consideration of any subject. He could not control the order of consideration. And he could neither punish nor reprove any member for saying anything whatever on "Parliament-business."

Nor was this a right of discussion only. Parliament could "propound, treat, reason, and bring to conclusion" its subjects of debate—that is, pass laws on them. The House of Commons had petitioned the King against the marriage of Charles and the Infanta of Spain. By the logic of its position, the next step was to pass a law forbidding it. The King, naturally, could veto such a law. But the very act of passing it would effectively veto the policy. Thus Parliament would gain a practical negative in foreign affairs—to mention only a single obstructive possibility.

Were the Commons, then, so entirely deluded about the nature of their Protestation? Could their intentions have been so innocent when the result virtually usurped the monarchy?

The best way to answer these questions is to consider the opposite case. Where would the Commons have stood had they *not* made their Protestation? If they challenged the King's position, the King's letters equally challenged theirs. The Commons did possess an ultimate veto in their power of the purse. But without the power to debate as well, this "veto" was worthless. The Commons could do no more than refuse to vote money. They could not justify themselves to the country, or argue for an alternative policy. Such a position was not politically tenable. But it was quite unnecessary to dramatize the issue even this far. If the Commons would not swallow the King's policy whole, he could simply present it in pieces, like the bill for Frederick's army. As the Commons themselves had recognized, there was no practical option not to pay such bills. Without the right to debate, therefore, what was the taxing power but a rubber stamp? And that power gone, what would be left to Parliament but the impotent chatter of continental assemblies, the fate of the French Estates, the Spanish Cortes, the Polish Sejm.

Thus the Protestation represented the irreducible minimum basis of Parliament's survival as the bulwark of the subject's right. That right, as defined by law and custom, was essentially the right to property. It was for this reason that the Apology had declared "this High Court of Parliament" to be the supreme court of the land:[171] it was the place of final resort for the subject's defense of his property. This, too, in the last analysis, was why the rights of Parliament were held to be inherent and inalienable. They were an aspect of the subject's right, and if the subject held his land by right and not grace, then Parliament must have its privilege by the same tenure. Property was a meaningless fiction if the right to defend it were not as firmly grounded as the right to hold it.

The Protestation is then simultaneously innovative and conservative. Which aspect one prefers to stress depends chiefly on one's point of view. Ours is simply to remark it, finally, as evidence of a society in the process of a profound and disquieting shift in the locus of political power.

The Protestation thrust upon James the most fateful decision of his reign. If he dissolved Parliament, he put himself powerless into the hands of the Spanish, for Parliament, in the words of John Chamberlain, was "the only ordinarie, auncient, and plaine highway"[172] to supply the King's wants, and without supply, there would be no army for the Palatinate. If he failed to dissolve it, however, the Crown of England and the person of James would suffer international scandal and disesteem. Worse, the Crown would risk irreparable internal damage as well. For James, with all his theories of monarchy, knew that the safest basis of power is the active and undiminished maintenance of it.

During the Christmas holiday, there was passionate debate in the inner circles of the King's government. Pembroke and Hamilton, the leading anti-Spaniards on the Council, fought as hard as they dared against dissolution.[173] So did Cranfield—James later recalled that he pleaded for Parliament on his knees[174]—but for different reasons. He neither supported nor opposed the Spanish match. He simply disliked the idea of foreign policy altogether.[175] War on top of debt, in his opinion, was bad enough; but with no Parliament to boot, how were bills to be paid by Lionel Cranfield, lord treasurer?

Cranfield, and everyone else as well, were ordered to find answers to this question. The only apparent options were a fresh benevolence and an increase in the rate of impositions. Lando reported the desperate proposal that the King levy taxes on his own authority. Precedents for raising money without Parliament were searched back to the Domesday Book.[176] There was also the usual quota of unsolicited suggestions from sympathetic cranks. One "Jhon Milton" wrote asking fifteen minutes with the King to explain how he might raise money "to the valluing and estimate of two subsidyes" by a method "sure, certayne, and infallible." He could be found, a note added, in his "poore lodging" near "the wharfe of London."[177]

If there was strong opposition in the Council to dissolution, those closest to James—Buckingham, Gondomar, and Charles —urged it strongly. Gondomar taunted the King that England was turning into a republic,[178] but the very vehemence of the favorite and the heir may less have influenced James than merely reflected him. Charles, certainly, was still no more than his father's shadow.[179] In the end, as Chamberlain observed sensibly, the King made up his own mind.[180]

James took his first step after Christmas. He had waited ten months to put his hands on Edward Coke. On St. John's Day, December 27, while the King was at the christening of Cranfield's new son, a guard of eight men seized Coke in his house on Broad Street and took him to the Tower.[181] The great jurist was jailed in what had once been a kitchen, above which was now unkindly scrawled, "this room needs a cook."[182] Coke's house and law chambers were sealed up, and his papers impounded. Sir Robert Cotton, Sir Thomas Wilson, and John Dickenson were assigned the formidable task of sifting them for incriminating material.[183] On the twenty-ninth, Coke was brought before his fellow councillors as a prisoner. They told him that he had forgotten the duty of a servant and a councillor, "and as might be thought the dutie of a Subject." Coke replied only that he hoped he had failed in none of these, "but Gods will and the Kings be don."[184]

The next day brought the end of Parliament. Although the fatal blow fell behind closed doors, the execution was staged with full formalities. The clerk of the Commons, John Wright, was summoned to Whitehall with his Journal. There, in full council and in the presence of six judges—all those available on such short notice—James, after pronouncing a lengthy anathema on the Protestation, tore it out of the Journal with his own hand, and ordered his act to be inscribed on the register of the Privy Council. The King carefully reiterated that he would protect all the lawful privileges of Parliament. But this document, he declared, was a willful invasion of royal prerogative, and therefore "fitt to be razed out of all memorials and utterly to be annihilated . . . invalid, annulled, and of noe effect."[185]

The question of Parliament itself was then put. "Proposed by the King & Councill, this parliament to be dismissed." There was no discussion. "We have come here not to debate but to vote," said Pembroke, "since the King has declared his will."[186]

The country remained in ignorance of this decision for a week. On January 6, the news broke with the publishing of a formal proclamation of dissolution. Lando quickly dubbed it James's anti-protest,[187] but it is more in the nature of a *pièce justificative*. "Albeit," it began,

> the assembling, continuing, and dissolving of Parliaments be a prerogative so peculiarly belonging to our Imperial Crown, and the times and seasons thereof so absolutely in our own power that we need not give accompt thereof unto any yet, according to our continual custom to make our subjects acquainted with the reasons of all our public resolutions and actions, we have thought it expedient at this

> time to declare not only our pleasure and resolution therein,
> . . . but therewith also to note some especial proceedings
> moving us to this resolution.

A résumé of the Parliament followed. It had begun auspicious-
ly, "and proceeded some months with such harmony between
us and our people as cannot be paralleled by any former time."
After Easter, the Commons had wandered into sterile controversy
and neglected their duty to make good laws, "yet we gave them
time and scope for their parliamentary proceedings ... [and]
indeed we must do them this right that at the ... recess [in June],
. . . they did with one unanimous consent, in the name of themselves and the whole body of the kingdom, make a most dutiful
and solemn protestation."

But at their last sitting, "some particular members" of the
Commons began to treat matters "that were no fit subjects to
be treated of in Parliament" and "to speak with less respect of
foreign princes our allies than were fit for any subject to do of
any anointed King, though in enmity and hostility with us."
When they were reproved for this, "some evil-affected and discontented persons ... descanting upon the words and syllables
of our letters and messages," disrupted the business of the House.
Despite the offer of a session and a pardon, and the assurance
of all reasonable guarantees for the maintenance of their privileges, they pretended further ground for discontent, and made
thereon "a protestation for their liberties in such ambiguous
and general words as might serve for future times to invade
most of our inseparable rights and prerogatives annexed to
our Imperial Crown whereof, not only in the times of other
our progenitors but in the blessed reign of our late predecessor
that renowned Queen Elizabeth, we found our Crown actually
possessed, an usurpation that the Majesty of a King can no means
endure."

For this reason, the Proclamation concluded, the present Parliament was "not to continue ... any longer," and it was further
declared "that the said convention of Parliament neither is,
nor after the cessing and breaking thereof shall be nor ought,
to be esteemed, adjudged, or taken to be or make any session
of Parliament."[188]

With these words the King ended the Parliament which had

begun with such high expectation fourteen months before. There remained only a last melancholy ceremony, enacted in the House of Lords on February 8:

> Dyvers LL. beinge come, as well the Commissioners as other Lordes, and a many of the Comons,
> Prayers were sayd.
> The Lordes syttinge all in their due places, the Comission was reade.
> Which beinge reade, the Comissioners sate upon the midle bench, and dissolved this late assembly of Parlement.

Et sic dissolutem est dictum Parliamentum.[189]

EPILOGUE:
THE WINTER OF 1622

The arrest of Coke was soon followed by others. Phelips was seized on his Cornish estate " 'ere he had finish'd his Christmas ... with as much terror as belongs to the apprehending of Treason itself,"[1] and Sir William Mallory was taken prisoner in Yorkshire.[2] Phelips' confinement was as harsh as Coke's; he was kept close prisoner without examination or charge, and denied all access to his family and friends.[3] Less rigor was needed with Mallory, who was "much dejected" at his seizure.[4] In addition, John Pym was placed under house arrest in London; Crew, Perrot, Rich, and Digges[5] were sent as commissioners to Ireland—an employment not much preferable to prison—and Sir Peter Heyman was sent to the Palatinate.[6]

But Coke's plight was the most serious. Here, and here alone, the Crown sought a court conviction—sought, that is, not merely to intimidate or punish, but to discredit and ruin. It could afford to do no less. James was said to have remarked that Coke was "the fittest instrument for a tyrant that ever was in England;"[7] but no man could more easily become a martyr either.

The case chosen against Coke was neither a parliamentary nor a judicial matter,[8] but the execution of a thirty-year-old wardship on behalf of his deceased father-in-law, Sir Christopher Hatton. Hatton, the old Elizabethan courtier, had left debts of £50,000 to the Crown at his death. Coke was accused of defrauding the Crown of its repayment by withholding the usufruct from his estate.[9]

To cast the Crown in the role of injured party was a stroke worthy of Jacobean statecraft. But the case must have been woefully misconceived because, despite strong royal pressure,[10] Coke's judges—Hobart, Ley, and Tanfield, the chief justices of the courts of common law—were unable to find him guilty. On August 8, 1622, Sir Edward was set free from the Tower. The next day, Phelips and Mallory were also released.[11]

The Crown's most urgent problem, however, was now as in the very beginning, to raise money for the Palatinate. After much deliberation, it fell back at last on the tested expedients of imposition and benevolence. The impost on wine was doubled, and an extraordinary tax of ninepence in the pound was levied on all goods imported by aliens.[12] The third benevolence of the reign was begun with little fanfare—there was no pretending it would be popular—but much firmness. One merchant of eighty who refused to rate himself at the Council table was threatened with service in the Palatinate. Sir John Strangways reluctantly put himself down at fifty pounds; the Council rated him for a hundred. This treatment was meted out as general policy to former MPs, who thus learned, or at any rate suffered, the error of their ways.[13]

Nonetheless, the benevolence was a failure. After a full year of grim persuasion, scarcely more had been collected than the value of a single subsidy.[14] And with this failure, all hope of reinforcing the Palatinate was abandoned. England could do no more than to send another ineffectual embassy to Brussels,[15] and, finally, the famous mission to Madrid. The war ground on inexorably; the last bastions in the Lower Palatinate fell one by one; and in February, 1623, the Diet of Ratisbon—convened after eighteen months' delay—conferred Frederick's electoral title on Maximilian of Bavaria. Frederick himself remained an exile in the Hague until his death nine years later; Elizabeth survived him to see her son Charles Lewis restored to the electorate by the Treaty of Westphalia and died, the last actor in the great drama, in 1662.

But these events seemed very far from England as the winter of 1622 set in. The weather was hard, and the depression was deepening. In London, political unrest was expressed in sermon and pamphlet. In the West Country, hungry weavers stripped meat openly from public stalls, and ranged the countryside in bands of fifty, extorting food and money from the local gentry.[16]

The Council racked a laywer's servant for prophesying rebellion, and condemned a poor simpleton who had muttered threats against the King.[17]

As for James, the end of his Parliament was the end of his reign. Nothing remained to him but to follow out the bitter failure of his hopes, and end in a pointless war with Spain which he was unable to avoid. But the end of the Parliament of 1621 was nearly the literal end of James as well. On January 6, the day the dissolution was published, he was thrown from his horse headfirst into a canal, so "that nothing but his boots were seen." A courtier pulled him out gushing water.[18] It is perhaps not a very fair point at which to leave James. But there was always something of the ridiculous about him, and the temptation is irresistible.

APPENDIX

A Declaration of the Commons howse of parliament,

June 4, 1621.

The Commons assembled in Parliament, takeinge into ther serious consideracion the present estate of the kings children abroad and the generall afflicted estate of the true professours of the same christian religion professed by the church of England in forraine parts, and being touched with a true sence and fellow feeleing of ther distresses as members of the same bodie, Doe with one unanimous consent in the name of them selfes and the whole bodie of this kingdome (whom they represent) declare unto his most excellent Majestie and unto the whole world ther hartie griefe and sorrow for the same; And doe not onelie Joyne with them in their humble and devout praiers unto almightie god to protect his true church and to avert the daingers now threatned, but also with one hart and voyce Doe solemnly protest that if his Majesty's pious endeavours by treatie to procure their peace and saftie shall not take that good affect that is desired in the treatie, whereof they humbly beseech his Majesty to suffer no longer delaye, that then, upon significacion of his Majesties pleasure in Parliament, they shalbe readye to the uttermost of their powers, bothe with their lyves and fortunes, to assist him. So as by the divine helpe of almightie god (who is never wantinge unto those who in his feare shall undertake the defence of his owne cause) Hee maye be able to doe that by his sword which by peaceable courses shall not be effected.

Examinatur per John Wright.[1]

NOTES

Introduction

1. James Spedding, *The Letters and the Life of Francis Bacon* (London, 1861–1874), VI, 18.

2. A. F. Pollard, *The Evolution of Parliament* (London, 1926); Sir John Neale, *Elizabeth I and Her Parliaments* (London, 1953, 1957); Wallace Notestein, *The Winning of the Initiative by the House of Commons* (London, 1924).

3. The organic analogy is built into the writing of institutional history. I think it requires no apology, but a word of caution may be in order. To say that the Jacobean House of Commons was a single coherent body tending to impose certain behavioral patterns on its members and a congeries of 450 separate sets of wills, intellects, and interests, is to make two true statements. Neither precludes or subsumes the other, and if it is the former that is the controlling image of this study, this is in no way to claim for it a superior or determining reality.

4. Notestein, *op. cit.*, p. 40.

5. On the new boroughs, see *C.J.*, pp. 572, 576, 624, 643, and Evangeline de Villiers, "Parliamentary Boroughs Restored by the House of Commons 1621–1641," *E.H.R.*, LXVII (April, 1952).

6. Nor was it a coincidence that the Stuarts, for their part, were making a strenuous effort to bring the common-law courts under royal control, especially on major constitutional questions. For a most lucid presentation of this "battle for the courts," and the parliamentary response, see Margaret A. Judson, *The Crisis of the Constitution 1603–1645* (New Brunswick, N.J., 1949).

7. Quoted in G. R. Elton, *The Tudor Constitution* (London, 1960), p. 16.

8. Wentworth's speech is in Sir Simond D'Ewes, *The Journals of all the Parliaments during the Reign of Queen Elizabeth* (London, 1845), pp. 236–241.

9. There was one "right" or function Parliament clearly possessed apart from the king's grace, the power to tax; but this was essentially a power delegated from the primary right of the subject's property, not one inherent in Parliament itself. On this question see Francis D. Wormuth, *The Royal Prerogative 1603–1649* (Ithaca, N.Y., 1949).

10. This statement does not apply to the House of Lords. On the general relationship between the two houses, see chapter iv.

Chapter I: The Summoning of Parliament

1. Actually, the Parliament of 1604–1611 sat, in five sessions, a total of 437 days, against 413 for the five parliaments of the 1620s combined. The Addled Parliament, however, the only session in the decade 1611–1621, sat a mere 43 days. These figures are taken from Williams M. Mitchell, *The Rise of the Revolutionary Party in the House of Commons 1603–1629* (New York, 1957).

2. Anton Gindely, *Geschichte des dreissigjahrigen Krieges* (Prague, 1869–1880), II, chaps. 4 and 5.

3. From "The Trew Law of Free Monarchies," in C. H. McIlwain, ed., *The Political Works of James I* (Cambridge, Mass., 1918), p. 60.

4. S. R. Gardiner, ed., *Letters and Documents Illustrating the Relations between England and Germany at the Commencement of The Thirty Years War, 1618–19* (Camden Society, Vol. XC), p. 13.

5. Doncaster's Instructions, in S. R. Gardiner, ed., *Letters and Documents . . . 1619–20* (Camden Society, Vol. XCVIII), p. 64 (Spanish), p. 69 (English retranslation).

6. Gardiner, *Letters and Documents . . . 1618–19*, p. 81.

7. Viscount Doncaster to Sir Robert Naunton, August 7/17, 1619, *ibid.*, p. 188.

8. S. R. Gardiner, *History of England from the Accession of James I to the Outbreak of the Civil War 1603–1642* (London, 1886) III, 311–313, henceforth cited as Gardiner.

9. Digby to Cottington, September, 1619, in Gardiner, *Letters and Documents . . . 1619–20*, p. 62.

10. Gardiner, III, 313–314; *Cabala*, p. 2.

11. Digby to Cottington [?], February 25, 1620, B.M. Add. MSS 36444 (Aston Papers).

12. Gindely, *Geschichte*, II, 368–381.

13. Garrett Mattingly, *Renaissance Diplomacy* (London, 1955), chap. xxvi; Charles H. Carter, "Gondomar: Ambassador to James I," *Historical Journal*, III, 2 (1964).

14. Quoted in A. H. Bullen, ed., *The Works of Thomas Middleton* (London, 1886), I, 26, n. 1.

15. Anthony Weldon, *The Court and Character of King James* (London, 1650); Arthur Wilson, *The History of Great Britain, Being the Life and Reign of James the First* (London, 1653).

16. Mattingly's phrase: *Renaissance Diplomacy*, p. 262.

17. Carter, *op. cit.*, p. 205.

18. But even that the wily ambassador could turn to account. He writes of one audience, "I therefore entreated the King to consider what a small achievement it would be to ruin a gentleman, who had done his best to

serve him as truly as I had done, and who trusting to his words had assured your Majesty of his good intentions" (Gondomar to Philip III, April 2/12, 1620, P.R.O. 31/12/21).

19. Gondomar to Ciriza, November 21 / December 1, December 19/29, 1619; January 8/18, 1620, P.R.O. 31/12/21.

20. Gondomar to Philip III, March 25 / April 4, 1620, *ibid.*

21. Same to same, April 2/12, 1620, *ibid.*

22. Same to same, May 22 / June 1, 1620, *ibid.*

23. Rumor had it in August that Mansell was to rendezvous with a large Dutch fleet for an attack on Spain. Tillières to Puisieux, August 15/25, 1620, P.R.O. 31/3/54. Gondomar was alarmed: see Gondomar to Philip III, October 11/21, 1620, B.M. Add. MSS 31111, p. 336.

24. For the Spanish reception of Mansell and the story of his voyage, see B.M. Add. MSS 36444 and 36445 (Aston Papers), *passim.*

25. See Julian S. Corbett, *England in the Mediterranean 1603–1713* (London, 1904).

26. The records of the Conway-Weston mission are principally in the State Papers Germany, S.P. 81/17, 18. A copy of their instructions may be found in B.M. Add. MSS 35832, ff. 11–12 (Hardwicke Papers). There are also letters scattered through other of the S.P. foreign, in B.M. Harleian MSS 1581, etc. For a typical gibe at the two ambassadors, see "Note from Vulcano," August 1, 1620, in S.P. 77/14/165. For the escape from Prague, Harl. MSS 1580, f. 281.

27. Chamberlain to Carleton, September 16, 1620, in N. E. McClure, ed., *The Letters of John Chamberlain* (Philadelphia, 1939), II, 317, henceforth cited as *Chamberlain;* Gardiner, III, 370.

28. Spain had in fact considered sending Spinola to Bohemia, and up to the very end Spinola tried to keep Europe guessing about where he would go; but the firm negative of Maximilian, Duke of Bavaria and leader of the Catholic League, had closed this course to Madrid.

29. Buckingham to Gondomar, October, 1620, S.P. 94/24/46. For the audience, Tillières to Puisieux, October 4/14, 1620, P.R.O. 31/3/54.

30. H. G. R. Reade, *Sidelights on the Thirty Years War* (London, 1924), I, 364–366, citing the dispatches of Gabaleone, the ambassador of Savoy.

31. Trumbull to Calvert, October 5/15, 1620, S.P. 77/14/224. *Cf.* Lando to the Doge and Senate of Venice, October 2/12, 1620, *Calendar of State Papers Venetian,* XVI, 429, henceforth cited as *C.S.P.V.:* " . . . many ministers continually spur him [James] on and they have shown him letters from his representatives abroad, from lords and individual Englishmen, who write that they wish they were dead, so that they might not hear the opprobrium and the unworthy attributes cast upon their nation throughout the world."

32. Rudyard to Nethersole, S.P. 81/18/55; *C.S.P.V.,* XVI, 431.

33. Locke to Carleton, December 2, 1620, S.P. 14/118/2.

34. See chap. v.

35. Spedding, VII, 114.

36. *Chamberlain*, II, 320.

37. *Ibid.*, p. 221.

38. See S.P. 14/117, 118, *passim.*

39. S.P. 14/117/30, 64; 14/119/14.

40. Salvetti Newsletter, November 2/12, 1620, B.M. Add. MSS 27962: "But, although many and perhaps most of them [the nobles] are most ready and willing to aid the Elector, nonetheless they are afraid of being compelled to pay more money by a Parliament later on, and, above all, are generally determined to force his Majesty to summon one." I am indebted to Miss Caterina Maddalena for permission to use the translation of Salvetti she is preparing for the years 1616–1629.

41. Nicholas Burton to William Carsnew, November 4, 1620, S.P. 14/117/55.

42. Spedding, VII, 114–117.

43. *Ibid.*, VI, 13–56, 61–71, 73–75, 181–193; VII, 70–72.

44. *Ibid.*, VI, 65, 184 ff.

45. Presumably there was such a list, as there is for the Parliament of 1614 (Spedding, VI, 14–18). On December 23, 1620, Bacon wrote to Buckingham, enclosing a paper in which he had broken down the "main of the Parliament business into questions and parts"; this, too, according to Spedding and D. H. Willson, appears to be lost. A list of sixteen bills prepared by Sir Robert Heath pertaining to London survives in S.P. 14/118. It includes proposed acts against the making of gold foliate and gilding and against transportation of ordnance, both of which became substantial issues in Parliament.

46. For the development of the rich and many-sided hatred between Bacon and Cranfield, see Robert C. Johnson, "Francis Bacon and Lionel Cranfield, *H.L.Q.*, XXIII, 4 (August, 1960).

47. See the analysis of trade and political conditions drawn up by Cranfield in November, 1619, in Sackville MSS 6774, partially printed in R. H. Tawney, *Business and Politics under James I: Lionel Cranfield as Merchant and Minister* (Cambridge, 1958), pp. 296–297. Most of his program is here in embryo, a year before Parliament was called.

48. J. V. Lyle, ed., *Acts of the Privy Council of England*, V, *passim*, henceforth cited as *A.P.C.*

49. On the patent system, see W. Hyde Price, *The English Patents of Monopoly* (London, 1913); Harold G. Fox, *Monopolies and Patents of England* (Toronto, 1947); J. U. Nef, *Industry and Government in France and England* (London, 1962); W. R. Scott, *Joint Stock Companies* (New York, 1951); George Unwin, *Industrial Organization in the Sixteenth and Seventeenth Centuries* (Oxford, 1904); William Holdsworth, *History of English Law* (London, 1922–1939), IV, 344–354; E. R. Foster, "The Procedure of the House of Commons against Patents and Monopolies," in W. A. Aiken and B. D. Henning, *Conflict in Stuart England: Essays in Honour of Wallace Notestein* (London, 1960); S. R. Gardiner, "On Four Letters from Lord Bacon to Christian IV . . . ," in *Archaeologia*, XLI, 1867; E. W. Hulme,

"The Early History of the English Patent System," *Law Quarterly Review*, 12, 16 (1896, 1900); Barbara Malament, "The 'Economic Liberalism' of Sir Edward Coke," *Yale Law Journal*, LXXVI, 7 (June, 1967).

50. For Yelverton's case in Star Chamber (November 9–11, 1620), see Spedding, VII, 98–99, 133–140; S.P. 14/117/57, 71, 76; *Chamberlain*, II, 322.

51. Spedding, VII, 145–148.

52. *Ibid.*, VII, 148–149.

53. Bacon, Montagu, and Naunton to James, November 15, December 12, 1620, Gibson MSS, Lambert MS 936, ff. 134*b*, 136. I am indebted to Professor Roy Schreiber for this reference. The first letter is printed in Spedding, VII, 140–141. A rather misleading excerpt is printed in Wallace Notestein, Frances Relf, and Hartley Simpson, eds., *Commons Debates 1621* (New Haven, 1935), VII, 469–470, henceforth cited as *C.D.* See also *Chamberlain*, II, 322.

54. For a view of the patent system as a considered part of a general commercial policy, see Gardiner, "On Four Letters from Lord Bacon to Christian IV . . . ."

55. Spedding, VII, 151–152.

56. *Ibid.*, p. 152.

57. *Ibid.*, p. 155.

58. Bacon urged a Parliament in 1613, and even more strongly in 1615, after the intervening fiasco (Spedding, IV, 363–373; V, 176–191), "For nothing [he wrote] is to a man a greater spur or a greater direction to do over a thing again, than when he knows where he failed" (V, 177). Bacon was proud of his parliamentary record: "I ought not to be novice-like or ignorant, having now served twelve full Parliaments" (*ibid.*). Christopher Hill, in his *Intellectual Origins of the English Revolution* (Oxford, 1965), p. 99, concludes that "Bacon was right to think of himself as a good House of Commons man." He also argues, less convincingly, that the Commons thought so too.

59. In his speech of March 10 in the House of Lords, James averred of the patent of inns that "I was soe troubled with complaints in this kind at Newmarket as they were brought unto me when I was in my bed." See below, pp. 67–71.

60. "On Saterday the Lord Chauncellor was created Vicount St. Albanes with all the ceremonies of robes and coronets, whereas the rest were only don by Patent" (*Chamberlain*, II, 339).

61. *Vox Populi* is printed in the *Somers Tracts* (London, 1809), II, 508–524, and partially in the first volume of Smeeton's *Historical and Biographical Tracts* (London, 1820), from which I have taken a variant quotation (p. 15).

62. Calvert to Buckingham, November 28, 1620, in S. R. Gardiner, ed., *The Fortescue Papers* (Camden Society, n.s., Vol. I), p. 143, henceforth cited as *Fortescue Papers;* Digby to Aston, December 15, 1620, B.M. Add. MSS 36444, f. 248.

63. Gondomar to Ciriza, December 11/21, 1620, P.R.O. 31/12/21.

64. Gondomar to Philip III, November 11/21, 1620, P.R.O. 31/12/21; Tillières to Puisieux, November 10/20, 1620, P.R.O. 31/3/54; Locke to Carleton, November 11, 1621, S.P. 14/117/71.

65. Van Male to de la Faille, November 30 / December 10, 1620, B.M. Add. MSS 31111, p. 342. The Venetian Lando is almost identical: "Tears, sighs and loud expressions of wrath are sent and heard in every direction" (*C.S.P.V.*, XVI, 496).

66. Calvert to Buckingham, December 4, 1620, *Fortescue Papers*, p. 144; Sir Simonds D'Ewes, *Autobiography and Letters* (London, 1845), I, 160.

67. *Chamberlain*, II, 331. Dr. John Everard of Cambridge was one of the most persistent of the anti-Spanish divines. He was imprisoned on February 25, 1621, for a sermon at the Paul's Cross against the "craft and crueltie" of Spain. Released unrepentant, he promptly repeated the offense and was jailed again. Dr. Samuel Ward of Ipswich was committed about the same time, not for a speech, but for a lampoon. Ralph Clayton went to prison for preaching against the importation of a Spanish ewe. For other anti-Spanish sermons, and a discussion of political sermons in the early Stuart period in general, see Louis B. Wright, "Propaganda against James I's 'Appeasement of Spain,' " *H.L.Q.*, VI, 2 (February, 1943); Godfrey Davies, "English Political Sermons 1603–1640," *ibid.*, III, 1 (October, 1939); and Millar Maclure, *The Pauls Cross Sermons* (Toronto, 1958).

68. Printed in Spedding, VII, 156–157.

69. Salvetti Newsletter, December 29, 1620/January 8, 1621.

70. Spedding, VII, 152.

71. *Ibid.*

72. A phrase James had inserted into the Proclamation for the Parliament, despite the pleas of Bacon and the Earl of Pembroke against it (*Chamberlain*, II, 328).

73. Lawrence Stone, "The Electoral Influence of the second Earl of Salisbury 1614–1668," *E.H.R.*, XXI, 280 (July, 1956), p. 388. Richardson was a serjeant, Shute a minor officeholder. See D. H. Willson, *Privy Councillors in the House of Commons 1604–1629* (Minneapolis, 1940), p. 156, n. 49, henceforth cited as Willson, *Privy Councillors*.

74. A good biography of Sandys is one of the most conspicuous lacunae in the early Stuart period. Professor Theodore K. Rabb, who is preparing one, has written a thorough account of "Sir Edwin Sandys and the Parliament of 1604," *A.H.R.*, LXIX, 3 (April, 1964). See also Wallace Mosher's study of the same subject (Philadelphia, 1940). John W. Osborne, "The Parliamentary Career of Sir Edwin Sandys, 1614–1621," in the *Bermuda Historical Quarterly*, XIX, 4 (1962), makes pleasant tropical reading, but is otherwise of little value.

75. *D.N.B.*, Sandys.

76. Richard Marsh to Edward Nicholas, January 8, 1621, S.P. 14/119/11.

77. *Calendar of State Papers, Domestic Series (1619-1623)*, p. 200, henceforce cited as C.S.P.D.

78. Locke to Carleton, December 16, 1620, S.P. 14/118/30; W. Knowler,

ed, *The Earl of Strafforde's Letters* . . . (London, 1739), I, 10–13; Willson, *Privy Councillors*, pp. 70–72.

79. Tillières, the French ambassador, viewed the delays of Parliament as "un essay pour le rompre." (Tillières to Puisieux, January 19/29, 1621, P.R.O. 31/3/54. The first prorogation, issued December 28, set Parliament back from January 16 to January 23. The second one prorogued it to January 30 (S.P. 14/118/61; 14/119/30). Lando, too, was alarmed at the second prorogation: "Such a thing has never happened before" (C.S.P.V., XVI, 544). In fact it was quite common; Neale points out that the Parliament of 1581 was prorogued no less than twenty-six times before it finally met *(Elizabeth I and Her Parliaments 1559–1581,* p. 369).

80. Sir John Neale, *The Elizabethan House of Commons* (London, 1949), p. 353.

81. Except Pembroke and the decrepit Hertford, too old to march, but spied hobbling along by D'Ewes *(Autobiography,* I, 170).

82. For the opening of Parliament, see: *Journals of the House of Commons,* I, 507, henceforth cited as *C.J.*; Edward Nicholas, *Proceedings and Debates in the House of Commons in 1620 and 1621* (Oxford, 1766), I, 2–3, henceforth cited as *P.D.*; C.D., V, 424–425; D'Ewes, *Autobiography,* I, 169–171; *Chamberlain,* II, 338.

83. *C.D.,* IV, 4, gives a figure of £350,000. But, as Bacon pointed out in 1615, Elizabeth had "reigned twenty-seven years before she had so much as a subsidy; and that by half-payments in four years" (Spedding, V, 178).

84. I have used two versions of the King's speech, *C.D.,* II, 2–13, and *P.D.,* I, 3–11. For the manuscript origins of these, see *C.D.,* II, 2, n. 2.

85. Tillières to Puisieux, February 3/13, 1621, P.R.O. 31/3/54.

Chapter II: 'The Happiest Parliament That Ever Was'

1. Spedding, VII, 173–179; *C.D.,* V. 431–432.
2. *C.D.,* IV, 11.
3. *C.D.,* IV, 12; II, 18; *C.J.,* 508.
4. See below, n. 53.
5. *C.D.,* II, 21.
6. By making itself a grand committee, or "committee of the whole" as it was commonly called, the House was able to waive its normal rule of one speech to one subject per member, and to bypass the Speaker, who was frequently able to curtail debate that might prove embarrassing to the Crown. See Wallace Notestein, *The Winning of the Initiative by the House of Commons, op. cit.*

7. *C.D.,* II, 25; IV, 17. This is a quotation from the Apology of 1604. See above, p. 179.

8. *C.J.,* 509.

9. *C.J.,* p. 511; *C.D.,* II, 34; V, 441; VI, 356; and see Willson, *Privy Councillors,* p. 224.

10. *C.J.*, pp. 511, 520; *C.D.*, II, 22, 42. See also Sackville's motion of May 4, *C.D.*, III, 169; V, 141–142. For a similar motion by Sandys in 1614, See *C.J.*, p. 465.

11. *C.J.*, p. 513; *C.D.*, II, 42.

12. *Chamberlain*, II, 341.

13. *C.D.*, II, 52–53; IV, 37–38.

14. *P.D.*, I, 32.

15. 4 H. 8 (Strode's case). *C.D.*, II, 59. Alford, who favored a bill, objected that this act did not extend to the privileges of Parliament (*C.J.*, p. 517).

16. This argument is conflated from two speeches delivered by Coke at a short interval. *C.D.*, II, 56–57, 57–58; *C.J.*, p. 517.

17 *P.D.*, I, 32.

18. *C.D.*, II, 60.

19. Sir George Chaworth, a courtier, complained "that Mr. Speaker made not the Petition for Liberty of Speech, as usual; and the Answer with more Caution than usual; almost a *Nosce teipsum*" (*C.J.*, p. 518).

20. For the full debate, see *C.D.*, II, 56–63; IV, 39–40; V, 7-8, 448–451; *C.J.*, pp. 517–518; *P.D.*, I, 32.

21. The King's letter is in *C.D.*, VII, 575–576. Cf. Wentworth's notes of Calvert's relation to the House (V, 462–463).

22. *C.D.*, II, 83, n. 11.

23. *C.D.*, II, 37, n. 18.

24. *C.D.*, V, 6; II, 37.

25. *C.D.*, II, 37–40; IV, 27–28; V, 6, 441–442; *P.D.*, I, 24–25; *C.S.P.V.*, XVI, 577.

26. First introduced in 1584. One passed in 1614 (*C.J.*, p. 492).

27. The royal proclamation of May 24, 1618, licensing certain Sunday sports.

28. *C.D.*, II, 82: "gins and snares."

29. *C.D.*, IV, 53.

30. *C.J.*, p. 524.

31. Mead to Stuteville, March 10, 1621, in Thomas Birch, ed., *The Court and Times of James the First* (London, 1849), II, 237, henceforth cited as Birch. It was rumored that Shepherd would try to reenter the House "by his Majesty's letters" *(ibid.)*. He did not.

32. *C.D.*, II, 96, n. 19.

33. *C.J.*, p. 524; *C. D.*, V, 501–502.

34. The text of the petition is in *C.D.*, V, 458–460. For that of 1610, see S. R. Gardiner, *Parliamentary Debates in 1610* (Camden Society, Vol. LXXXI), p. 43.

35. *C.J.*, p. 519.

36. *C.D.*, V, 460.

37. Gondomar to Philip III, February 8/18, 1621, B.M. Add. MSS 31111, pp. 353–358.

38. For the presentation of the petition and the King's speech, see *C.D.*, IV, 69–75; cf. V, 470–472; VI, 282–283.

39. *C.D.*, IV, 75, n. v; V, 472.

40. *C.D.*, VI, 362; cf. II, 104; IV, 75–76; V, 257. Mr. Chudleigh grumbled that the "Book of Sports" was "but a probationer," and was confident that the King would recall it when he saw how it was abused by the ungodly. The House, however, referred the sabbath bill to a committee to "make it so, as it cross not with his Majesty's Book" (*C.D.*, II, 104–105; *P.D.*, I, 60).

41. *C.D.*, II 103–104; IV, 75; II, 114; IV, 81–82; V, 477.

42. *C.D.*, II, 133.

43. Neale, *Elizabeth I and Her Parliaments 1584–1601*, pp. 419–422.

44. The Council had in fact taken serious note of the smuggling of ordnance. On October 18, a commission consisting of Greville, Coventry, Crew, and Clement Edmonds was appointed to investigate the matter, interrogate suspects, and prosecute in Star Chamber. On November 22, another commission was appointed to investigate the shipping of a large quantity of ordnance from Lewes under pretext of a warrant to Gondomar. The Lord Privy Seal was meanwhile instructed to keep the real warrant in hand, pending the result of the investigation. On December 4, a supplementary order put a freeze on the exportation of all ordnance under any warrant whatsoever. On December 8, a culprit was found, one Stephen Aynscombe, a gunfounder of Kent. His arsenal was confiscated and brought to the Tower Wharf. This was presumably the ordnance referred to by the Commons. *A.P.C.*, V, 287–288, 289, 316–317, 320, 321–322, 334, 336–337.

45. *C.D.*, V, 9. For the full debate, see *C.D.*, II, 69–74; IV, 45–47; V, 453–455; *C.J.*, 519–520; *P.D.*, I, 36–37.

46. *C.D.*, VII, 614–615.

47. *C.S.P.V.*, XVI, 590; Salvetti Newsletter, February 9/19, 1621; Tillières to Puisieux, February 11/21, 1621, P.R.O. 31/3/54.

48. Gooch and Roe clearly spoke from expert knowledge (*C.J.*, p. 519; *C.D.*, II, 71).

49. Caesar computed a subsidy at £82,000, a fifteenth at £29,000 (*P.D.*, I, 49).

50. *C.D.*, II, 24: "After dinner the Committee being assembled, they called upon Sir Edward Coke to take the Chair at the Committee which, when with some seeming unwillingness he had accepted, Sir Carew Raleigh said that it was never seen that a Privy Councillor was called to the Chair. But answer was made that being all members of one House there was no difference and therefore the House might set up anyone whom they pleased."

51. *Ibid.*: "Then the first question being alone propounded by Sir Edward Coke, he desired that they would not enter into any other until that were ended, which was agreed."

52. *C.D.*, II, 84–86.

53. *C.D.*, IV., 57. The Council of War, set up by James in January, estimated the cost of maintaining 25,000 foot and 5,000 horse on the Continent for one year at £900,000 ("Report of the Council of War," S.P. 14/-119/93).

54. *C.D.*, II, 88–91; V, 465.

55. *C.D.*, V, 498, 466.

56. *C.D.*, V, 467; cf. VI, 351–352.

57. *C.D.*, II, 22, 92–93; *C.J.*, 523.

58. *C.D.*, II, 89–90; *P.D.*, I, 75. *C.D.*, IV, 32; *C.J.*, p. 514. *C.J.*, p. 528.

59. *C.J.*, p. 518.

60. *C.D.*, II, 44; IV, 31–32; *C.J.*, p. 514.

61. *C.J.*, p. 514; Digges to Carleton, February 15, 1621, S.P. 84/99. *C.D.*, IV, 54, n. 2; *P.D.*, I, 66.

62. *C.D.*, II, 19–20; IV, 13–14; V, 435–436; *C.J.*, p. 509. *C.D.*, II, 22–23; IV, 15–16; V, 437; *C.J.*, p. 509.

63. *C.D.*, II, 90.

64. Coke was still attending Council meetings; his name appears on the register March 1 and 4. There is no further record of his attendance between April and August, but he appeared again in the fall on at least three occasions, September 26, October 5, and December 20, the last just a week before his arrest. He is still recorded as "one of the King's Privy Council" in the Nicholas Diary on June 4. *A.P.C.*, V, 358, 359; VI, 49, 54, 55, 103, 104–105; *P.D.*, II, 174.

Menna Prestwich, *Cranfield: Politics and Profits under the Early Stuarts* (Oxford, 1966), suggests that Coke consciously exploited his "nuisance-value" in Parliament as a lever to gain high office. This was doubtless one of the options in his mind at the beginning of Parliament, and perhaps his primary strategy, but he was soon playing for far higher stakes; and though this never-quite abandoned goal may account for his occasional lapse back into the role of loyal councillor, Coke could have had few illusions about what was really in store for him after the crisis of March.

65. Mandeville, then Sir Henry Montagu, had succeeded Coke on the bench in 1616, which was doubly salting the wound.

66. *P.D.*, II, 284; *C.J.*, 665.

67. *C.D., IV*, 399; cf. III, 376.

68. See above, pp. 75, 91–92.

69. Willson, *Privy Councillors*, p. 151.

70. Diary of John Pym, April 16, 1624.

71. *C.D.*, IV, 19–20.

72. *C.D.*, V, 4.

73. *C.D.*, II, 90.

74. The so-called "Book of Bounty"; see chap. i, p. 22.

75. *C.D.*, IV, 78; *P.D.*, I, 63. Cf. *C.D.*, VI, 249–250; V, 257–258.

76. *C.D.*, IV, 79–81; VI, 249–251; V, 258, 475–476; *P.D.*, I, 65–66.

77. *C.D.*, VI, 253; II, 108.

78. For the debate and condemnation, see *C.D.*, II, 108–111; V, 478–481; VI, 254–257; *P.D.*, I, 69–72.

79. *C.D.*, II, 118.

80. *C.D.*, II, 122–123; VI, 262–263, 285–286.

81. *C.D.*, II, 146–147.

82. *C.D.,* II, 147; *C.J.,* 530.

83. *C.J.,* p. 530; *C.D.,* II, 146; IV, 115–116. *P.D.,* I, 108–109; *C.D.,* II, 148.

84. Gardiner, IV, 68–69; cf. Spedding, VII, 217, 219.

85. Lawrence Stone, "The Inflation of Honors 1558–1641," *Past and Present,* 14 (November, 1958), p. 57.

86. John Hacket, *Scrinia Reserata: A Memorial Offered to the Great Deservings of John Williams D.D.* (London, 1692), p. 39.

87. *Ibid.,* p. 64. But cf. F. C. Dietz, *English Public Finance 1558–1641* (New York, 1932), p. 179; and C. R. Mayes, "The Sale of Peerages in Early Stuart England," *J.M.H.,* XXIX, 1 (March, 1957).

88. Arthur Wilson, *The History of Great Britain, being the Life and Reign of King James the First* (London, 1653), p. 187.

89. I have computed this using a table given in Stone, *op. cit.,* p. 69.

90. *A.P.C.,* V, 352–353; Frances Relf, ed., *Notes of the Debates in the House of Lords 1621–1628* (London, 1929), pp. 10–11, henceforth cited as L.D.R.; cf. *L.J.,* pp. 41–42.

91. Published 1657. See Vernon P. Snow, "Essex and the Aristocratic Opposition to the Early Stuarts," *J.M.H.,* XXXII, 3 (September, 1960), p. 227; and on the general subject of parliamentary technique, E. R. Foster, "Procedure in the House of Lords during the Early Stuart Period," *Journal of British Studies,* V, 2 (May, 1966).

92. *L.J.,* p. 21; Evangeline de Villiers, ed., "The Hastings Journal of the Parliament of 1621," *Camden Miscellany,* XX (1953), pp. 20–21, henceforth cited as H.J. Southampton and Sandys, for example, were close business associates (the Virginia Company). Dorset and Sackville were brothers. Essex' steward was related to Coke; Selden was his lawyer; Sir John Eliot, a correspondent.

93. *L.D. R.,* pp. 5–7, 11.

94. See chap. iii, pp. 91–92.

95. For the meeting of February 28, see *P.D.,* I, 109–112; *C.D.,* VI, 272–275, 292–295.

96. Birch, II, 232.

97. *C.D.,* VI, 303–304. *Ibid.,* II, 161; V, 270; *C.J.,* p. 537.

98. See chap. i, p. 30.

99. *C.D.,* II, 164–167; V, 272; VI, 29–30, 309–311; *P.D.,* I, 120–121; *C.J.,* p. 538.

100. *C.D.,* II, 167; *C.J.,* 538.

101. *C.D.,* II, 167–168; V, 272; *P.D.,* I, 122.

102. *C.D.,* II, 168; IV, 124–125; V, 272; VI, 31, 305; *C.J.,* p. 539.

103. *C.D.,* II, 169; V, 272; VI, 31; *C.J.,* p. 539.

105. *C.D.,* V. 272.

106. *C.D., II,* 193–199; IV, 134–137; V, 284; VI, 43–45.

107. *C.J.,* p. 546; *P.D.,* I, 135–136. *Chamberlain,* II, 351–352. Digges wrote to Carleton that Coke had "behaved himself like the last of the Romans" (S.P. 84/100/45).

108. *C.J.,* p. 547; *C.D.,* II, 200–201; V, 284.

109. *C.J.*, p. 547; *C.D.*, II, 201.

110. "White Crow" was a snipish reference to one of the precedents cited by Coke before the Lords on March 8: 4 Henry IV, the case of Brangwyn or White Crow. Coke was accused of having falsified this precedent. This reference indicates, among other things, how thoroughly well informed the King was about what had transpired at the conference that day.

111. *H.J.*, pp. 26–31; *L.D. R.*, pp. 12–16; *L.J.*, 42.

112. Worth about £60,000 altogether, according to Coke (*C.J.*, 543), or less than a single parliamentary subsidy.

113. This the lawyers of the Commons had debated on the seventh. Locke to Carleton, March 12, 1621, S.P. 14/120/15; *C.D.*, II, 177; IV, 132–133; V, 279; VI, 37, 358–359; *C.J.*, p. 544; *P.D.*, I, 131.

114. *C.J.*, p. 544; *C.D.*, IV, 132.

115. *L.D. R.*, p. 16.

116. Salvetti Newsletter, March 16/26.

117. *C.D.*, II, 205; IV, 143; V, 34; *C.J.*, p. 541.

118. *C.D.*, VII, 577–578.

119. *Chamberlain*, II, 352.

120. Gardiner, IV, 50.

121. Hacket, *op. cit.*, p. 50.

122. *C.J.*, p. 542.

123. *C.D.*, V, 43.

124. *C.D.*, V, 272.

125. *C.J.*, pp. 549, 555. Prestwich, *op. cit.*, pp. 289–291, takes a less ambivalent view of Sackville's behavior, and firmly characterizes him at one point as an "unrelenting enemy" of Bacon. His apparent aid to Bacon in negotiating the sale of York House in 1622 is put down as the act of "a smart intriguer confusing the trail." But why should Sackville have bothered to pose as the friend of a man who could do him no harm?

126. These were injunctions for the staying of debts. In conception a humane modification of England's barbaric debt laws, they aroused the violent opposition of London merchants. Cranfield's haste to attack them stemmed partly from the fact that his court, as well as Bacon's, had a hand in issuing them (Locke to Carleton, March 3, 1621). Bacon, ironically, had planned to do away with them himself in Parliament.

127. *C.D.*, II, 221–223; IV, 152–155; V, 40, 296–297; VI, 62–64; *P.D.*, I, 157–160.

128. Spedding, VII, 212; Gardiner, IV, 65.

129. *P.D.*, I, 162.

130. One can only conjecture who brought the two men forward, but it is clear that they were well sponsored. Presumably Coke was involved, and Phelips; possibly others.

131. *P.D.*, I, 163–164.

132. *P.D.*, I, 163.

133. *C.D.*, II, 224.

134. *C.D.*, II, 226–227; V, 299; *C.J.*, p. 554.

135. Spedding, VII, 213.

136. *C.J.*, p. 555; cf. *C.D.*, II, 230.

137. *C.D.*, V, 301.

138. *L.D. R.*, p. 24.

139. *C.D.*, IV, 160–161; V, 44–45,301–302; VI, 66–68; *P.D.*, I, 171–174.

140. *C.D.*, IV, 162; cf. VI, 70.

141. *C.D.*, V, 303.

142. *C.D.*, IV, 163.

143. For the debate, see *C.D.*, II, 232–235; IV, 162–164; V, 45–48, 302–303; *C.J.*, pp 557–558; *P.D.*, I, 176–178.

144. *C.D.*, II, 237–239; IV, 166–167; V, 306; *P.D.*, I, 183–185; *C.J.*, p. 560.

145. The Earl of Suffolk's case (1449). See F. W. Maitland, *The Constitutional History of England* (Cambridge, 1909), p. 246.

146. *C.J.*, pp. 560–561; *C.D.*, IV, 167.

147. *P.D.*, I, 187. There was some precedent for this in the examination of Lord Chancellor Wriothesley in 1547 by an *ad hoc* commission of lawyers and judges appointed by the Crown. I am indebted to Professor Donald Slavin for this reference.

148. *C.J.*, p. 561; *P.D.*, I, 187–188; *C.D.*, II, 239–242; IV, 168. Cf. Coke's argument on March 9, when it was objected that there was insufficient evidence for naming the referees: "If we cannot come to the Originals, let us take the Confession of Sir H. Yelverton, who *particeps criminis*" (*C.J.*, p. 547).

149. *C.J.*, p. 561; *P.D.*, I, 188.

150. Only Finch held out to quash the charges altogether. *C.J.*, p. 561; *P.D.*, I, 187.

151. *C.D.*, II, 244–245; IV, 170; V, 301, 501; VI, 73, 384–385; *C.J.*, p. 563; *P.D.*, I, 193–194.

152. *P.D.*, I, 193–194.

153. *L.J.*, pp. 52–55.

154. *L.J.*, p. 55; *L.D. R.*, pp. 28–29.

155. Birch, II, 239.

156. Salvetti Newsletter, March 23 / April 2; *Chamberlain*, II, 356; *P.D.*, I, 186; Birch, II, 241–242; Spedding, VII, 225–226.

157. *C.D.*, IV, 184–185.

158. *C.J.*, p. 568.

159. *C.D.*, IV, 203.

160. *C.D.*, V, 71.

161. *C.D.*, IV, 207–209; V, 327–328; VI, 88–89, 388–390.

Chapter III: Popery and Prerogative

1. Locke to Carleton, March 23, 1621, S.P. 14/120/36.

2. Sir Henry Mainwaring to Lord Zouch, April 6, 1621, S.P. 14/120/69.

3. For this incident, see *Chamberlain*, II, 360–363; Birch, II, 245–249; *C.S.P.V.* XVII, 31–32; *A.P.C.*, V, 373–374; B.M. Add. MSS 36445, ff. 94–95.

4. Spedding, VII, 238.

5. *L.J.*, pp. 79–80.

6. *L.J.*, pp. 84–85.

7. "Neither will I trouble your Lordships by singling out those Particulars, which I think may fall off . . . . Neither will I prompt your Lordships to observe upon the Proofs, where they come not home, or the Scruples touching the Credits of the Witnesses; neither will I represent unto your Lordships how far a Defence might, in divers Things, extenuate the Offence, in Respect of the Time or Manner of the Gift, or the like Circumstances, but only leave these Things to spring out of your own Noble Thoughts . . . and to submit myself wholly to your Piety and Grace" (*L.J.*, p. 84). For the Lords' dissatisfaction with this answer, see *L.D. G.*, pp. 14–15.

8. *L.J.*, pp. 98–101.

9. *L.J.*, p. 101; *L.D. G.*, p. 41.

10. *L.J.*, p. 104; *L.D. G.*, p. 54.

11. *L.J.*, p. 106; *L.D. G.*, p. 64. Buckingham alone dissented.

12. Spedding, VII, 280–281; Gardiner, IV, 132.

13. Spedding, VII, 288–291.

14. *Cabala*, pp. 262, 263. Williams wondered how Parliament would react at being thus "mocked and derided."

15. Spedding, VII, 347; *D.N.B.*, Bacon (by Gardiner).

16. Bacon's fall inspired an extraordinary number of quite brutal satires. Of his entourage, only his secretary, Meautys, apparently remained faithful to him.

17. Spedding, VII, 225. See, for example, the irregularities in the patent drawn by Attorney Bacon for Alderman Cockayne's project, cited in Astrid Friis, *Alderman Cockayne's Project and the Cloth Trade* (London, 1927), pp. 279–280. I am indebted to Professor Wallace Notestein for this reference and for the benefit of his shrewd judgments on Bacon's character in general.

18. *C.D.*, III, 327.

19. E. R. Foster, ed., *Proceedings in Parliament 1610* (New Haven, 1966), I, 280–281; II, 71.

20. *C.J.*, p. 507; for the content of the bill, see *C.D.*, VII, 3. It was read only four days before the dissolution of Parliament, and so got no further.

21. *C.D.*, VI, 272–273, 292–295; II, 153–154; IV, 117.

22. *C.D.*, II, 90.

23. *C.D.*, VI, 273.

24. John Finch (1584–1660), MP, 1621, 1624, 1625; Attorney-General to the Queen, 1626; Speaker of the House of Commons, 1628–1629; Chief Justice of the Common Pleas, 1634–1640; a baron and Lord Keeper, 1640. Forced by Parliament to flee that year to Holland. Finch had other worries in 1621. His father, Sir Henry, published a book that year predicting the temporal dominion of the Jews (*D.N.B.*).

25. *C.D.*, VI, 273–274; cf. VI, 20; V, 264.

26. *C.D.*, VI, 24; V, 20, 533–534; *C.J.*, p. 535.

27. *C.D.*, V, 48–49.

28. Ironically, it was Cranfield himself who asserted that "The lower howse of parliament hath not authoritie to determine iurisdiction of Courts, it belongs to the prerogative of the Kinge. Wee maye enquire and complaine, as in case of grievances, but reformation can onelie be by the kinge" (*C.D.*, V, 20). His every action in the Hall-Fuller case belied these words of warning.

29. *C.J.*, p. 559.

30. George Norbury, "The Abuses and Remedies of the High Court of Chancerye," S.P. 14/122/56. Cf. William Jones, *The Elizabethan Court of Chancery* (Oxford, 1967); Louis Knafla, *New Model Lawyer: The Career of Thomas Egerton, 1541–1616* (unpublished doctoral thesis, U.C.L.A., 1965).

31. See chap. ii, p. 62.

32. *C.D.*, II, 242.

33. According to the petition attached to it (*C.D.*, VII, 204–207), the bill called for the reviving and strengthening of the statute of 15 H. 6 (still in force), which provided "that no subpena should be granted without suertie first bound to pay costes and damages to the partie greaved if the suggestions of the Bill proved not true." What the old statute lacked was a penalty for nonperformance, in view of "The experience of greavances of many poore subiectes in this age and at this instant with crying Complaintes . . . [of] the tedious and chargeable proceedinges in the said Court, by Leingth of Bills grounded uppon untrue Suggestions displeasing to god the aucthor of truth, multiplicitie of needles suites breeding referrences, charges of reportes and many orders thereuppon, chargeable mocions, excessive fees and other intollerable dilatorie expences."

34. *P.D.*, I, 277.

35. There is no mention of it in the records of the Parliament after the original reference (*C.D.*, IV, 232; V, 72), but a bill "To regulate jurisdiction of Courts" is referred to in the State Papers Domestic as being in the Lords at the breakup of Parliament.

36. For Coke's views, see *C.D.*, II, 223; IV, 154; V, 39.

37. Writs empowering private persons to order constables to seize prohibited merchandise or manufacture.

38. "An act concerninge dayes of hearinge and orders in the Court of Chauncery and other Courts of equitie" (*C.D.*, VII, 264–265).

39. 1) "For avoydeinge Exactions of Undue Fees in Courts of Justice"; 2) "An Act for Moderateing Fees for Orders in Courts of Equitye"; 3) "An acte to establish two Judges Assistantes in the Court of Chancery and to lessen the charge of Suites in that Courte"; 4) A bill against extortion by proctors [of wills]; 5) "An Act to prevent Exaction of Fees by Ecclesiasticall Judges and Courtes" (*C.D.*, II, 255–256).

40. *C.D.*, VII, 519–521.

41. *C.D.*, IV, 196; *P.D.*, I, 226–227; *C.J.*, p. 574.

42. *C.D.*, III, 3.

43. *P.D.*, I, 302–305; *C.D.*, II, 315–316.

44. See the reply to the Masters' petition, *C.D.*, *VII 521–526*.

45. *C.D.*, III, 97–98; V, 103–104; VI, 433–434; *C.J.*, p. 594; *P.D.*, I, 334.

46. James Spedding, ed., *The Works of Francis Bacon* ... (London, 1857–1874), VII, 759–774.

47. *C.D.*, IV, 194.

48. *P.D.*, I, 351–352; *C.D.*, II, 331; IV, 274; V, 355; VI, 111.

49. *C.D.*, VII, 244–248.

50. *P.D.*, I, 274.

51. *C.D.*, IV, 194.

52. *C.D.*, IV, 199–200.

53. *C.D.*, III, 28, 31; V, 240–241; *P.D.*, I, 284; *C.J.*, p. 587; *Chamberlain*, II, 363–364. Sandys called Bennet "his fellow scholler and ancientest frend."

54. *C.D.*, II, 32; cf. V, 84.

55. Locke to Carleton, April 23, 1621, S.P. 14/120/107.

56. John Dodderidge, Justice of the King's Bench, 1612–1628.

57. *C.D.*, V, 111; cf. II, 331; IV, 274; V, 354; VI, 108; *P.D.*, I, 347–348.

58. *C.D.*, III, 99.

59. *C.D.*, III, 108.

60. *C.D.*, III, 100.

61. *C.D.*, V, 181.

62. G. E. Aylmer, *The King's Servants: The Civil Service of Charles I 1625–1642* (New York, 1961), p. 190. Aylmer's discussion of fees is brief but excellent.

63. Digges to Carleton, April 18, 1621, S.P. 14/120/98.

64. *Chamberlain*, II, 363.

65. An office in the Exchequer.

66. *C.D.*, II, 303–306; cf. V, 84–86.

67. *C.D.*, III, 30; cf. II, 303: "The high court of parliament is the great eye of the kingdom to find out offences and punish them." See also *C.D.*, V, 83; *P.D.*, I, 283; *C.J.*, p. 583, for this interesting and significant speech. Pym wanted the Commons to examine Bennet, "and so leave nothing but Judicature [i.e., the verdict] to the Lords." See above, p. 110.

68. *C.D.*, VI, 70.

69. Among the more striking examples: *C.D.*, II, 37, 95; III, 354; V, 107, 206, 219, 240.

70. *C.D.*, II, 305.

71. Louise Fargo Brown, "Ideas of Representation from Elizabeth to Charles II," *J.M.H.*, XI, 1 (March, 1939), argues that the use of "country" in the modern sense of nation, as opposed to its old synonymy with "county," first clearly emerges in 1621. It is in the 1620s that the idea of Parliament as the representative of the nation too gains general acceptance. As Miss Judson concludes, "In the eight years between 1621 and 1629 . . . the idea of parliament's responsibility to the nation became one of the most common arguments used by leaders in the Commons" *(The Crisis of the Constitution, op. cit.,* p. 285).

72. Edmondes to Carleton, June 12, 1621, S.P. 14/121/96.

73. *C.D.*, III, 78.

74. Henry Elsing, *Notes of the Debates in the House of Lords . . . A.D.*

1621, ed. S. R. Gardiner (Camden Society, Vol. CIII), p. 11, henceforth cited as *L.D. G.; C.D.,* IV, 241–243; III, 38.

75. "Purveyance" was the term used to describe the requisitioning of local labor and vehicles for the transport of the royal entourage during the King's progresses. Grievances arising from this practice were chronic; as Sir Humphrey May resignedly expressed it, "There be somm diseases incurable, and in som things we can never take the abuse of things from the use" (*C.D.,* III, 307). On the general problem, see Allegra Woodworth, "Purveyance for the Royal Household in the Reign of Queen Elizabeth," *Transactions of the American Philosophical Society,* n.s. XXXV, i (1945).

76. *C.D.,* III, 306. Fleetwood retorted "that no Prerogative may extend to take away the Hire of the Labourer, which is due both by the Law of God and Man." The House passed the bill.

77. See above, pp. 95–96.

78. Originally pegged at £1,095, its cost had fallen by 1622 to £220–250. Stone, "Inflation of Honors," *op. cit.,* p. 53.

79. *C.D.,* III, 104.

80. *C.J.,* p. 494; *C.D.,* VII, 645.

81. See chap. ii, pp. 60–61.

82. *C.D.,* III, 111.

83. *C.D.,* III, 112; V, 124–125; VI, 116.

84. *C.D.,* III, 113; cf. VI, 116.

85. *C.D.,* II, 121–122, 135, 141–142; IV, 100; V, 489; VI, 7–8. For the complete history of the Virginia lottery, see Robert C. Johnson, "Lotteries of the Virginia Company 1612–1621," *Virginia Magazine of History and Biography,* LXXIV, 3 (July, 1966).

86. For Sandys' role in the Virginia Company, see Wesley Frank Craven, *Dissolution of the Virginia Company* (Massachusetts, 1964).

87. *C.D.,* V, 516; II, 139.

88. *P.D.,* I, 296–297; *C.D.,* IV, 261; III, 305.

89. *C.D.,* V, 528; *P.D.,* I, 106–107. The Treaty of London (1604) had ended the Elizabethan wars with Spain.

90. The text of the bill is in *C.D.,* VII, 202–204. For Sandys' West Indian interests, see Prestwich, *op. cit.,* pp. 305 ff, and Theodore K. Rabb, *Enterprise and Empire: Merchant and Gentry Investment in the Expansion of England, 1575–1630* (Cambridge, Mass., 1967), *passim.*

91. *C.D.,* IV, 256. This view was not likely to find much sympathy in the House, 79 of whose members were members also of the Virginia Company. Rabb, *op. cit.,* p. 128.

92. *C.D.,* IV, 256; cf. III, 83.

93. *C.D.,* III, 3. On the depression, see J. D. Gould, "The Trade Depression of the Early 1620's," *Ec.H.R.,* 2d ser., VII, 1 (August, 1954), and Barry E. Supple, *Commercial Crisis and Change in England, 1600–1642* (Cambridge, 1959). Gould argues that a temporary price differential enjoyed by England under Elizabeth, owing to her distance from the center of European inflation, was lost under James, so that English goods rose sharply in price

on the Continental market. "It would doubtless have been possible [writes Gould], given correct policies and resolute action, to have cut English costs; but it is impossible to avoid the conclusion that the period during which English exports enjoyed a price-advantage was largely wasted in a scramble for privileges, and that as that advantage disappeared, England was left saddled with a rigid, oligopolistic, high-cost economy, ill-fitted to cope with a competitor who throve on low costs, adaptability, and up-to-datedness." Supple emphasizes the role of currency debasement, especially in Germany and Poland, which discouraged English exports to those traditionally important markets.

94. *C.D.*, II, 375–377, 385–387; III, 276–277, 297, 300–301. Coke remarked sympathetically of the Cinque Ports' petition against the Merchant Adventurers that there was "no greater Cause in all this Parliament" (*C.J.*, p. 620).

95. *C.D.*, III, 157.

96. *P.D.*, II, 67. For other examples of the striking radicalism of this little-known figure, see *P.D.*, I, 32; *C.D.*, II, 120; III, 42, 164.

97. See chap. v.

98. *C.J.*, p. 592; *C.D.*, III, 87. For the state of legislation at that date, see *C.D.*, IV, 261–264.

99. *D.N.B.*, Floyd; *C.S.P.D.*, pp. 64, 65, 67, 169; *A.P.C.*, V, 42–43, 94, 97, 262. "Goodman" and "Goodwife" were terms of great derision and contempt, used only of the lowest peasantry.

100. *P.D.*, I, 42; *C.J.*, p. 521.

101. *C.D.*, IV, 281–282; V, 366.

102. *C.D.*, V, 117; IV, 278.

103. *C.D.*, III, 120–121; IV, 286. The tract against Coke concerned the patent of John Lepton. For this, see *C.D.*, III, 121; V, 128, 359; II, 261; and above, pp. 157–158.

104. *C.D.*, V, 360; cf. *P.D.*, I, 372.

105. *C.D.*, VI, 120.

106. *P.D.*, I, 374. Cf. *C.D.*, V, 130: "[It was thought] not fitt, though they sent for him, to discharge him of the prison themselfes without the Consent of the Lords of the Counsell."

107. For the entire scene, see *C.J.*, pp. 601–602; *P.D.*, I, 370–374; *C.D.*, II, 335; III, 120–128; IV, 286–287; V, 128–130, 359–361; VI, 119–123.

108. Locke to Carleton, May 5, 1621, S.P. 14/121/13.

109. *C.D.*, III, 134–135; IV, 290; II, 337; VI, 398; *C.J.*, p. 603; *P.D.*, II, 5. The perplexities of Cranfield's dual role are well expressed in this speech: "Yow may thinke that I was ielouse because I desyred presidents [the previous day]. We aboute the chaire, have a heavy burthen for we are Questioned for all things in the house by the King. I received this paper from the King which is a record delivred, I know not by whom, By which it seemes we are much mistaken" (*C.D.*, III, 135).

110. *C.D.*, III, 138–140; *C.J.*, p. 603.

111. *C.D.*, III, 143–146; II, 340; *C.J.*, p. 604; *P.D.*, II, 8–9.

112. *C.D.*, III, 152; cf. V, 138, which confirms the use of the word. Note,

too, the Commons' stated intention to use Floyd as an exemplary warning to all Catholics—precisely the effect James wished to avoid.

113. *C.D.*, III, 152.

114. *C.D.*, III, 137.

115. *C.J.*, p. 606; *C.D.*, III, 152; VI, 132; *P.D.*, II, 14.

116. *C.D.*, IV, 296.

117. *C.J.*, p. 606.

118. Coke, for one. *C.J.*, 604.

119. *C.D.*, III, 155, n. 52.

120. *C.D.*, II, 342–343; III, 155–158; IV, 298.

121. *C.D.*, III, 163–164; *P.D.*, II, 19–20; cf. *C.J.*, p. 607; *C.D.*, V, 366.

122. *C.D.*, VI, 400. The B diarist is an anonymous diarist of the Parliament, so called by Professor Notestein in his seven-volume edition of the records of the House of Commons for 1621. It is not known for certain whether or not he was a member of Parliament.

123. *C.J.*, p. 608 (More); *C.D.*, IV, 304 (Sandys); and cf. *C.J.*, p. 608; *C.D.*, III, 167. Gooch asserted the next day that the House had "the substance of an oth from the witnesses" (*C.D.*, III, 176).

124. *C.D.*, II, 346; III, 168; V, 141; *C.J.*, p. 608; *P.D.*, II, 22.

125. See above, n. 67.

126. *C.D.*, IV, 304.

127. *C.J.*, pp. 608–609; *C.D.*, V, 367.

128. *C.D.*, III, 173.

129. See above, pp. 116 ff.

130. Relf (*L.D. R.*, p. xviii) suggests Noy. Coke and Sandys, who favored going to the Lords from the beginning, had close connections in the Upper House. Sandys was a friend and business associate of Southampton, the leading "opposition" peer. Hakewill, too, had had grave misgivings from the outset of the Floyd affair, and had been at various times a legal consultant to the Lords. John Selden might also have been a go-between; see above, p. 61.

131. *L.D. G.*, p. 66: "Pembroke: 'not to aggravate against them.' Abbot: 'A conference in a temperate, kynde manner.' Saye: 'the caryage of this buissines to be such as may not distast them.'"

132. This was clearly perceived by Sir Thomas Roe in the debate of May 4. "If by this Means the King send this Business to the Lords," he warned, "we shall then exclude ourselves, and the Lords will hence forth deal in such Business without us, and so we shall lose that Privilege" (*P.D.*, II, 21).

133. Chap. ii, pp. 82–84.

134. *P.D.*, II, 26; *C.D.*, III, 173–174.

135. It was Sandys who had suggested that the House ground its case on "reason and precedent" (*C.D.*, III, 155, n. 52). Sandys was reprimanded for this by the Court: "And though I have suffred for useing the word reson, I hould me unto it, for it is that which only makes a man differ from the other creatuers" (*ibid.*, 174).

136. *C.D.*, III, 179–183; IV, 311–314; *P.D.*, II, 30–31. "Note that the Lordes seemed to goe awaye unsatisfied" (*C.D.*, V, 147). Upon returning to the Upper

House, Lord Sheffield commented that "The most parte of the Commons did disavow the most parte what Sir Ed. Cooke spake" (*L.D. G.*, p. 67). It is not clear, however, whether this referred to Coke's speech or his passage with Pembroke. Cf. *C.J.*, pp. 613–614; *C.D.*, V. 155.

137 *L.D. G.*, pp. 69–71; *L.J.*, p. 113. See *L.D. G.*, pp. 74–75, for further debate on the subcommittee.

138. *C.D.*, III, 209–210.

139. *C.J.*, p. 614. Only Noy dissented.

140. *C.J.*, pp. 613–614; *C.D.*, V, 155.

141. *C.D.*, V, 155.

142. *C.D.*, III, 208–209; IV, 320; VI, 401–402; *P.D.*, II, 45–46; *C.J.*, p. 614.

143. *C.D.*, 209–211; *C.J.*, p. 614; *P.D.*, II, 46–47.

144. *C.J.*, p. 619.

145. *Ibid.*

146. *C.D.*, III, 232; *P.D.*, II, 63.

147. *C.D.*, III, 238–240; II, 304; *P.D.*, II, 63–64.

148. *C.J.*, p. 619; *C.D.*, VI, 470. See *C.D.*, III, 203–204, VI, 144–145 for an account of the altercation. Even this interlude was not without its constitutional aspects. The Commons debated earnestly whether or not to examine Coke and Morrison on oath, and Sir Samuel Sandys objected that, by complaining to the Marshal's Court, Morrison had jeopardized the right of the House to punish its own members (*C.J.* p. 612; *C.D.*, III, 187–188).

149. See, for example, *P.D.*, I, 308–309; *C.D.*, III, 68.

150. *L.J.*, p. 134; *C.D.*, V, 386.

151. *Chamberlain*, II, 377.

152. Salvetti Newsletter, June 1/11, 1621. This sentiment had been much in evidence during the Commons' "sentencing" of Floyd. Goring remarked on that occasion, "In civilitie to an Embassadour of a forraine prince of late punished with whippinge, much more this scorne and indignitie to princes themselfes"; and Sir Henry Anderson, "the apprentices whoope at him if theay will" (*C.D.*, V, 129; III, 126).

153. See above, p. 141.

154. *D.N.B.*, Floyd. Despite their disclaimer, the Commons continued to take judicial action against all manner of persons in the 1620s. Yet their procedure was no better defined at the end of the decade than at the beginning. On May 9, 1628, the Commons committed a "scandalous minister," Richard Burgess, Vicar of Whitney, for refusing to answer questions about his conduct to the committee for religion. A debate followed on punishing him. Some suggested petitioning the King; others, sending him to the Lords; others still, to Convocation. His guilt was simply assumed from his refusal to answer; Sir Thomas Wentworth declared that he was "as guilty of the fact, as at common law."

Three days later, a group of Cornish gentry who had conspired against the elections of Sir John Eliot and Sir William Coryton were brought to the bar of the House. The Commons debated whether to grant counsel to the accused. Eliot himself argued that "We cannot deny counsel in any cause but matter of treason." Phelips, however, replied that there was "Neither a necessity for counsel . . . [nor] witnesses . . . but only to view what they have written." Coke assured the Commons that they might so proceed. The defendants were examined, and debate resumed. Selden maintained that they had been in contempt of the House in ignoring a previous summons to appear, and "if a man commits a contempt in any court in the face of the judges: there counsel never allowed." Sir Giles Estcourt was indignant at the very idea: "To ask counsel: both intimate an injustice in this House: as though the justice of this House might be mitigated by counsel." This was a remarkable conception of justice indeed. Ultimately, the House did grant counsel; but these debates are recommended to those who think of Parliament as the bulwark of personal liberty and judicial independence in Stuart England. No more political a court could be imagined. Journal of Sir Richard Grosvenor, III, 109–113, 128–138 (collection of the Yale Parliamentary Diaries Project, Yale University).

Chapter IV: Private Men and Public Good

1. Tillières to Puisieux, April 3/13, 1621, P.R.O. 31/3/54; Salvetti Newsletter, March 30 / April 9; S.P. 14/120/69; Gardiner, IV, 85–87.

2. Sir James Whitelocke, *Liber Famelicus* (Camden Society, 1858), p. 55; *L.D. G.*, p. 47; Spedding, VI, 247.

3. Bacon presided at his trial (November 9–11, 1620). What sort of trial he had may readily be gathered. When one of his lawyers tried to point out that several of the King's learned counsel had had a hand in drawing the patent, he "was snapt up short by my Lord Chanceller And he said that he was ill kept to conclude the cause . . . [and] that it was fitt some wiser man should speake." Bacon rushed the trial to conclusion in an eight-hour sitting; "I have almost killed myself," he reported, " . . . but things passed to his Majesty's great honour." For the trial, see Harl. MSS 6055; S.P. 14/117/71; Spedding, VII, 133–140.

The most violent of Yelverton's judges, however, was Coke, who "made the matter verie fowle," and wanted to fine him £10,000. There had never been any love lost between the two men. In 1617, Yelverton had complained that Coke was plotting against him; he was to denounce him in the Lords on April 30, and later took part in the Lepton plot. Spedding, VI, 247; *L.D. G.*, p. 43; *C.D.*, II, 477; VI, 423.

4. Chap. ii, pp. 63–64.

5. *L.D. R.*, pp. 14–15.

6. A warrant dormant, as the name suggests, was a warrant drawn without a name, a blank check for arrest.

7. *L.J.*, p. 70.

8. *L.J.*, pp. 76–77, 78.

9. Yelverton was accused of having issued 3,400 *quo warrantos* to compel innkeepers to procure licenses from Mompesson. It was confessed, however, that only two of these had ever been prosecuted.

10. *L.J.*, p. 78.

11. *Chamberlain*, II, 366.

12. *C.D.*, II, 309; III, 42–45; IV, 243–245; V, 87; *C.J.*, p. 586; *P.D.*, I, 291–292.

13. *L.J.*, p. 82.

14. *Ibid.*

15. Salvetti Newsletter, April 27 / May 7.

16. See p. 45. Jephson was a close associate of Southampton's. See C. C. Stopes, *The Life of Henry, Third Earl of Southampton . . .* (Cambridge, 1922), pp. 406–409.

17. *C.D.*, III, 89. Coke presented on this occasion one of the most classic formulations of English isolationism ever made: "Lett us looke to make Irland the back doare safe, the Navy well rigd, and the Low Countries our freinds; and we shall not need to Care for Turke, Pope, nor Devill."

18. Cf. the B diarist: "It is thought the Marquis of Buckingham is aimed at" (*C.D.*, VI, 401).

19. *C.D.*, V. 118–119, 356; *P.D.*, I, 356–357.

20. *C.J.*, p. 598; *P.D.*, I, 358–359.

21. Hugh le Despencer, of course, the notorious paramour of Edward II, had gone to the gallows.

22. *L.D. G.*, pp. 42–49; *L.J.*, p. 121; *Chamberlain*, II, 369.

23. *L.D. G.*, p. 52.

24. *L.D. G.*, pp. 54–59; *L.J.*, p. 104.

25. *L.J.*, p. 114.

26. *L.D. G.*, pp. 58, 59.

27. *L.D. G.*, pp. 72–75; S.P. 14/121/15.

28. *Chamberlain*, II, 374–375.

29. *Ibid.*

30. *L.D. G.*, p. 91; *Chamberlain*, II, 375; Salvetti Newsletter, May 18/28, May 25 / June 4, June 8/18; Locke to Carleton, May 26, 1621, S.P. 14/121/54.

31. *L.D. G.*, p. 84. For the entire hearing, *ibid.*, pp. 79–85; *L.J.*, p. 121.

32. *L.D. G.*, pp. 85–86; *L.J.*, p. 123.

33. Yelverton testified on May 14 "that by his closse imprisonment he knewe not of the buissiness on this day" (*L.D. G.*, p. 83). He had been allowed to consult his papers from April 18 to 30 (*ibid.*, p. 78).

34. Thomas Emerson, on May 8. He had been employed as a messenger by Buckingham. Not surprisingly, he contradicted Yelverton's testimony. *L.J.*, p. 115.

35. Sir James Ley, Chief Justice of the King's Bench, had replaced Bacon as Speaker of the Lords in March.

36. *L.D. G.*, pp. 88–90.

37. *L.J.*, p. 125. Buckingham declined the fine.

38. *Chamberlain*, II, 374.

39. See Willson, *Privy Councillors*, pp. 179–188.

40. See the table of peers in office in Lawrence Stone, *The Crisis of the Aristocracy, 1558–1641* (Oxford, 1965), p. 774. Thirty-eight percent of the Tudor-Stuart aristocracy held political positions. Stone quotes Harrington's remark that "A monarchy divested of its nobility has no refuge under Heaven but an army" (*ibid.*, pp. 13–14). The reverse is equally true, as renegade peers were to discover in the 1640s.

41. Stone, *op. cit.*, pp. 479–480.

42. In December, 1621, the Lords refused to receive a petition that came, not from the Commons, but from a plaintiff in the Chancery, Sir John Boucher (*L.J.*, pp. 179, 180, 189; *L.D. G.*, pp. 106–109). The Lords later reversed themselves, however, and "By the time of the third Parliament of Charles, petition had become a regular way of redress against a decree in an inferior court" (*L.D. R.*, p. xxx). In this they were heartily encouraged by the Commons. But, meeting infrequently and uncertainly as they did, and dependent as they were on expert legal advice, the Lords soon found their judicial chores onerous and unrewarding. When in April, 1628, they refused to accept the Commons' resolutions on the Five Knights' Case, they were refraining in effect from overturning a decision in the King's Bench. From this point, the peers decidedly cooled on their role as a judicial cat's-paw for the Commons. The extreme difficulty the Commons had in gaining the Lords' support for the Petition of Right further illustrates this point. See Miss Relf's masterly introduction to the Lords' debates, cited above.

43. With the lone exception of Lewis Bayly, Bishop of Bangor, a man with a mind most emphatically his own.

44. As Arthur Wilson put it, the presence of Charles "did cast an awe" (*History of Great Britain, op. cit.*, p. 161). Compare the reaction, for example, to two almost identical statements by Arundel and Charles in the debate over Yelverton (see above, p. 121). When the Earl said, "That that [*i.e.*, allowing Yelverton to speak] is not necessary, for we have his wordes," he was personally challenged. When the Prince said, "*E contra;* for we have his wordes and are to judg uppon him," there was a murmur of approval: "Agreed per many," noted the Clerk in his margin (*L.D. G.*, pp. 72, 73). Charles's attitude toward Parliament may well have been largely formed by his experience of the Lords in 1621; it is certainly well illustrated in this letter to Buckingham: "The lower house this day has been a little unruly, but I hope it will turn to the best, for before they rose they began to be ashamed of it; yet I could wish that the King would send down a commission here, (that if need were,) such seditious fellows might be made an example to others by Monday next. . . . I have spoken with so many of the Council as the King trusts most, and they [are] all of this mind; only the sending of authority to set seditious fellows fast is of my adding" (Charles to Buckingham, December 3, 1621, Godfrey Goodman, ed., *The Court of King James the First* [London, 1839], II, 209–210).

45. Phelips and Mallett opposed reviving the referee issue (*P.D.*, I, 292).

46. To secure Frederick's compliance in the forthcoming negotiations for the restitution of the Palatinate. Villiers returned in the train of Lord Digby,

who had gone to Brussels in March to lay the groundwork for the negotiations. See chap. v, pp. 142–144.

47. Against the strong advice of Dean Williams, who urged him to remain in Germany for the duration of the session (John Hacket, *Scrinia Reserata: A Memorial Offered to the Great Deservings of John Williams, D.D.* [London, 1692], p. 49).

48. *C.D.*, III, 129–130; IV, 288–289; VI, 124; *C.J.*, pp. 602–603; *P.D.*, II, 2–3.

49. *C.D.*, III, 132 (Sandys); III, 133 (Wentworth); III, 132 (Giles).

50. Dickenson to Carleton, May 7, 1621, S.P. 84/101/21; *C.S.P.V.*, XVII, 53–54; cf. Salvetti, May 11/21.

51. *C.D.*, III, 158.

52. Calvert to Carleton, May 16, 1621, S.P. 84/101/54. On one occasion, Calvert tried to leave the Commons, pleading other business, but was angrily restrained (*C.D.*, VI, 137).

53. The fate of court reform was exemplary. On April 25, the House appointed a new committee "To regulate the Court of Chancery, by Bill"; presumably, its function was to prepare the bills Heath had reported out of the general committee for courts of justice. To this was added the consideration of some compensation claims against the Chancery, and the still-dangling case of Churchill and his fellow registrars. The new committee consisted of Coke, Alford, Thomas Wentworth, Phelips, Hoby, Giles, Sir Miles Fleetwood, Sackville, Rich, Ashley, Roe, Neville, Sir Edwin Sandys, More, May, Withrington, Ravenscroft, Mallory, Wardour, Brooke, Palmes, Carvile, Cavendish, Pym, Sir Francis Barrington, Sir Samuel Sandys, and Poole. Its first meeting was scheduled for April 27, in the Star Chamber (*C.J.*, p. 591).

No record of such a meeting appears. On April 30 it was reassigned for May 2, in the Inner Temple Hall (*C.J.*, p. 596). Once again it failed to meet, for on May 5, another meeting was assigned, "to be upon Tuesday next peremptorily, in the Star-Chamber" (*C.J.*, p. 609). Nevertheless, it was reassigned again on May 9: "Regulating the Court of Chancery:—This afternoon, in the former Place" (*C.J.*, p. 615). Needless to say, this meeting did not take place either.

What happened? On April 27, the House considered the petition of the masters of Chancery for confirmation of their fees. Enraged by the masters' insolence, it appointed a special committee to deal with them, which met that very afternoon. This new committee included Coke, Alford, Phelips, Roe, Poole, and Samuel Sandys, all members of our committee of April 25. Coke and Phelips, moreover, were unable to attend the new committee either, for they were both present that afternoon at the committee for grievances (of which Coke, of course, was chairman). *C.J.*, p. 594; *P.D.*, I, 336–344.

On May 2 and 5, the rescheduled committee meetings were put off by Floyd's case. On May 9, according to John Smyth, there were "Dyvers Comittees, as Mr. Horsemans [a private bill], Against Cart takyng [purveyance], and others." One of the others, as Barrington informs us, was the committee for a bill for standardizing the production of arms *(C.D.,* V, 372; III, 219).

Horseman's committee included Poole, More, and Carvile, all members of the Chancery committee. The committee against cart taking included Coke, More, and Phelips. The committee for arms had eight members of the chancery committee: Coke, Alford, Giles, Carvile, More, Cavendish, Sackville, and Withrington *(C.J.,* pp. 563, 585, 543). All of these committees had seniority on the chancery committee; all had been postponed at least once; and one, the committee for arms, had been waiting for two months. In the crush, the Chancery committee evidently lost out again.

This conclusion is confirmed by Alford's motion for the committee on May 28. He was seconded by Giles, Phelips, and Sandys, who agreed warmly that the committee meet before the end of the session. Coke called it the most pressing business in the House *(C.D.,* III, 326–327, 329). But the phantom committee never did meet. On May 30, its fifth assigned date, the House was once again deep in controversy. A few days later, it was adjourned.

54. There were two standing committees for trade, one chaired by Cranfield, the other, by Sir Edwin Sandys. As Cranfield was an unabashed supporter of the London companies, and Sandys the champion of the Outports, the committees were often at cross-purposes. Coke's committee for grievances, which of course dealt heavily with economic matters, was occasionally able to throw its weight behind Sandys (see above, p. 103). Cranfield held the clear, if not correct, position that England was suffering from an excess of luxury imports *(C.D.,* II, 89). Sandys, of course, blamed all on the London monopolists. Before their respective committees came an endless babel of frightened businessmen, each with a scheme to save his own neck. "There are 75 Lawes for clothing," Cranfield pleaded, "lett us make one good law oute of all them." But in truth, neither one law nor seventy-five would have mattered much. See p. 209, n. 93.

55. *C.D.,* V. 190. The bill for Welsh butter was to free that commodity from a monopoly.

56. See above, p. 65.

57. "Penned by Coke" *(C.D.,* V, 290), but Noy and Crew also had a hand in it *(C.D.,* IV, 160).

58. *H.J.,* p. 26.

59. *C.J.,* p. 533.

60. Printed in *C.D.,* VII, 491–496.

61. *L.D.,* G. p. 151.

62. *C.D.,* II, 228–229.

63. W. Hyde Price, *The English Patents of Monopoly, op. cit.,* p. 24.

64. *C.D.,* II, 219.

65. *C.J.,* p. 554.

66. Sir Edward Coke, *The Third Part of the Institutes of England* (London, 1660), chap. lxxxv, p. 181.

67. *C.D.,* IV, 197. This change does not appear in the House of Lords manuscript printed by Gardiner *(L.D. G.,* pp. 151–155), which states that

proscribed grants and proclamations "ought to be and shalbe for ever hereafter examyned, hard, tryed, and determyned by *and according to the common lawes* of this realme, and not *otherwyse.*" The emphasis is Gardiner's, and is used to denote interlineation. It would thus appear that this manuscript represents a stage of the bill prior to March 26.

68. *C.D.,* IV, 197.

69. Price, *op. cit.,* p. 17, n. 4; p. 27.

70. *C.D.,* IV, 198; *C.J.,* 575.

71. Hacket, p. 49.

72. *P.D.,* II, 240.

73. *C.D.,* III, 193.

74. What made this incident possible was the rather careless practice of letting members "borrow" bills in preparation from the Clerk. But it produced an order that engrossed bills could henceforth be read only in the Clerk's presence *(C.D.,* II, 354).

75. *C.J.,* p. 619.

76. Lord Keeper Williams asked "Whe[ther] the clause for the future trenches into the Prerogative of his Majestie? Conceaves veryly yt dothe." Statutes might declare such and such an act illegal; they could not declare the royal power behind that act illegal.

77. See above, p. 163.

78. For the Lords' debate, see *L.D. G.,* pp. 102–105, 106.

79. *C.J.,* p. 794 (May 25, 1624). The text of the Act is printed in Price, pp. 135–141.

80. C. H. McIlwain, *Constitutionalism, Ancient and Modern* (Ithaca, 1940), p. 138. For an account of the monopoly bill's enactment, see E. R. Foster, "The Procedure of the House of Commons against Patents and Monopolies, 1621–1624," in W. A. Aiken and B. D. Henning, eds., *Conflict in Stuart England: Essays in honour of Wallace Notestein* (London, 1960), pp. 57–85. Associated with the 1621 bill was a smaller one to confirm Magna Carta, *cap.* 29. This had grown out of the imprisonment of those who resisted the thread patent. It serves as an interesting commentary on the evolution of Coke's thought. When the bill was brought for its second reading on May 5, Coke noted that it "trenches so deepe that a man for any cause of State not be imprisoned but theay must shew ther reason" *(C.D.,* III, 172). This, he thought, was "very dangerous, for matters of state ought not to be inserted in a *mittimus*" (IV, 139–140). It exceeded the reasonable interpretation of Magna Carta, and controverted the rule set down in Poynges' Case (33 H. 6) : "Yf a man be Committed by the bodye of the Counsell he is not to be bayled, neither are they to set downe the Cause in the *Mittimus* (IV, 308; see also *C.J.,* pp. 609–610).

Here again, Alford is in advance of Coke. His words ring prophetically of 1628: "That we may explain what shall be matters of State, for if proclamations may committ a man or the least matters of state unknowne, *pereat Res[publica]* and lett us be Villaines" *(C.D.,* III, 324; cf. *P.D.,* II, 109).

81. And not only the mob; the Privy Council chastised the city govern-

ment for harassing members of the diplomatic corps as if they were subject to English recusancy laws *(A.P.C.,* V, 360–361).

82. Mead to Stuteville, February 10, 1621, Harl. MSS 389.

83. First published in 1599. The book was translated into Italian by Paolo Sarpi, the famous historian of the Catholic Reformation, with whom Sandys became friendly on his travels. *D.N.B.*

84. *C.D.,* III, 161.

85. See above, pp. 44–45.

86. *Public General Acts, James I, 1604–1624.*

87. *L.J.,* p. 122. The text of the bill is in *C.D.,* VII, 61–65.

88. Pym provides a clear summary of the draft provisions of the bill *(C.D.,* IV, 214).

89. *C.D.,* II, 276.

90. *C.S.P.V.,* XVII, 54.

91. Salvetti Newsletter, May 25 / June 4.

92. *Ibid.*

93. *Chamberlain,* II, 379. Cf. Lando, *C.S.P.V.,* XVII, 66.

94. Rudyard to Nethersole, April 13, 1621, S.P. 14/120/82.

95. Cf. the B diarist: "Some great reason of state there is for this sudden breaking of, if we knew it. A gesse there is that the King wold not have such strict lawes yet to come forth against the Papists as the house is in hand with and that he wold not willingly deny to passe them. Only, in policie of state, his desire may be to stay them for some time to see what will be done by faire meanes for the Palatinate and for the Match. For it were better the King of Spaine shold breake without cause then with pretext of cause, that his Sister and her Servants of that religion might by the hard usage of our own Papists (as they will call it) feare such a measure toward themselves. But these things are supra Nos, and so leave them" *(C.D.,* VI, 406).

96. *C.D.,* IV, 383. A month later, Sir Richard Weston still wrote of "the sudden, & much wondered at" adjournment. Weston to Aston, June 25, 1621, B.M. Add. MSS 36445, f. 148.

97. *C.D.,* III, 329.

98. *Ibid.*

99. *C.D.,* III, 329–334; II, 399–400; IV, 384–385; V, 181–182; *P.D.,* II, 114–115; *C.J.,* p. 629.

100. *C.J.,* p. 631; *C.D.,* II, 405; IV, 399.

101. *C.D.,* III, 344.

102. *Ibid.*

103. *P.D.,* II, 122.

104. *C.D.,* III, 347–348; cf. *P.D.,* II, 123–124.

105. *C.D.,* II, 408–409 (Gooch); III, 354 (Alford); II, 410 (Crane).

106. *C.D.,* III, 352–355; *C.J.,* pp. 631–632.

107. An apparent reference to James's statement that he could no longer spare his councillors for duty in Parliament.

108. *C.D.,* III, 355; cf. II, 410; *P.D.,* II, 128; *C.J.,* p. 632.

109. *L.J.,* p. 153.

110. *C.D.*, III, 403–404; *C.J.*, p. 637.

111. *P.D.*, II, 165–166; *C.D.*, II, 427.

112. *C.D.*, III, 385; cf. II, 419–420; IV, 403. Noy claimed that it would be "a Determination of the Sessions" (*P.D.*, II, 148; cf. *C.D.*, III, 385; *C.J.*, p. 635.

113. See above, p. 54. *C.D.*, III, 373–376; IV, 399; *P.D.*, II, 140–143; *C.J.*, p. 634. On May 8, Cranfield warned those whom he claimed had misrepresented certain remarks of his that "I will in dew time call them to accompt for it." His assertion was aimed at Sandys, who replied: "It pleased this honorable person to deliver somwhat in the Clouds that touches upon me. We argewd pro and con, and it is not fitt to Question any thing afterward. I would Answer heear. I spake as an honest man and so I will defend it" (*C.D.*, III, 206–207). On May 29, Cranfield was cried down in the House when he tried to speak after a speech by Sandys (*P.D.*, II, 122). His very presence in the House had become an all but intolerable irritant by this time. A friend and fellow MP, Sir Arthur Ingram, wrote him next day: "Let me entreat your honour to be at the house today and that you will likewise be pleased to be careful that if you speak, it may be with such moderation as may give no cause of exception. . . . hearing what I have, I could not do less out of the true respect I bear you than to write these few lines to you" (*C.D.*, III, 358, n. 19). Nonetheless, Cranfield began that day: "If any man have a mind to discontent the King and the country and to hinder all good, he may further us to this discontented departure. . . . I thinke many wise men in the house know how and by whom we are now interrupted and diverted" (*C.D.*, III, 363).

114. *C.D.*, III, 390; IV, 406–407. Cf. Phelips: " . . . I hope every man stands upon the strength of his owne innocence, and if the King heear, he hath 2 eares, one to receive information, another to receive trew information" (*C.D.*, III, 392).

115. *C.D.*, V, 392.

116. Delbridge lamented that "he had rather he were in heaven than to carry such news to the country" (*C.D.*, II, 406). Sir Samuel Sandys would not go that far, but averred "that, if he had any other Place to go, he would not go into his Country with empty Hands" (*P.D.*, II, 116). The sense of having been duped was especially bitter. If the 1614 Parliament had gotten nothing, said Sandys, at least it had given nothing up, whereas now Parliament would be "a Mock and a Scorn to the Country."

117. *P.D.*, II, 168–169.

118. *P.D.*, II, 169–170; *C.J.*, p. 639; *C.D.*, IV, 415.

119. *C.J.*, p. 639. See the Appendix for the text of this declaration.

120. *C.J.*, p. 639; *P.D.*, II, 163.

121. *P.D.*, II, 174.

122. *C.D.*, II, 430. When James first heard of the declaration, he flew into a rage, taking it as a parting shot at his religious policy, and a wanton interference in his conduct of foreign affairs. But, on reading a copy, he changed his mind. It was respectfully framed, and would make excellent propaganda. It would also help keep Gondomar and the Spanish on their toes.

Chamberlain, II, 381; *C.S.P.V.*, 67, 71; Calvert to Aston, June 26, 1621, B.M. Add. MSS 36445, f. 151.

123. "The Report of the Royal Commission on Clothing," S.P. 14/131/55 and Stowe MSS. 554, f. 45 ff.

124. S.P. 14/121/122, 125. Solicitor Heath found 79 patents not mentioned in Parliament, as well as 17 mentioned but never considered.

125. The proclamation is printed in Price, *op. cit.*, pp. 166–168. Some of those condemned in Parliament were spared, for example, Sir Robert Mansell's glass patent and John Lambe's extortion racket in the Prerogative Court of Canterbury. Mansell was exempted for his service at sea (above, pp. 15–16). See *A.P.C.*, V, 400–401; VI, 8, 17–18; S.P. 14/121/11. Lambe had a friend at Court, Williams. The new Lord Keeper not only got the charges against Lambe dropped, but had him made a doctor at Cambridge, and shortly thereafter a knight. Sir Edward Montagu, who had brought the complaint against Lambe first to Parliament and then before the Council, at last dissuaded his clients from further effort: "If we tamper the third time, his great friend that hath already made him a Doctor and a Knight, I fear will make him a Baron" (Hacket, p. 37). Even Hacket, Williams' idolatrous biographer, admits that in this case his hero shielded a skunk. Lambe lived to turn on his patron, achieve high office himself, and in his old age nearly suffer impeachment with Laud. *D.N.B.*, Lambe. For the petitions against Lambe, see *C.D.*, VII, 471–476; for parliamentary debate and action, *ibid.*, III, 262–266; IV, 346–349. Lambe's defense before the Council is in VII, 606–609. For his knighthood, see *Cabala*, 260.

126. See above, p. 69.

127. Proclamation of February 14, 1623. Printed in Price, pp. 169–170.

128. Birch, II, 259–261. Rumor had Hakewill and Samuel Sandys arrested, and it was said that Coke had been sequestered from the Council. But the arrests were confined to three. James would clearly have loved to deal with Coke, but Sir Edward was still too powerful. For awhile James toyed with the idea of sending him on a commission to Ireland. It was also rumored that Sir Edwin Sandys would go (Locke to Carleton, September 29, 1621, S.P. 14/122/152). In the end, he decided to wait.

129. Southampton's Interrogation, S.P. 14/121/136 (printed in *P.D.*); Birch, II, 266; Salvetti Newsletter, June 22 / July 2; Calvert to Aston, June 25, 1621, B.M. Add. MSS 36445, f. 151.

130. Birch, II, 260, 265, 267–268.

131. Stone, *Crisis of the Aristocracy, op. cit*, p. 480; Williams to Buckingham, November 13, 1621, *Fortescue Papers*, p. 166. Apparently, Williams was a moderating influence on Southampton, Buckingham, and the King alike: Hacket, pp. 68–69; *Cabala*, 259–261; *Chamberlain*, II, 390, 411.

132. Hacket, pp. 69–70.

133. Birch, II, 264.

134. Mansell to Aston, July 25, 1621, B.M. Add. MSS 36445, f. 187.

135. Craven, *Dissolution of the Virginia Company, op. cit.*, pp. 95–96, 236–237.

136. Southampton on July 18, Sandys and Selden on July 20. The for-

mer two were confined to their estates, Southampton at Tichfield (under the surveillance of Sir William Parkhurst), Sandys at Kent. *A.P.C.*, VI, 21, 23, 24.

137. Williams was sworn in on July 10 (*ibid.*, pp. 11–12). He also became Bishop of Lincoln.

138. Hacket, pp. 69–70; *Chamberlain,* II, 389–390, 395; *C.S.P.V.*, XVII, 108.

139. *Chamberlain,* II, 396: "The common people . . . continue to take no notice of yt."

140. *C.S.P.V.*, XVII, 117.

Chapter V: The Dissolution

1. Princes of the Union to Ferdinand II, January 29 / February 8, 1621, S.P. 81/20/108; to Maximilian of Bavaria, same date, *ibid.*, f. 125; and so forth. The ban is printed in M. C. Londorp, ed., *Acta Publica . . .* (Frankfurt-am-Main, 1668), II, 307 ff.

2. The treaty is in B.M. Add. MSS 35832, f. 71 (Latin), f. 73 (English).

3. *Ibid.* Digby had negotiated this arrangement on a visit to Brussels in March (Gardiner, IV, 189).

4. Digby to the Lords Commissioners for the affairs of Germany, July 26, 1621, in O. Ogle and W. H. Bliss, *Calendar of the Clarendon Papers* (London, 1872), I, Appendix, p. vi.

5. The above analysis is based on Digby's correspondence from Vienna (S.P. 80/4), and is set out in greater detail in a forthcoming paper, "Interest of State: James I and the Palatinate."

6. Frederick to James, April 2/12, 1621, S.P. 81/20/331.

7. Digby to Calvert, August 12, 1621, S.P. 80/4/162.

8. Gardiner, IV, 219; S.P. 81/22/82, 109–111; 84/103/56–8, 61.

9. Digby to Calvert, October 21–24, 1621, S.P. 77/14/524; James to Philip IV, November 12/22, 1621, P.R.O. 31/12/21.

10. Digby to Calvert, October 21–24; same to same, September 5, S.P. 80/4/216.

11. Calvert to Carleton, November 5, 10, 1621, S.P. 84/103/211, 243; Digby to Carleton, November 6, S.P. 84/103/215.

12. Earl of Leicester to Viscount Lisle, September 3, 1621, H. M. C. *Buccleuch,* III, 425.

13. Proclamation, October 6, 1621, S.P. 14/123/17.

14. Gondomar's account of Parliament bore down heavily on this; James had ordered his justices of assize to be especially lenient with recusants on their summer circuits. Gondomar to Philip IV, July 9/19, 1621, P.R.O. 31/12/24; Calvert to Aston, June 26, 1621, B.M. Add. MSS 36445, f. 151.

15. Gardiner, IV, 294.

16. Proclamation, November 3, 1621, S.P. 187, no. 98.

17. Locke to Carleton, November 3 1621, S.P. 14/123/85.

18. Speaker Richardson and about 200 MPs assembled at nine o'clock

on November 14, to hear Parliament formally put off until the following Tuesday. A motion was made to issue writs for elections to replace three newly created barons, Cranfield, Greville, and Montagu. Horsey also moved to have a preacher selected to deliver a sermon on the twentieth, but the House refused to consider business. *C.J.*, p. 640; *C.D.*, IV, 417–418.

19. *C.S.P.V.*, XVII, 168; *Chamberlain*, II, 408, 411.

20. Cranfield was elevated to the peerage as Baron Cranfield in July, and replaced Mandeville as Lord Treasurer in September.

21. In fact, as a royal investigation had revealed, it was on the verge of rebellion, and the Lord Deputy was desperately appealing for arms (*A.P.C.*, VI, 84–85, 88–91, 93–94).

22. *C.D.*, III, 415.

23. *P.D.*, II, 189; *C.D.*, VI, 418.

24. In fact, with the approach of winter, the government was bracing itself for food riots. *A.P.C.*, VI, 77–78, 87–88.

25. *P.D.*, II, 185; *C.D.*, IV, 425.

26. *P.D.*, II, 189; *C.D.*, IV, 428.

27. For Williams' speech, see *P.D.*, II, 183–186; *C.D.*, III, 414–418; IV, 423–425; for Cranfield's, see *P.D.*, II, 188–190; *C.D.*, III, 424–426; IV, 428–429; for Digby's, see *P.D.*, II, 186–188; *C.D.*, III, 419–424; IV, 426–428. Notes for Cranfield's speech appear in *C.D.*, VII, 617–619. His official optimism "was thought somwhat straunge," observed Chamberlain, "when all or most of the hearers knew the realme was never so bare and poore since he was borne." He had little better to say of the Lord Keeper or the Ambassador Extraordinary. Williams spoke "more like a divine than a statesman or an orator"; Digby "not with that confidence that was expected from a man of so great employment" (II, 410).

28. *P.D.*, II, 197–198; *C.D.*, II, 441; III, 434–435.

29. *C.D.*, III, 430.

30. "I am required to tell you," Calvert wrote him, *"that it is his Majesty's pleasure* yow faile not to be at the Lower howse tomorrow morning [italics in original]." Calvert apologized in a postscript for the harshness of the directive, saying that he was merely transmitting it as he had received it. Caesar Papers, B.M. Add. MSS 34324, f. 290. With the departure of Cranfield and Greville, and the defection of Coke, the number of councillors in the Commons had fallen to four. Weston replaced Greville in a special election, but was of little help.

31. *P.D.*, II, 210–213; *C.D.*, III, 490–492; IV, 437. Cf. V, 211: "Bavier is but a pettie prince and cannot move but by that great engine of Spaine." Phelips certainly knew better than this. He was scarcely a Puritan, for all the poses he struck in the House, and was well versed diplomatically—had, indeed, been a part of Digby's entourage in Spain in 1618, and was to be again in 1623. For the twists and turns of this enigmatic figure, see K. S. van Eerde, "The Spanish Match Through an English Protestant's Eyes," *H.L.Q.*, XXXII, 1 (November, 1968).

32. For the Puritan-Country view of foreign affairs in general, see Martin

Arthur Breslow, *A Mirror of England: English Puitan Views of Foreign Nations, 1618–1640* (Cambridge, Mass., 1970).

33. *C.J.*, p. 646; *C.D.*, V, 214.

34. Tillières identified the three leaders in Parliament in December as Coke, Phelips, and *"un certain nommé Criou"* (Tillières to Puisieux, December 4/14, 1621, P.R.O. 31/3/55).

35. *C.D.*, VI, 199.

36. *C.D.*, II 451.

37. *C.D.*, V, 214.

38. *C.D.*, V, 405, 214; cf. *P.D.*, II, 217.

39. *C.D.*, IV, 441; *C.J.*, p. 647; *P.D.*, II, 217; *C.D.*, III, 459–460. A draft of Edmondes' speech is printed in *C.D.*, VII, 619.

40. *C.D.*, IV, 441–443; V, 216; II, 453, n. c. Note also the crucial speech by Neale which preceded Pym's, and cleverly smudged the issue raised by Edmondes: *ibid.*, IV, 441; V, 215; *P.D.*, II, 218.

41. *C.D.*, V, 215.

42. *C.D.*, IV, 443.

43. George Goring (1583?–1663) began life as a gentleman pensioner at Elizabeth's Court and ended it as Earl of Norwich. Thirty-four of his letters to Buckingham are extant in the Harleian MSS. He felt bold enough in Buckingham's favor to reprove Sackville for flirting with the "opposition" in March on his own initiative, even threatening him with the Marquis' displeasure (Harl. MSS 1580, f. 422). It was Goring too who, perhaps carried away by the spirit of the occasion, devised the most sadistic punishment of all for Floyd (above, p. 105).

44. Harl. MSS 1580, f. 428.

45. *P.D.*, II, 230–241. Pym's diary breaks off in the middle of his speech (*C.D.*, IV, 447–448). See also *C.D.*, II, 461–464. Chamberlain reported that Pym "had great attention and was excedingly commended both for matter and manner" (II, 412). James ordered a copy of the speech.

46. *P.D.*, II, 241.

47. *C.D.*, V, 214; *C.J.*, p. 654. Wentworth's remark was made on November 26, Mallory's on December 1. Cf. John Glanville: "And not to have adiourning and calling and adjourning one upon another withoute any thing donn, to our sham[e] in future ages" (*C.D.*, III, 456).

48. *C.D.*, V, 214.

49. Harl. MSS 1580, f. 401; cf. *C.J.*, p. 652.

50. "Accordinge to your Lordship's last directions, I did with all care and dilligence I possibly coulde, make this proposition" (Goring to Buckingham, November 29, 1621, Harl. MSS 1580, f. 401).

51. Gardiner, IV, 265, n. 2.

52. *C.D.*, II, 474–476.

53. Calvert to Doncaster, December 27, 1621, B.M. Egerton MSS 2595, f. 7.

54. *C.J.*, p. 655; *P.D.*, II, 267; *C.D.*, V, 228; VI, 220.

55. How much James learned, and through whom, is uncertain. It is diffi-

cult to see how he could have failed to learn, sooner or later, that Buckingham's minion was responsible for the Commons' petition, yet neither Goring nor Buckingham appear to have ever suffered from such a disclosure.

56. *C.D.*, VII, 625.

57. *C.D.*, II, 487–488; VI, 220; *P.D.*, II, 269; *C.J.*, 655.

58. *C.D.*, VI, 220: "He was hemmed at."

59. *C.J.*, p. 656.

60. *C.D.*, II, 488–489, 492–493, 494–495.

61. *P.D.*, II 274; *C.D.*, II, 497.

62. *C.D.*, II, 493.

63. *C.D.*, II, 491; *P.D.*, II, 271.

64. *C.D.*, II, 498.

65. *C.J.*, p. 657.

66. *C.D.*, II, 498–499. The Journal gives Compton, Manners, and Villiers for Clifford, Fane, and Vane. Professor Notestein argues for the list
given in the X diary *(C.D.*, II, 499, n. 33). Nicholas gives fourteen members,
omitting Vane and adding Sir Thomas Howard, Sir John Hayward, and
Lord Compton *(P.D.*, II, 276).

67. *C.J.*, p. 658. For the petition, see John Rushworth, ed., *Historical
Collections* (London, 1721–1722), I, 40–43, henceforth cited as Rushworth.

68. Rushworth, I, 43–44.

69. *P.D.*, II, 278–279; *C.J.*, 658; *C.D.*, VI, 224.

70. *C.D.*, II, 491.

71. *C.D.*, III, 195. The House confirmed this *(ibid.*, 245). See *C.D.*, VII,
394–395 for a schedule of the patent, 508–511 for complaints against it. The
history of the patent is summarized in R. R. Reid, *The King's Council in
the North* (London, 1921), pp. 383–385.

72. *C.D.*, V, 319.

73. The patent was referred to a committee consisting of Falkland, Edmondes, Cranfield, and Calvert. There is no record of their proceedings, if
any, and in November the patent was reported to be still functioning (S.P.
14/121/110; *C.D.*, II, 473).

74. The eleven charges in the suit are listed in *C.D.*, VI, 422.

75. *Ibid.*, 422–423; *C.J.*, p. 654.

76. *C.J.*, p. 644; *P.D.*, II, 201.

77. *C.D.*, II, 471, 511. The other counsel were Serjeant Ashley, Sir Henry
Yelverton, and one William Hudson, who claimed to have been dragooned
into the plot against his will (VI, 423). Yelverton was no doubt being given
a chance to redeem himself, and doubtless too he welcomed the chance to
settle scores with the man who had persecuted him in Star Chamber a year
before.

78. Calvert read the King's letter in the House on December 7 *(P.D.*, II,
294). It had been in his possession, however, since the morning of the
fourth *(C.D.*, VII, 621), and James had alluded to its contents in his message on the Commons' petition that day as well.

79. *C.D.*, V, 206; III, 436–438.

80. *C.D.*, II, 483–486; VI, 218; *C.J.*, p. 654; *P.D.*, II, 259.
81. *P.D.*, II, 279.
82. *Ibid.*, 279–281; *C.J.*, p. 658.
83. *P.D.*, II, 283. It may well have been a punishment. The House was irked with Noy, perhaps for his moderation on December 3, certainly for an ironic remark about the papist son of the Archbishop of York, Tobie Matthew, which, reported Chamberlain, gained him "nothing but the reputation to favor or savour of that sect" (*Chamberlain*, II, 412). In any event, it silenced a moderate voice. Digges had also been forcibly hoisted into the Chair on one occasion (November 26), and "tooke it as a Reprehencion of his too much speakeinge that they would put him into a place of silence" (*C.D.*, IV, 447).
84. *P.D.*, II, 284.
85. *Ibid.*, 286.
86. *Ibid.*, 286–287.
87. *P.D.*, II, 287; *C.D.*, II, 504; VI, 225; V, 234.
88. *P.D.*, II, 288.
89. I.e., the right to punish its own members.
90. *Ibid.*, 289; Rushworth, I, 44–46.
91. *C.D.*, III, 112–113.
92. *C.J.*, p. 659.
93. Above, pp. 145–146.
94. *P.D.*, II, 305.
95. *C.D.*, II, 510.
96. *C.D.*, VII, 625. It was a sad commentary on the decline of royal influence in the House. James had taken deliberate care that all eligible members of the Privy Council should secure seats in the Commons. Eight were elected, the highest number of any Jacobean parliament, but only six actually served. Henry Cary was raised to a Scottish peerage as Viscount Falkland on the eve of Parliament, and when his eligibility was questioned in the Commons, he did not contest it (*C.D.*, II, 32, 36–37; IV, 25–26; V, 5–6; VI, 438; Goodman, II, 201; Willson, *Privy Councillors*, p. 65; "Note on Falkland," February 6, 1621, S.P. 14/119). Sir Robert Naunton was suspended from office in mid-January under clouded circumstances and placed under house arrest. The Commons talked of investigating his restraint as a breach of privilege, but the horrified secretary begged the House to make his situation no worse by angering the King (*C.D.*, IV, 18; Goodman, II, 225–227. By autumn, the six councillors had dwindled to four, and the dutiful Calvert was the only one who could really be counted on (see above, note 30).

Below the conciliar level, there were a few officials of high rank—for example, Sir Humphrey May, Chancellor of the Duchy of Lancaster and later a councillor himself—whose adherence to the government line, when there was one, could be counted on. But even this was not certain; Solicitor Heath took some startlingly "popular" positions in the House (*e.g.*, above p. 79), and was nearly dismissed for his behavior at the end of Parliament (*Chamberlain,* II, 549). And further down in the ranks, among the petty officeholders and marginal courtiers, there was, as G. E. Aylmer observes, "no assumption that all officials either should or would support the Crown's policy" (Aylmer, "Place Bills and the Separation of Powers: Some Seventeenth-Century Origins of the 'non-political' Civil Service," *T.R.H.S.,* V, 15 [1965], p. 46). The early Stuart period was thus a transitional one in terms of royal influence in the Commons. The mere presence of a privy councillor in the House no longer awed the Commons, as it once had, and the day of the placeman—the politically disciplined office-holder—had not yet come. What stymied the Crown in Parliament then was much less a failure of royal competence or will than a breakdown of the machinery for getting that will across.

97. *C.J.,* pp. 659–660.

98. *C.J.,* p. 660.

99. *Ibid.; P.D.,* II, 297–298.

100. *P.D.,* II, 296–299.

101. *P.D.,* II, 300.

102. *Ibid.; C.J.,* p. 661.

103. Maurice Berkeley, MP for Gloucestershire; Thomas Mallett, MP for Tregony Borough, Cornwall; Sir Henry Spiller, MP for Arundel Borough, Sussex, and an Exchequer official.

104. See chap. iii, pp. 129–130.

105. *C.J.,* 661; *P.D.,* II, 301–302; *C.D.,* II, 508.

106. " . . . there is no great good correspondencie between the two howses" (Locke to Carleton, December 8, 1621, S.P. 14/124/22). Cf. *C.J.,* p. 663; *C.D.,* II, 521.

107. Cranfield to Buckingham, December 4, 1621, Goodman, II, 210. Cf. Williams to Buckingham, December 16: "In our House his Majesty's Servants are very strong, and increase every day; nor is there the least fear of any malignant Opposition" (*Cabala,* 264).

108. *P.D.,* II, 302–303; *C.D.,* II, 508–509.

109. *C.D.,* VI, 230; cf. V, 413; *P.D.,* II, 303.

110. *C.D.,* VI, 230; *P.D.,* II, 304.

111. *C.D.,* II, 513–514; *P.D.,* II, 311.

112. *C.J.,* p. 661.

113. *P.D.,* II, 311; *C.D.,* V, 235.

114. *C.D.,* VI, 234; II, 514; *P.D.,* II, 311–312.

115. *C.J.,* p. 662; *P.D.,* II, 312; *C.D.,* V, 236.

116. *C.J.,* p. 662; *P.D.,* II, 313.

117. *C.D.,* V, 236.

118. *C.J.,* p. 662.

119. A reply to the King's order for Goldsmith's release had been drafted (*C.D.,* V, 236–237). But, in its indecision—and much to Pym's disgust (*C.J.,* p. 663)—the House could not decide whether to send it.

120. *Chamberlain,* II, 414.

121. *C.J.,* p. 663; *C.D.,* V, 237–238.

122. Rushworth, I, 46–52.

123. *C.J.*, p. 663. On the pardon, cf. *C.D.*, VII, 626; *A.P.C.*, VI, 101–102.

124. *C.J.*, p. 663.

125. *P.D.*, II, 328. Gardiner quotes this sentence *(History of England, IV,* 255) in such a way as to suggest that Phelips was supporting the King. In the full context of the speech, it is clear that he was doing just the reverse.

126. *C.J.*, p. 663; cf. *C.D.*, II, 520.

127. *C.J.*, p. 663; *P.D.*, II, 329.

128. *P.D.*, II, 330.

129. *Ibid.; C.D.*, II, 521; *C.J.*, p. 664.

130. *P.D.*, II, 331.

131. *C.J.*, p. 664; *P.D.*, II, 331–333; *C.D.*, II, 522–523.

132. *P.D.*, II, 333–335; *C.D.*, II, 524; VI, 238–239; V, 238–239; *C.J.*, pp. 664–665.

133. *P.D.*, II, 336. The Journal, however, had the walls blushing.

134. *C.D.*, V, 240. Cf. VI, 240: "I will not Contend with my soveraigne for words, but if he will not allowe me my Inheritance I must Fly to Magna Charta and entreat an explanacion of his Majestie of those words I doe not allowe."

135. *C.J.*, p. 665; *P.D.*, II, 335–336; *C.D.*, VI, 239.

136. *C.J.*, p. 666.

137. He arrived the night of December 15: "His Majesty cometh this Night to Royston" *(C.J.*, p. 666).

138. Williams to Buckingham, December 16, 1621, *Cabala*, 264.

139. The phrase "wrangling lawyers" was still, it will be noted, a favorite of James's. It was the same one Bacon had tried to get him to delete a year before from the original proclamation for Parliament (above, p. 28, n. 72).

140. *P.D.*, II, 339–341; *C.D.*, II, 528–530.

141. *P.D.*, II, 341–343.

142. *C.D.*, VI, 335. Cf. Crew: "This were to make us . . . tenants att will" *(ibid.).*

143. *C.J.*, pp. 666–667; *C.D.*, VI, 335.

144. *P.D.*, II, 347–350.

145. "Howe," asked Glanville, "shall this letter give more security for the tyme to come, Then the other, which Mr. Secretary brought for the tyme past" *(C.D.*, VI, 335).

146. *C.D.*, V, 241; VI, 243.

147. *C.D.*, VI, 244; *C.J.*, p. 667; *P.D.*, II, 347.

148. *P.D.*, II, 350–352, italics mine.

149. See above, p. 145.

150. *C.D.*, VI, 337. Cf. the final passage of the King's letter in B *(C.D.,* VI, 425): "But tell them, Mr. Speaker, from us, that if they shall not apply their time instantly and use that well, which is not theirs but ours, we will without expectation of any further answere from them construe their slacknes to no desire of any Session and lay the fault upon the committers of it."

151. *C.D.*, VI, 337; *P.D.*, II, 352–353.

152. *C.D.*, VI, 339.

153. *C.D.*, VI, 339–340; *P.D.*, II, 354.

154. *P.D.*, II, 354–355.

155. *P.D.*, II, 357–359; *C.D.*, II, 540–542; V, 244; VI, 342–343.

156. Rushworth, I, 54.

157. *P.D.*, II, 359–361.

158. *C.D.*, II, 539–540; V, 244.

159. *C.D.*, II, 543; *P.D.*, II, 361–362.

160. *P.D.*, II, 362.

161. *C.D.*, V, 243.

162. *C.D.*, II, 544–545; V, 245–246; *P.D.*, II, 363–364.

163. Rushworth, I, 53.

164. *C.D.*, II, 524, 525, 526, 533, 541; V, 239, 241, 242, 418; VI, 239–240, 243, 338, 341; *C.J.*, pp. 665, 667; *P.D.*, II, 334, 336, 338, 346–347, 355.

165. This fact is made much of in G. R. Elton's essay, "A High Road to Civil War?" in C. H. Carter, ed., *From the Renaissance to the Counter-Reformation: Essays in Honor of Garrett Mattingly* (New York, 1965). But the Apology was far from being esoteric, and Hakewill at least had a private copy which he brought to Parliament.

166. J. R. Tanner, *Constitutional Documents of the Reign of James I 1603–1625* (London, 1930), p. 221.

167. *Ibid.*, p. 222.

168. For a penetrating discussion of the seventeenth-century concept of fundamental law, see J. G. A. Pocock, *The Ancient Constitution and the Feudal Law* (Cambridge, 1957). For opposed views on the influence of Magna Carta, see Faith Thompson, *Magna Carta: Its Role in the Making of the English Constitution 1300–1629* (Minneapolis, 1950), and Max Radin, "The Myth of Magna Carta," *Harvard Law Review*, LX, 7 (September, 1947).

169. Above, p. 177.

170. Tanner, *op. cit.*, p. 224.

171. *Ibid.*, p. 221.

172. *Chamberlain*, II, 419.

173. Birch, II, 281, 287.

174. Diary of John Pym, April 16, 1624.

175. Calvert wrote to Aston on October 19, "Wee are growne to that passe now, that there was not within theese fewe dayes a penny to be had there for pacquetts eyther outward or homeward bound, insomuch as I havinge occasion to send an extraordinary to my Lord of Doncaster I could not procure any money at all from thence to dispatch him. I have called, and doe call withall . . . upon my Lord Treasurer, who must needes furnish the office of the Chamber Treasury better or hee will soone make me weary of my place" (B.M. Add. MSS 36445, f. 261). A month later, Cranfield held up £30,000 which James had ordered sent to Frederick (Calvert

to Carleton, November 17, 1621, S.P. 84/104/290). With Digby he quarreled violently about the cost of his embassy to Vienna (Birch, II, 390).

176. *C.S.P.V.*, XVII, 198; B.M. Add. MSS 34324, f. 149.

177. Sackville Transcripts 6871.

178. *C.S.P.V.*, XVII, 184.

179. *Ibid.*, 168.

180. "Yf the parlement to be dissolved, many [will] impute yt to some yll affected about the King; but he is too strong in his owne judgement, and of too great experience to be led along or to relie on private whisperers" (*Chamberlain*, II, 419).

181. *Ibid.*, p. 418; *A.P.C.*, VI., 106.

182. Birch, II, 281.

183. *A.P.C.*, VI, 107. Coke was to remark bitterly, years afterward, that if a man were committed and had his study searched, it was easy enough to find a charge against him. Thirty-seven bundles were removed from his house and chambers. Three were never returned: a breviate of all the records in the Tower, a collection of old Chancery orders, and a treatise on Ireland. "I would give for [the] 3 of them £300," Coke lamented (in Parliament, April 29, 1628: Journal of Sir Richard Grosvenor, II, 163; Bodleian MS 330, f. 136). Sir Robert Cotton, one of those who searched and seized Coke's papers, was to find himself in the same circumstances after the Parliament of 1629.

184. *Chamberlain*, II, 418.

185. *A.P.C.*, VI, 108–110; S.P. 14/124/83.

186. Gondomar to Philip IV, January 21/31, 1622, *P.R.O.* 31/12/26; Add. MSS 34324, f. 149; D. H. Willson, "Summoning and Dissolving Parliament 1603–1625," *A.H.R.*, XLV, 2 (January, 1940), pp. 294–295.

187. *C.S.P.V.*, XVII, 190.

188. Tanner, *op. cit.*, pp. 289–295.

189. *L.D. G.*, p. 127.

Epilogue: The Winter of 1622

1. *Cabala*, p. 311. The warrant for Phelips' arrest was dated December 28 (*A.P.C.*, VI, 107). His last speeches in the Commons (*C.J.*, p. 668; *P.D.*, II, 354) were querulous and almost toadying; he must have had a hint of what was in store for him.

2. Mallory's seizure was presumably connected with his part in the plot against Buckingham. See chap. iv.

3. *Cabala*, pp. 311–312; *Chamberlain*, II, 438, 444.

4. Birch, II, 288.

5. *Chamberlain*, II, 423.

6. *Ibid.*, 429, 437. Chamberlain suggests that Heyman was punished partly for his conduct in Parliament, partly for refusing the benevolence. There was considerable resistance to this in the country. Sir Jerome Horsey was

arrested for nonpayment, and Lord Saye not only for refusing personally, but encouraging his neighbors to do so as well (*ibid.*, p. 439).

7. James Howell, ed., *Familiar Letters* . . . (Aberdeen, 1753), p. 117.

8. The notoriety of Lepton's plot had made his charges impolitic; thus a lot of excellent legal research went out the window. But rumor had it at first that Coke was to be tried for treason (Birch, II, 284, 287).

9. Sackville Transcripts 8305, 8306. These fragmentary notes by Cranfield are the only source for this important event in Coke's career. An apocryphal story has it that James offered Coke eight learned jurists for his defense, but Coke declined them, saying that he knew as much law as any man in England, and would defend himself (Birch, II, 287). Coke was not likely to take the deepest trouble of his life with levity; and there is direct mention of his counsel in Sackville 2420.

10. *Chamberlain*, II, 445–446.

11. *Ibid.*, pp. 448–449. Coke was confined to a six-mile compass of his estate at Stoke for three months, but in November, he regained full liberty (*ibid.*, p. 463).

12. Gardiner, IV, 294.

13. Sackville 2421; S.P. 14/125/36.

14. Gardiner, IV, 295.

15. The story of this is in S.P. 77/15.

16. Birch, II, 291–292.

17. *Ibid.*, pp. 282–283; Gardiner, IV, 296.

18. Birch, II, 282.

Appendix: The Declaration of June 4

1. *C.D.*, V, 203–204.

INDEX